Interdisciplinary Systems Research
Analysis — Modeling — Simulation

The system science has been developed from several scientific fields: control and communication theory, model theory and computer science. Nowadays it fulfills the requirements which Norbert Wiener formulated originally for cybernetics; and were not feasible at his time, because of insufficient development of computer science in the past.

Research and practical application of system science involve works of specialists of system science as well as of those from various fields of application. Up to now, the efficiency of this co-operation has been proved in many theoretical and practical works.

The series 'Interdisciplinary Systems Research' is intended to be a source of information for university students and scientists involved in theoretical and applied systems research. The reader shall be informed about the most advanced state of the art in research, application, lecturing and metatheoretical criticism in this area. It is also intended to enlarge this area by including diverse mathematical modeling procedures developed in many decades for the description and optimization of systems.

In contrast to the former tradition, which restricted the theoretical control and computer science to mathematicians, physicists and engineers, the present series emphasizes the interdisciplinarity which system science has reached until now, and which tends to expand. City and regional planners, psychologists, physiologists, economists, ecologists, food scientists, sociologists, political scientists, lawyers, pedagogues, philologists, managers, diplomats, military scientists and other specialists are increasingly confronted or even charged with problems of system science.

The ISR series will contain research reports — including PhD-theses — lecture notes, readers for lectures and proceedings of scientific symposia. The use of less expensive printing methods is provided to assure that the authors' results may be offered for discussion in the shortest time to a broad, interested community. In order to assure the reproducibility of the published results the coding lists of the used programs should be included in reports about computer simulation.

The international character of this series is intended to be accomplished by including reports in German, English and French, both from universities and research centers in the whole world. To assure this goal, the editors' board will be composed of representatives of the different countries and areas of interest.

Interdisziplinäre Systemforschung
Analyse — Formalisierung — Simulation

Die Systemwissenschaft hat sich aus der Verbindung mehrerer Wissenschaftszweige entwickelt: der Regelungs- und Steuerungstheorie, der Kommunikationswissenschaft, der Modelltheorie und der Informatik. Sie erfüllt heute das Programm, das Norbert Wiener mit seiner Definition von Kybernetik ursprünglich vorgelegt hat und dessen Durchführung zu seiner Zeit durch die noch ungenügend entwickelte Computerwissenschaft stark eingeschränkt war.

Die Forschung und die praktische Anwendung der Systemwissenschaft bezieht heute sowohl die Fachleute der Systemwissenschaft als auch die Spezialisten der Anwendungsgebiete ein. In vielen Bereichen hat sich diese Zusammenarbeit mittlerweile bewährt.

Die Reihe «Interdisziplinäre Systemforschung» setzt sich zum Ziel, dem Studenten, dem Theoretiker und dem Praktiker über den neuesten Stand aus Lehre und Forschung, aus der Anwendung und der metatheoretischen Kritik dieser Wissenschaft zu berichten. Dieser Rahmen soll noch insofern erweitert werden, als die Reihe in ihren Publikationen die mathematischen Modellierungsverfahren mit einbezieht, die in verschiedensten Wissenschaften in vielen Jahrzehnten zur Beschreibung und Optimierung von Systemen erarbeitet wurden.

Entgegen der früheren Tradition, in der die theoretische Regelungs- und Computerwissenschaft auf den Kreis der Mathematiker, Physiker und Ingenieure beschränkt war, liegt die Betonung dieser Reihe auf der Interdisziplinarität, die die Systemwissenschaft mittlerweile erreicht hat und weiter anstrebt. Stadt- und Regionalplaner, Psychologen, Physiologen, Betriebswirte, Volkswirtschafter, Ökologen, Ernährungswissenschafter, Soziologen, Politologen, Juristen, Pädagogen, Manager, Diplomaten, Militärwissenschafter und andere Fachleute sehen sich zunehmend mit Aufgaben der Systemforschung konfrontiert oder sogar beauftragt.

Die ISR-Reihe wird Forschungsberichte — einschliesslich Dissertationen —, Vorlesungsskripten, Readers zu Vorlesungen und Tagungsberichte enthalten. Die Verwendung wenig aufwendiger Herstellungsverfahren soll dazu dienen, die Ergebnisse der Autoren in kürzester Frist einer möglichst breiten, interessierten Öffentlichkeit zur Diskussion zu stellen. Um auch die Reproduzierbarkeit der Ergebnisse zu gewährleisten, werden in Berichten über Arbeiten mit dem Computer wenn immer möglich auch die Befehlslisten im Anhang mitgedruckt.

Der internationale Charakter der Reihe soll durch die Aufnahme von Arbeiten in Deutsch, Englisch und Französisch aus Hochschulen und Forschungszentren aus aller Welt verwirklicht werden. Dafür soll eine entsprechende Zusammensetzung des Herausgebergremiums sorgen.

ISR 36

Interdisciplinary Systems Research
Interdisziplinäre Systemforschung

Hartmut Bossel
(editor)

Concepts and Tools of Computer-assisted Policy Analysis

Vol. 1   Basic Concepts

Foreword by Eduard Pestel

1977   Springer Basel AG

CIP-Kurztitelaufnahme der Deutschen Bibliothek

Concepts and tools of computer-assisted policy analysis /
Hartmut Bossel (ed.).

Vol. 1. Basic concepts. — 1. Aufl. — 1977.
  (Interdisciplinary systems research; 36)
    ISBN 978-3-7643-0921-3   ISBN 978-3-0348-5570-9 (eBook)
    DOI 10.1007/978-3-0348-5570-9
NE: Bossel, Hartmut [Hrsg.]

© Springer Basel AG 1977

Originally published by Birkhäuser Verlag Basel in 1977

C O N T E N T S

PREFACE

Change is the most pervasive characteristic of our time: technological change affects production, transportation, and living patterns, these in turn cause changes in existing ecological and social systems, these again influence decisions and behavior of the individual, and of the organizational entities at the various levels of the social system. It is these decisions and actions which control further change and with it the future living conditions on our planet.

In many domains of our experience - production, consumption, construction, transportation - we have become accustomed to annual average rates of change of around five percent, or a doubling in 14 years. Yet the social and political problems all around us seem to indicate that individuals as well as social structures are ill-equipped to deal adaptively and constructively with such rates of change - which may locally reach much higher values, such as 25 percent per year, or a doubling every three years. In many, if not most cases, such amounts require qualitatively different responses, or a constant review and adaptation of the normative principles controlling decision and action.

Change is never isolated. It is the result of, and it causes, other changes. Change often feeds back on itself. Causal chains are rarely self-evident and obvious. Even where causalities are known, the human brain is ill-equipped to project the dynamic consequences: the hog cycle, caused by the delayed effects of the stimulation of production in boom years, is the classical example. Unfortunately, the dynamics of most problems facing the globe today are more complex than those of the hog cycle.

Coping successfully with the challenges of dynamic and interconnected change requires more than anything else information, and the ability to process this information correctly. It is therefore only natural that due to their enormous information processing capability, computers are beginning to play their role in assisting man in the performance of the different tasks of policy analysis. This role will increase as we learn more about ourselves and the systems in which we are embedded, as computers become more widely and more easily available, as information must be increasingly applied to using scarce resources more efficiently, and as projective simulations will be increasingly used to protect our social and ecological systems from costly, if not catastrophic failures.

The book "Concepts and Tools of Computer-Assisted Policy Analysis" is a contribution by an interdisciplinary research group which has been actively involved in the field of computer-assisted policy analysis for several years. In constant confrontation with the limitations and short-comings of current tools of computer-assisted policy analysis, the group, led by H. Bossel, has focussed on three particularly important aspects: (1) the formulation of a theoretical framework for the description of societal systems and their behavior; (2) the development of interactive (conversational) instruments of computer-assisted policy analysis; and (3) the simulation of the cognitive/normative processes underlying all decision-making.

Theoretical framework: Most attempts at describing societal systems and their dynamic processes in computer simulation models have in the past been undertaken by researchers with a technical systems analysis background. While they have often made significant contributions to the formalized description of societal processes, all too often these projects have been accused by social scientists - and rightly so - of lacking a solid theoretical foundation, of re-inventing the wheel, or of altogether ignoring essential results of social science research.

A sound theoretical framework based on empirically confirmed elements is a precondition for a valid social system policy analysis tool. The book presents in its first chapters a review of relevant results and approaches from the social and the systems sciences and then settles on viewing processes in society as consequences of the interaction of information-processing actor systems. This point of view seems to me to be both appropriate and necessary: man's information processing capability enables him to cope effectively even with totally new and unknown situations. The behaviorist black box and stimulus-response models - so common in the economic sciences - therefore lose their applicability in situations of relatively rapid and qualitative change, as we experience them today.

Many sciences have traditionally dealt with man and his socio-technical system. It is only natural, then, that the valid description of the behavior of social systems must integrate the findings of systems theory with those of the social sciences. The framework presented allows this integration; it also facilitates a better view of the type and magnitude of research gaps still existing, and on which future research efforts should be concentrated.

Instruments of computer-assisted policy analysis: I have argued - as is done in this book - for the development of interactive (conversational) policy analysis tools which allow direct interaction of man and simulation model. This is such more than the technocrat's pipe-dream of a computerized board room. Most of us in computer-assisted policy analysis fully realize that most policy analysis will still remain a staff function - even assuming that fully interactive models are generally available and accepted. However, interactive policy analysis offers two very important benefits: (1) it can provide for an optimal match of the bookkeeping qualities of the computer and the heuristic and pattern processing abilities of the human interactor; and (2) it appears to be the only way to avoid technocratic manipulation by an elite of computer priests. Only the second point requires elaboration: Given the possibility of the development of valid models of processes in society, those who know how to develop and operate such models thereby control a central source of information, and with it, power. In a democratic society, such an information monopoly cannot be tolerated. Computer models for policy analysis, or at least the methods for constructing and operating them, must not be accessible to only a small elite, they must also be accessible to the decision-makers themselves, in order to avoid blind reliance on the model-builders; and to the opposition; and in fact, to any individual or group whose interests are potentially being affected, or who represent other interests which cannot represent themselves (i. e. future generations or ecological systems). Computer-assisted policy analysis must recognize its important potential role in the democratization of our societies through participatory planning. In particular, parliamentary democracy is threatened by the imbalance of information processing capabilities on the part of - and in favor of - the government. Only if a certain balance is restored, will parliament again be able to serve as a forum for a constructive dialog with the government, and to again assume a potent role in the legislative process.

The book reports on several significant advances in the development of interactive policy analysis tools: interactive programs for the construction of system models, for the flexible operation and scenario analysis of simulation models, for the assessment of subjective preferences, for the analysis and simulation of cognitive processes, and for the computation of changing goals and aspirations. Some of these add new instruments to the tool box of the model builder; all of them significantly contribute towards the goals of making computer-assisted policy analysis more flexible, more transparent, and more useful.

Simulation of cognitive/normative processes: In the conceptual foundation of our world model[+], M. Mesarovic and I have stressed the role of the normative system and of decision processes in the behavior of societal systems. A valid description of these elements seems to us absolutely crucial for the development of reliable tools of policy analysis. Although many would agree with this assessment, the prevalent neglect of normative and cognitive aspects in practically all social system models (in particular, econometric and other forecasting models), is disquieting, to say the least.

The issue has been squarely faced in this book; the research group has developed methods and programs to deal with the most important of them: the simulation of chains of reasoning leading to behaviorally relevant attitudes and decisions, the deduction of situation-specific normative statements from more general norms and a description of the given circumstances, the change of goals, values, and aspirations as a function of the state of the actor system and its environment, and finally the orientation of the behavior of the system in nonroutine situations by reference to a set of basic orienting dimensions ("basic orientors") equally applicable to all

---

[+] M. Mesarovic, E. Pestel, A Goal-Seeking and Regionalized World Model for Analysis of Critical World Relationships - The Conceptual Foundation. Kybernetes Journal, Vol. 1, 1972.

types of autonomous systems, including individuals and collectivities. In dealing successfully with these issues, the research group has opened new vistas for the analysis of social systems in general, and for the field of computer-assisted policy analysis in particular.

In the course of human history, man has been extraordinarily inventive and adaptive in dealing with the challenges of change. Computer-assisted policy analysis is one of the attempts for coping with some of today's and tomorrow's challenges, if not threats. This book is a stimulating, useful, and significant contribution to the development of computer-assisted policy analysis as a tool for better planning and decision-making.

                                                            Eduard Pestel

Hannover, December 1976

INTRODUCTION: BACKGROUND, PURPOSE, OVERVIEW

Computers and Policy Analysis

There can be little doubt that policy analysis and decision-making concerning the complex issues facing society today stand to benefit from the enormous information processing capability of the computer - if it is properly used. Proper use requires more than anything else an adequate understanding of the social, political, psychological, technological, ecological, and economic systems and processes of which a societal system is composed, as well as the availability of instruments which match the different information processing capabilities of man and computer in an optimal manner. Today we have not yet come close to fulfilling these requirements in a satisfactory manner.

Motivation and Origin

The work reported in CONCEPTS AND TOOLS OF COMPUTER-ASSISTED POLICY ANALYSIS has been performed in recognition on the one hand of the potential of computer-assisted policy analysis, and of the need for valid instruments for such analysis on the other. The 17 chapters of the book deal with both of the resulting challenges: that of developing valid formalized, computer-implementable descriptions of societal systems and processes, and that of optimally matching the powers of man and computer on the other. Most of the ideas, concepts, approaches, programs, and results are here reported for the first time in the hope that they will stimulate discussions and further research and development work.

Most of the work described in the book is the result of a three-year research and development effort[+] which involved some 19 people at one time or another, although most of them contributed during limited assignments only and the permanent core group consisted of a mere two people. The group represented the disciplines of sociology, social psychology, political science, systems analysis, computer and information sciences, psychology, engineering, philosophy, physics, management science, and linguistics. The project - occasionally referred to as "Project UTOPIA" (Undertaking To Operationalize Policy-directive Indicators of Action) - was funded by Stiftung Volkswagenwerk and carried out at Institut für Systemtechnik und Innovationsforschung (ISI) of the Fraunhofer Gesellschaft applied research organization of the Federal Republic of Germany. The work was

---

[+] exceptions are the articles by Schwember and Deissenberg.

the direct result of a research suggestion by Profs. Mihajlo Mesarović
(Case Western Reserve University, Cleveland, Ohio, USA) and Eduard
Pestel (Technical University of Hannover, Federal Republic of Germany)
to supplement their well-known global modelling research in the cognitive /
normative domain. In the course of the UTOPIA project work, close contact has been maintained with the Mesarović-Pestel global modelling teams
in Cleveland and Hannover - even though the UTOPIA research effort was
completely independent of that project. We have tried to learn and benefit
from the diverse experiences of these teams, as well as from those of many
other groups and individuals throughout the world involved in related projects.

Introduction to the Contents

The articles in this book are intended as contributions to the two important
aspects of computer-assisted policy analysis mentioned above: computer
simulation of societal processes, and man-machine interfacing. These
topics can be dealt with in a variety of ways; our presentation is strongly influenced by the research "philosophy" as it evolved in the course of the project. Leaving details and justifications to the different chapters, we will now
briefly state the essential elements of this "philosophy".

Our approach to the description and simulation of societal processes is
characterized by the following basic hypotheses:
- The various processes of conflict, coexistence, and cooperation in
  societal systems can be viewed as interactions of idealized "actors"
  or "actor systems" (individuals, organizations, power centers, nations;
  depending on the resolution required in the analysis).
- Actor systems consist of an information processing system and a
  certain material (causal) system providing for physical support and a
  certain amount of control over the system's environment. The information processing of the actor system is governed by a more or less
  homogeneous concept structure relating the needs and goals of the actor
  system to its decisions and actions. Actors are thus defined by their
  commonalities in perception and response which largely depend on the
  aspect of reality under consideration. By definition then, as soon as
  a conflict relevant to the aspect under study arises within the actor
  system, it can no longer be considered as o n e   actor, and must be
  split into as many actors as there are important parties to the conflict.
- Rational behavior of actors is controlled by their cognitive system,
  and in particular by the desire to remove differences between cognitions of the "Is" (the perceived state of the system) and the "Ought"
  (the normative concepts of the system). This amounts to a generalized
  cognitive dissonance concept.
- Where normative concepts fitting a given situation are not available,
  i. e. in nonroutine situations, recourse is ultimately made to a hand-
  ful of basic orienting dimensions (basic orientors) common to all autonomous systems, for deriving normative guide-lines.

With these few basic tenets, a coherent theoretical framework for the description of the behavior of interacting rational actor systems in a perturbed environment can be developed. This theoretical framework is the backbone of the simulation work reported in the book.

The following statements characterize our philosophy concerning the development of interactive policy analysis tools, i. e. the man-machine interfacing aspect:
- The division of labor between man and the computer must be such that those who are charged with policy development and decision-making are not burdened with rote, mechanical, and bookkeeping chores and routine programming tasks and can instead concentrate on the perceptive, creative, interpretative, evaluative, and subjective processes of reality description, policy development, and policy analysis and assessment - without having to undergo lengthy special training or to possess special computer and programming knowledge and skills.
- The language of communication between man and computer should not differ substantially from natural language, common symbols, and normal communication by graphical means (sketches and figures).
- The policy analysis tools developed should make use of a generally valid framework while allowing application to very specific problem settings. This requires the development of generic meta-programs for the generation of problem-specific policy analysis programs.
- These meta-programs must accommodate both the developer (model builder) of a new policy analysis program as well as the eventual user of this tool (planner and decision-maker). Ideally, the tools should be so well developed that valid models of reality can be constructed by the planner or decision-maker himself.

Arguments for these objectives are presented in several chapters of the book. The meta-programs developed and presented here represent attempts to adhere as closely as possible to these objectives.

It will be obvious from these statements of our research and development "philosophy" that we consider most current attempts at computer-assisted policy analysis to be deficient on two major counts:
(1) Practically all system models of societal systems developed to date concentrate on the representation of the material processes of these systems and all too often entirely neglect the cognitive/normative (information-processing) components of the real processes which dominate decision-making and action.
(2) Current simulation methodology was developed by and for the (technological and/or computer science) specialist and is not geared to the communication and analysis modes and requirements of those in applied policy analysis, development planning and decision-making.

The book represents an attempt to contribute in these two areas.

Organization of the book

CONCEPTS AND TOOLS OF COMPUTER-ASSISTED POLICY ANALYSIS
goes significantly beyond current trends in computer-assisted policy analysis
in specifically recognizing and accounting for the dominant role of information processing in all processes of society. Correspondingly, the three
parts of the book deal with (I) basic concepts of social systems representation and requirements of computer-assisted policy analysis, (II) representation of processes in the material system and corresponding policy analysis
tools, and (III) representation of information processes in the cognitive/
normative system and corresponding policy analysis tools.

Part I: Computer-Assisted Policy Analysis for Social Systems: Basic Concepts

The first six chapters of the book deal with basic theoretical and empirical
aspects of the formalized representation of societal systems and processes
and of computer-assisted policy analysis.

Chapter 1 "Systems Science and Social Science Foundations of Computer-
Assisted Policy Analysis" provides a representative survey of work in the
different sciences bearing on the development of tools of computer-assisted
policy analysis and their application to social systems. A great deal of
applicable work has already been done elsewhere, albeit in a diverse collection of disciplines, and usually without a direct policy-analysis objective.
The chapter also points to existing research gaps. Much of the theoretical
and empirical groundwork is applied in later chapters of the book.

Chapter 2 "Cybernetics in Government: Experience with New Tools for
Management in Chile 1971 - 1973" is a report on the most ambitious and
far-reaching application of the principles of cybernetics and computer-assisted
policy analysis to date under President Salvador Allende, by a participant
who had an active role in the development effort. The chapter provides an
overview of the theoretical framework of the system as well as details of
its implementation and the practical experience collected during its operation.
The chapter has a special authority borne of experience: It provides both
a damper for those who dream of solving all the world's problems by turning
them over to the computer, as well as encouragement to those who feel that
society stands to gain from a sensible application of computer-assisted
policy analysis.

Chapter 3 "Computer Models for Policy Analysis: Hierarchy, Goal Orientation, Scenarios" deals with the requirements which must be met by instruments of computer-assisted policy analysis. The different requirements
concerning the overall approach, the system description, and the planning
instrument are spelled out. The current state of the Mesarović-Pestel
global modelling effort is discussed with reference to these requirements.

Chapter 4 "A Modelling Framework for Societal Systems" summarizes an
information-processing approach to the description of the behavior of (rational)
actor systems embedded in an environment containing other mutually interacting
actor systems. The framework explicitly recognizes the role of cognitions
and cognitive processing, and the controlling influence of cognitive dissonances
and of basic behavior-orienting dimensions ("orientors" such as security,
freedom of action, adaptivity, etc.) which determine decisions and actions
especially in nonroutine decision situations.

Chapter 5 "Social Indicators and Quality of Life Measures" deals with one
particular aspect of the information-processing approach: the perception
of the system state (in this case the state of the social system) by the actor
system through a set of indicators. The chapter surveys the international
work on social indicators and quality of life measures and examines in particular its applicability to modelling efforts. It appears that social indicators to date do not meet the specific requirements of policy analysis models,
and considerable work remains to be done in this area.

Chapter 6 "Orientors of Nonroutine Behavior" deals with another major
aspect of the information-processing approach: the mapping of the often
large number of indicators of the perceived system state on the few basic
orienting dimensions by reference to which the actor system determines
proper behavior in nonroutine decision situations (where standard norms
do not apply). A set of basic orientors is derived by different approaches;
an empirical application to the determination of value priorities is presented.
The orientor concept is related to global system performance indexes (e. g.
"robustness"). Its importance lies in the fact that it allows the prediction
of likely (rational) system behavior even under circumstances requiring
abrupt qualitative changes in behavioral policy. The orientor concept is the
basis of the orientor satisfaction assessment program in Chapter 15 (Part III)
which determines the emergence of different priorities as a function of
changing system state.

Part II: Computer Tools for the Analysis of Material Systems

The next six chapters deal with computer-assisted policy analysis instruments
developed for the analysis of processes in the physical system. Most of these
programs are interactive in order to provide an adaptive and flexible division
of labor between man and computer.

Chapter 7 "Construction of Dynamic System Models Using Interactive Computer
Graphics" presents a powerful tool for the fast and efficient development of

dynamic system models: block diagrams are sketched on the graphic terminal of a minicomputer using a light pen and converted by the program into the corresponding state equations; functional relationships are specified, or sketched on the screen; the necessary parameters are entered; and the model output is generated automatically in a desired form, including time and phase plots. The GRIPS system also generates a full FORTRAN program for the simulation model, which can then be combined with other model programs to form a larger simulation model, and to perhaps be implemented on other computers. The system has particular significance for model development and for teaching purposes.

Chapter 8 "Sensitivity Analysis of Simulation Models" deals with the important problem of determining how sensitive a given model is to changes in the different input parameters. In all except very small models, experimentation to determine parameter sensitivity is out of the question. The chapter outlines a systematic approach applicable to all dynamic system models. The automatic sensitivity analysis of a model identifies the critical parameters, providing clues in particular for the determination of parameters which may either lead to large system perturbations, or which may be used for efficient system control.

Chapter 9 "Matching Man and Model: The GUIDE System for Interactive Model Handling" describes a program system for the development and use of interactive models. The system requires the model core equations (developed e. g. by using the GRIPS system), and specification of search hierarchies for the input and output parameters. The user can then access any of these parameters separately, input scenarios on different levels of aggregation, generate tabular or graphic output adapted to his requirements, perform operations on the output variables, and perform many other functions designed to allow maximum interaction with the model with a minimum of user effort and no special programming or computer knowledge.

Chapter 10 "An Interactive Model for Energy Policy Assessment" describes in some detail the structure and features of a medium-size interactive policy analysis instrument, and presents sample applications. The program allows the interactive development of policies concerning the energy supply system. To assist the user in policy development, it offers the flexible input of scenarios, forward and backward stepping in time, presentation of the results in different forms (standard printout, summaries grouped according to the different sectors of the energy model, summaries of decision-relevant indicators, and focussing on any one of over 700 individual variables), and subjective assessment of the results for evaluation and comparison of policies.

Chapter 11 "Man-Machine Interaction as an Answer to the Multiple-Goal Problem" deals with the central issue of policy analysis: the identification of the (in some sense) most efficient policy to achieve given objectives. In most real policy analysis problems, competing criteria must be considered simultaneously.

The chapter discusses three interactive approaches which assist the program user in developing a satisfactory policy for given constraints by progressive extraction of his preferences in a dialog with the program. Preferences stated are used by the program to obtain improved solutions. In this
manner a satisfactory (suboptimal) solution can be reached in a few iterative
steps. The procedure has special significance for larger models, where the
trial-and-error search for a good policy becomes very inefficient.

Chapter 12 "Systems Analysis on Programmable Pocket Calculators" recognizes the fact that small programmable calculators are becoming available
whose storage capacity allows the analysis of small to medium size systems.
Programming methods for dynamic systems, for preference assessment,
and for scenario development are described by developing examples. The
use of pocket calculators for system models having a modest number of
state variables opens the use of systems simulation and policy analysis to
a much wider group of potential users. It may contribute in particular to
a more widespread appreciation of the characteristic behavioral properties
of dynamic systems, in particular their tendency for "counterintuitive behavior" as a result of feedbacks and delays.

Part III: Computer Tools for the Analysis of Cognitive Systems

The final five chapters deal with methods of representing aspects of information processing in the cognitive system of an actor. As rational behavior is
the outcome of information processing, its correct description assumes a
central role - so far not properly recognized - in all attempts at simulation
and policy analysis concerning societal systems.

Chapter 13 "Modelling of the Cognitive Processes Determining Nonroutine
Behavior" provides an introduction to the problems, requirements, and
possibilities of the simulation of cognitive processes taking place in the
conceptual systems of actors. The representation of conceptual systems,
and of cognitive processes, requires nonnumerical simulation. The chapter
introduces to the application of the predicate calculus for the representation
of conceptual systems and the simulation of processes of deduction resulting
in normative statements requiring certain behavioral modes and constraining
others. The formalized representation of conceptual systems, and the simulation of cognitive processes following given information inputs, provides
an extremely important policy analysis tool for determining the behavioral
potential of an actor system, and in particular possible conceptual deficiencies
which may lead to self-induced catastrophic response.

Chapter 14 "Cognitive Systems Analysis: An Interactive Program for the
Modelling of Deduction" presents in some detail the interactive program
DEDUC which has been developed for the formalized representation of conceptual systems, and of deductive processes taking place following a given
information input. The program is implemented in the multi-place predicate
calculus. It requires the specification of the object structures and causal

relationships between objects representing the actor's perception of the world around him concerning the aspect under investigation. Using the connectives "and", "or", "not", and "when ... then ..."., and the object classifier "is", the program is capable of representing and operating with natural language statements, once they are transformed to the required form. The main areas of application are the representation of cognitive processes, the deduction of situation-specific normative statements from more general orientors, and qualitative simulation.

Chapter 15 "An Interactive Program for Orientor Satisfaction Assessment" presents a flexible policy analysis tool based on the orientor approach of Chapter 6. The program allows the problem-specific mapping of the system and environmental state on the respective orientor state. The necessary parameter and data inputs are obtained from the program user in an interactive session making full use of computer graphics and the light pen in addition to the terminal keyboard. The program can be used in several modes: (1) issue assessment (e. g. the assessment of value rankings, or the assessment of the relative importance of political issues); (2) scenario assessment (here scenarios for quantitative indicators are sketched on the display screen using the light pen); or (3)alternative assessment (here the values of representative indicators characterizing the alternatives are supplied to the program). The program produces a complete documentation of the analysis process. Applications of the three modes are presented.

Chapter 16 "Computer Implementation of Social-Psychological Hypotheses Connected to Decision-Making" develops a coherent simulation approach which contains the elements of the orientor approach (orientors, resp. values, indicators, loadings, satisfaction scales, etc.) but in addition includes policy search and assessment processes and adjustment of aspiration levels by the mechanisms of cognitive dissonance reduction. The approach is implemented in a general simulation program (COGDIS). In order to run the program, it has to be loaded with problem-specific information. Details of the structure and the different features of the program are presented.

Chapter 17 "A Simulation of the Change of Political Values and Goals in the Federal Republic of Germany" reports on the application of the program COGDIS to the modelling of the changes of political priorities in West Germany from 1950 to 1975. The data base consisted of the time series for selected social indicators covering the spectrum of political concerns. The agreement with recorded political emphasis is good, despite the fact that for lack of empirical data subjective quantification of the qualitative social-psychological hypotheses had to be employed.

Acknowledgements

I owe a deep debt of gratitude to Mihajlo Mesarović and Eduard Pestel for suggesting and encouraging the research on which this book is based, to Stiftung Volkswagenwerk for supporting it, to the colleagues who contributed to Project UTOPIA with their research (cf. the list of UTOPIA reports in the appendix), to those who provided comments and criticism on the way (too numerous to name here), to those whose ideas we have used (see the references), and to the efficient typing and organizational skills of Mrs. Dietlind Dippel. I thank my wife Rika Gerlind for her understanding co-operation.

The book is dedicated to those who are children today.

December 1976   Hartmut Bossel

1

SYSTEMS SCIENCE AND SOCIAL SCIENCE FOUNDATIONS OF COMPUTER-ASSISTED POLICY ANALYSIS

Hartmut Bossel and Edelgard Gruber

Survey

Originally developed in the technical sciences, computer simulation has over the past decade been increasingly used for the simulation of proces- ses in societal systems and as a tool of policy analysis. New scientific and socio-political problems arise in this connection, to which solutions are for the greater part still in their infancy. The article provides a survey of the specific requirements of simulations of societal systems, in particular with respect to their use in computer-assisted policy ana- lysis, of foundations available in the social and the systems sciences, of research gaps, of the problems of application, and of the relevant literature.

1   INTRODUCTION: THE SIMULATION OF SOCIETAL SYSTEMS - PROGRESS AND PROBLEMS

Development of computer simulation

The basic feasibility of computer simulation[+] of societal processes has become almost common knowledge following the publication of the world model studies sponsored by the Club of Rome[1]. These studies have per- formed a historic service by stimulating - in addition to a flood of often justified criticism - fundamental discussions and new research approaches which will only bear fruit in coming years. This contribution also is a product of this discussion.

At the time of their publication the world model studies were neither the first, nor in some respects the scientifically most advanced attempts at simulation of societal processes. The beginnings of this field of scienti- fic study reach back to approximately the year 1950 when electronic com- puters began to become available[2]. To the year 1969 the number of annual

---

[+] In the following, the terms "computer simulation" or "simulation" are applied exclusively to computer studies using programmed simulation models. "Societal Systems" is used to denote systems possibly having political, technological, economic, ecological, psychological etc. com- ponents as well as social components.

publications had increased to several hundred per year[3]. The applications reached from microanalytic models of human problem-solving to the macro-analysis of the dynamics of development processes in countries of the Third World[4]. The surveys given in these references are still representative today.

Reasons for the application of simulation

The main reasons for the application of simulation for the description of societal processes are based on the following insights:
- The processes, resp. their component processes, are subject to certain regularities (which however rarely reach the reliability of e. g. the natural laws of physics).
- Processes of individual or social behavior are the result of the interconnection of many component processes.
- The human mind can comprehend and projectively describe isolated component processes and their dynamics and consequences reasonably well, but falters in assessing the dynamics and consequences of complex systems composed of many interconnected component systems.

It suggests itself to entrust the computer as an 'incorruptible book-keeper' with this last task, as an aid to policy analysis, in the hope of reducing the risk of producing the wrong decisions in minor or major applications.

Applications of computer simulation

From the multitude of applications to date of simulations of individual or societal processes the following major areas of application stand out[5]:
- Applications in research and teaching:
  Description of processes; explorative and speculative application; heuristic tool in the development of theory; experimental test bed for controlled experiments; training instrument for familiarization with the response dynamics of complex coupled processes (analogous to a flight simulator for a new aircraft); teaching tool to demonstrate e. g. dynamics of an economic system.
- Application in policy planning:
  Forecasting of probable developments; consequence analysis; study of alternatives; planning; systems synthesis; model for parallel simulation of real processes for the purpose of short term forecasting and anticipative control.

The applications so far have mostly focussed on explorative uses in research, and on the development of decision aids for (mostly) industrial management[6]. Despite its very considerable potential as an instrument of planning, simulation gains a foothold only very slowly in the area of political policy analysis and decision-making[7]. In view of the potential consequences of misjudgments in this area reservations concerning this new tool should perhaps be applauded at its current state of development;

they should be given up, however, to the degree that the problems still
open find acceptable solutions.

The problem of subjectivity

A simulation - like any description of reality - is always a simplified
representation of reality. This image is obtained by a cognitive process
representing reality for a certain given purpose, taking into account certain aspects only, i. e. those seen as relevant for the task. There is no
other way to obtain the reduction of complexity required for the model. As
a result, a model is always an image of reality tinged by the subjective
point of view of the model builder. In a purely technical field this aspect
rarely causes difficulties, as there generally exists intersubjective
agreement concerning the mode of description, performance criteria,
etc. But even here the models constructed by different authors of one
and the same process (e. g. a process of chemical engineering) may differ
to a certain degree, as each author - on the basis of his personal experience - may feel he should neglect different parameters as having only
insignificant influence. In addition, one and the same author will model
the process differently, depending on whether the task calls for e. g.
process optimization, a study of the energy flows, or an investigation
of control problems.

Within the domain of societal systems the problem of subjectivity is substantially aggravated for several reasons: there are hardly any solidly
validated and generally accepted theories which could be used for description; as a result of circumstances, experience, and role, the actors
within a societal system see reality through different filters; the criteria
of analysis differ: One man's owl is another man's nightingale. Since it
is impossible, on principle, - simply on account of age differences - to
attain intersubjective agreement concerning social reality (except through
coercion and hypocrisy), the simulation of social reality must live with
the problem of different subjective assessments. Concretely this means
that during the construction of models which are to be used in policy
analysis the interests of those potentially affected by decisions must be
represented. Otherwise simulation-assisted decision-making will de-
generate into technocratic patronizing, if not manipulation. The same
reservations obviously also apply to political decision-making in general;
but they apply to simulation with particular severity, since the construction of simulation models requires expertise and expense generally available only to specialists in well-financed institutions. For the most part,
decision-makers will have no alternative but to accept the conclusions of
the experts, unless they want to wholly forego the benefits of simulations.

There are possible ways out of this dilemma, which have however so far
hardly been taken:
- Models which are to be used in decision-making are constructed
  in collaboration with all parties affected, or with proper repre-

sentatives of their interests (this applies in particular to the representation of interests of future generations).

- Models are made available to all parties affected resp. to their representatives (this requires a certain amount of expertise on the part of at least the representatives).
- Parallel models are developed representing the different points of view of the parties involved.
- Independent 'ombudsmen' examine models in the case of disagreements.
- Simulation languages and methods are developed to such a stage that working with them is no longer reserved exclusively to experts.

We have discussed these problems here, as they must be solved simultaneously with the development of simulation methods, for policy analysis and decision-making, in order to avoid the possibility of serious setbacks in the processes of democratization. This problem area is discussed more fully by Harbordt[8]. Compared to the dangers of technocratization the following objections concerning formalization, mathematization, and quantification of societal processes are of relatively minor importance. We here summarize the more important concerns[9].

Problems of formalization, mathematization, and quantification

The traditional manner of description of the social sciences (with the major exception of econometrics) is the verbal statement. In the course of formalization in a simulation language, important conceptual elements may get lost. In addition, communication with non-experts is made more difficult. The same is true for mathematization. Reference to the large number of nonquantifiable variables in the social sciences is no argument against mathematization; mathematics can deal with such sets. Rather, the crucial criterion of "mathematizability" is whether the objects and structures of the reality to be simulated have mathematical structures and objects as counterparts, on which they can be mapped. This may not be the case; thus additions to the collection of mathematical instruments may be required ("fuzzy analysis" is a case in point).

Quantification is n o t a unique characteristic of simulation: Many dynamic processes can only be represented using nonnumerical (list) processing. This is particularly true for cognitive processes. Problems of quantification arise where variables must be quantified although data of the required precision or reliability are not available (e. g. the table functions of many DYNAMO simulations).

Problems of validity

A conclusion of the philosophy of science is the finding that the validity of a theory can never be verified, only falsified[10]. At best, a theory can therefore be provisionally valid for lack of falsification. The same conclusion obviously also applies to simulation models. In the case of

simulation models we may define "validity" as (in some way sufficient)
agreement between the model and the real system or process which is
being mapped. In this case the proof of validity is rendered even more
difficult by the fact that systems of different structure may show identical behavior. Harbordt differentiates between three types of validity[11]:

- Formal validity refers to the precision with which the
  model reproduces the data which have been used in its construction.
- Empirical validity refers to the precision of the mapping relation between model and the real system mapped; in this
  case one has to differentiate between the similarity of the behavior
  and the similarity of the system structure.
- Pragmatic validity refers to the degree to which the
  model meets the goals and purposes of the model construction
  exercise.

An assessment of these three aspects of validity is possible only through
application of subjective elements (assessment criteria, requirements
of precision, assessments of pragmatic validity). A critical methodological gap presently exists concerning methods of testing structural
validity; extensive sensitivity tests are the most appropriate method.
Problems of validity are more fully discussed e.g. by Harbordt[12].

Preliminary conclusions and survey

The potential of computer simulation is often overvalued, but very often
it is also not accorded the proper respect - partly as a result of not
always fully scientifically respectable applications in the past. The remarks so far were intended to give a brief survey over the possibilities,
limits, and problems of the method, before we embark on a closer study
of its application in the social sciences. In many respects, the method
is still in its infancy and therefore offers rich potential for research.
In the following we shall point out some of the almost unplowed fields.

In the next section we turn to those components of individual and social
behavior which must be mapped in simulations of societal processes.
From these components the analysis leads to individual research areas
which can make available the elements needed for the simulation of
societal systems. In the following section, the major part of this contribution, we will discuss these elements briefly, with reference to the relevant literature. In the last section we list some major unsolved research
problems.

2 COMPONENTS OF SOCIETAL SYSTEMS

Information processing and actor

A comprehensive and complete theory of societal systems which would
permit the construction of valid simulation models does not exist. Rather,
for the description of most societal processes one has to fall back on

different, only more or less well validated, often even controversial approaches.

As mentioned above, the simulation approach depends on the point of view and is therefore - on principle - not free of subjective components. In order to have a uniform frame of reference, we here choose the point of view of information processing. Different points of view (e. g. theories of exchange, or of conflict, dialectic materialism, etc.) are possible. It seems reasonable to us, however, to anchor the frame of reference at a place where a multitude of system components are indisputably located. Humans are more or less autonomous systems, whose behavior is controlled by information processes. Societal processes can be viewed as the consequences of interaction of individuals. From this interaction may result new qualities of behavior not found in the individual component (e. g. group and mass phenomena); the dominant structural component of the subsystems remains that of information processing, however.

In the following we employ the term societal "actor", by which we mean a collection of individuals which behave in a similar fashion with respect to a given ordering aspect, while exchanging information among themselves. In this sense, a soccer club, a government, or a labor union are seen as actors as far as matters of soccer, government, or labor are concerned. In the following, the actor is viewed as an information processing system requiring certain system components to enable it to function; these components are to be determined first. As a special case, the actor may obviously be composed of a single individual; in this case the consideration of certain qualities of behavior which may result from the interaction of individuals does not apply. The societal system as a whole is then understood as a system of interacting actors (in the sense defined), where the resolution into actors follows from the aspects and requirements of the simulation task. A comprehensive survey of the information processing approach is given by Kirsch[13].

System components of the actor

Our approach to the modelling of actor systems is outlined in more detail elsewhere in this volume. We here summarize some essential aspects. Following the terminology of Mesarović and Pestel[14] we distinguish between the e n v i r o n m e n t of a system, its c a u s a l s t r a t u m, its d e c i s i o n s t r a t u m, and its n o r m a t i v e s t r a t u m. We count as environment that part of the universe which can be influenced to a significant degree by the behavior of the actor (in the sense of the simulation task), or which can exert significant influence on the actor. The causal stratum is composed of those processes which represent the material functioning of the system and follow certain laws or pseudo-laws (e. g. economic "laws"); of the effectors of the system, by which instructions for actions originating from the decision stratum are translated into processes in the causal stratum, or influence on the environment; and of the receptors by which information is received from the environment. The causal stratum is therefore the controlled system.

The decision stratum combines the processes of state analysis, policy synthesis, and decision; it represents the controller. In performing these operations it has to refer back to normative references from the normative stratum. A special difficulty of the analysis of societal system results from the constant change of these normative references (value changes, changes in attitudes, priorities, preferences, etc.). Normative change manifests itself via the decision stratum and the causal stratum, not merely in the behavioral changes but in particular in changes of the causal structure ("structural change"; the entire process is referred to as "social change").

The interaction of two or more actors may take place either indirectly via the environment, or directly via the exertion of influence on the causal stratum of the opposite party. This influence may be of a physical nature (e. g. the application of sanctions), or it may be applied through the transmission of information (e. g. the threat of an application of sanctions). A characteristic of the interaction is that at least one of the actors affects, resp. considers consciously or unconsciously the interests of the other actor. The framework of analysis therefore also takes into consideration aspects such as that of structural power where the freedom of action of one actor is reduced disproportionately (with or without his conscious knowledge); or of verbal conflict, where actors attempt to influence the actions of the opponent by emitting information intended to influence the opponent's cognitive process; or of physical conflict, where the opponents strive for direct or indirect control of the opponent's causal stratum.

The information processing sequence leading to an action, resp. to a certain behavior of the actor proceeds roughly as follows (we present here a preliminary and certainly not generally accepted conceptual approach which will serve as a framework for the further discussion[15]):

State changes in the causal system and the environment: As a result of the characteristic dynamics of the system, of the actions of the different actors, or of perturbations, state changes take place in the causal system of the actor, resp. in the environment.

Simulation aspects: Description of deterministic or indeterministic (stochastic or probabilistic) continuous or discontinuous processes.

Reception of information from the causal system and the environment: From the information available in the causal system and the environment, and potentially receivable by the actor, he selectively receives only a subset. Part of this information may consist of symbolic information (written documents, spoken language, gestures, implications).

Simulation aspects: Decoding, selection, filtering, storage of information and codes, selection norms, influences of affect and emotions.

Recognition of information content: A precondition for the absorption of information relevant for or of interest to the actor is the recognition of the information content in the widest sense.

Simulation aspects: Pattern recognition, concept recognition, state recognition, classification, recognition of interconnections, cognitive processes, perception, discrimination, threshold analysis, perception norms, influences of affect and emotions.

Updating and complementation of the state image: The newly acquired information is used to update the image of the state of the causal system and the environment, resp. to change, enlarge, supplement and complement memory content.

Simulation aspects: Short term and long term memories, storage of quantitative and qualitative (nonnumerical) information, change of perception patterns and cognitions, change of memory storage content and forgetting, norms for the change of memory content, learning, influence of affect and emotions.

State analysis: The new state image ("Is") is compared with the normative concepts concerning the desired system goal state ("Ought"). The comparison of the two cognitions results in more or less pronounced dissonances[16] with respect to certain aspects of the current system state. The motivation for the reduction or dissolution of these dissonances determines the subsequent problem solving behavior and the choice of actions.

Simulation aspects: State description by selection of relevant indicator variables (e. g. "social indicators"), derivation of the respective goal state from basic operational requirements of the actor (e. g. "security"), resp. from values or goals derived from these, deduction of normative statements, emergence and change of cognitive dissonances, influences of affect and emotions.

Policy synthesis: If on the basis of the state perception the application of an existing response program (e. g. escape response) appears advisable, this program is activated without further problem-solving behavior via the effectors of the causal system. If no applicable response program is available in the long term memory, the dissonance vector generated during the state analysis guides the corresponding problem-solving process. In the course of this process, trial solutions are formulated and tested with respect to their likely consequences, using the internal model. A set of measures promising success is selected and implemented via the effectors of the causal system.

Simulation aspects: Learning of response programs, perception of the situation, problem-solving, heuristic search, decision behavior, decision criteria, subjective utility, subjective probability, selection norms, internal model and projection using the internal model, time horizon and weighting of the future, learning and self-organizing systems, influences of affects and emotions.

Change of normative statements: From the state analysis and the policy synthesis may result the necessity of changing or supplementing certain normative statements concerning e. g. the state perception, the state analysis, or the policy synthesis (e. g. observation of new indicator variables, reduction of aspiration levels, consideration of measures not employed so far, generation of new subsystems within the causal system (structural change) in order to ensure adequate coping with respect to new requirements).

Simulation aspects: Deduction and induction, manipulation of concepts, linguistic simulation, cognitive processes.

Learning: The actor may learn new recognition classifiers, new (general) information, new response programs, new problem-solving approaches, new normative statements, as well as structural system changes in a variety of ways.

Simulation aspects: Learning mechanisms, long term memory, forgetting.

With this brief survey we have been able to cover the different aspects of information processing in individuals or societal systems only in a very superficial way[17]. Nevertheless, the survey has produced an indication of the wide range of aspects which will have to be considered in simulations of societal processes within the information processing framework. The next section will be devoted to a discussion of the contributions of different fields of science to the simulation tasks. For literature on the information processing approach we refer to the bibliography in Kirsch.[18]

Contributing research areas

The successful simulation of societal systems and processes requires multidisciplinary if not interdisciplinary contributions from a multitude of research areas scattered over a wide range of disciplines within the social and the systems sciences:
- concepts from the philosophy of science
- social science systems theories
- theories of social psychology
- sociological behavioral theories
- conflict research
- research on pluralism and elites

- organization sociology
- social indicators and quality of life research
- systems theory
- mathematics
- simulation approaches
- simulation languages and user adaptation
- economics
- decision theory
- cognitive processes and system adaptation

We shall now discuss these contributions in sequence.

3 CONTRIBUTIONS OF DIFFERENT SCIENTIFIC AREAS

We can only devote a small amount of space to the individual contributions
of the different scientific areas. Our presentation is itself only a model
of scientific reality and is subject to the restrictions of unavoidable subjectivity mentioned above. This subjectivity is partially a result of our
incomplete knowledge of a given scientific area, partially it is a consequence of our own research approach and corresponding bias, and partially it is determined by the need to be selective. Our comments should
be understood merely as hints and suggestions; a broader and deeper
study of the subject matter will be possible using the literature cited in
the text and listed in the appendix. Very often we have not cited primary
references, but rather contributions which seemed to us especially useful as introductory references, and in which references to the primary
literature can easily be found. Our apologies therefore to authors who
have made significant contributions and are not directly referenced in
this paper. We are reasonably certain, however, that their names will
not escape the reader who studies the references cited.

Contributions of the social sciences: an introduction

Simulations in the social area are difficult mainly because a multitude
of different fields has to be considered. Knowledge concerning technical
or economic relationships is much better developed than sociological
theories, as certain types of problems occur almost exclusively in the
social sciences[19] and complicate empirical theory construction.

The use of simulation methods in the social sciences requires comprehensive, empirically well confirmed theories which can serve as components of models reflecting the development of social processes. The deductive-nomological method so common in sociology concentrates more
on an individualistic approach to social phenomena than on the concept of
the social system functioning as a whole.

The systems approach is by no means in contradiction to the deductive-
nomological method. Systems analysis also needs formulation and em-

pirical validation of general laws. The difference between both orientations lies mainly in the different emphasis of systems analysis: in lieu
of verbal, qualitative theories it prefers formalized theories; in lieu of
fundamental research we find a more pragmatic orientation with emphasis on prognosis and application; at the same time the inclusion of as
many aspects as possible is favored over the theoretical in-depth study
of individual aspects of the object under investigation.

Today one meets both orientations to a similar extent: A large part of
the theories of sociology and the political sciences is founded in a systems
concept, while the empirically better grounded theories of social psychology have more of a deductive-nomological character. The linking of
both approaches, in particular on the basis of computer simulation, is
still in its infancy.

Concepts from the philosophy of science

At the center of attention of the theoretical social sciences are attempts
today to explain social events and occurrences. According to the deductive-nomological method[20] - as represented primarily by Popper, Albert,
and Hempel - such an explanation consists of the logical deduction of a
conclusion from nomological hypotheses, i.e. from general assertions
of a law-like character[21] which are empirically rich and can be tested,
and of certain statements describing a given system state to which the
nomological hypothesis applies. The following example may clarify this
explanatory scheme:

Behavior complying with given norms is rewarded by the social environment	(general hypothesis)
Person A complies with the given norms	(circumstance, state description)
Deduction Person A is rewarded by the social environment	(explanandum)

The same scheme can be used for prognoses as well as for "social
technologies"; only the question will be different[22]: A prognosis corresponds to the question concerning the event which will take place given
a certain law applies and a certain system state occurs. A technology
answers to a question concerning possible courses of action; in the
example above: How should person A behave in order to be rewarded by
the social environment?

There is general agreement that the general laws found in the empirical
sciences have the character of preliminary hypotheses. An absolute
claim to the truth does not exist. Inductively determined generalizations
therefore have to be tested by application of deductive procedures. A
hypothesis must prove itself again and again in systematic and strict

attempts at falsification; only in this manner can one approach the truth[23].

As obvious as these concepts may be from the point of view of the natural sciences, they are not accorded the proper attention in the social area and are questioned again and again[24]. Fundamentally, the concern is about the unity of the empirical sciences.

Classical rationalism already showed that man and nature are subject to the same laws and can be understood by application of identical principles of knowledge (e. g. Spinoza, Grotius, Kant). This idea was lost during diverse attempts to save the free will and uniqueness of man by claiming inapplicability of science. Later the unity of the experiential sciences was again strengthened as a result of Darwin's theory of evolution. More recent objections to this unity - which originated especially around the turn of the century - were aimed at giving the social sciences a distinctive methodological position among the empirical sciences. The special characteristic of the sciences of human behavior was seen in the fact that man belongs to "two worlds" simultaneously, the physical world and the world of the mind. In addition he is both subject and object of science at the same time. From these circumstances were drawn several conclusions important for methodology: The distinction of social phenomena compared to natural phenomena was established by asserting the indeterminism of human behavior. One expects to find room for free will where there is no determination through causes or laws. The psychologist Münsterberg and the economist Stammler maintain, for example, that occurrences in nature are characterized by cause-effect relationships, where the present determines the future, while human behavior is characterized by means-ends relationships where the future determines the present[25]. However, the determinate course of human activity does not encroach upon freedom. Necessity as cause, and freedom as causelessness are the wrong alternatives. Rather, we may never consciously pursue a given purpose unless we know and use natural laws concerning means-ends relationships. Human actions are certainly also determined by free will which represents one factor among many other determinants[26].

It is sometimes stated that the social sciences are not about causal relationships, but rather about relationships of meanings. Natural phenomena are to be explained, social relationships, on the other hand, are to be understood. This point of view lead - in particular subsequent to Dilthey - to an independent development in the social sciences which is still active today and is commonly referred to as "historicism". It holds the view that processes having to do with human actions are unique. One is altogether opposed to the establishment of general theories for the explanation of social phenomena[27]. However, in each empirical science the facts are always unique in their full concreteness. The more precise the observation, the smaller the chance of finding two exactly equal objects. This "uniqueness" does not make the natural sciences impossible. Why then should it call in question the social sciences?

The assertion that laws basically different from natural laws matter in human behavior, i. e. relationships involving meanings, is hardly maintained any more today[28]; at best the category of meaning serves as a heuristic means of understanding behavioral relationships, e. g. in the writings of Max Weber[29].

Finally the thesis is often proposed that the social sciences cannot be practiced in a value-free manner, i. e. that in contrast to the natural sciences they cannot avoid containing value judgement, since humans have to orient their actions with respect to values. Max Weber poses the problem explicitly[30]; he asks whether it is proper for the experiential sciences to state "objective" value judgements. He formulates the principle of "value-freeness" which applies to all empirical sciences and which has lead to the so-called value judgement controversy[31].

It is absolutely necessary to consider three facts in this connection[32] (1) Values are social factors. They belong into the object range of the social sciences. (2) No scientific research is "value-free" in the sense that it is without preconditions. Interests and decisions are reflected in the selection of the material to be studied and in the problem definition. (3) The task of an empirical science is the understanding of reality. It contains only cognitive statements informing about the possibilities. Valuations are not required[33]. A value-free, empirically rich social science theory has much wider applicability than generally assumed. On the basis of the identity of the logical structure a theory can analytically be transformed into a technology. A technology in this sense does not have a prescriptive character. It merely informs about the possible paths of actions and their consequences, and answers e. g. to the question by what means a certain goal could be reached. In this respect there is no difference between the natural and the social sciences.

A large part of more recent attempts to construct a unity of the empirical sciences - in particular on the part of the social sciences - originates from so-called critical rationalism which is connected in particular with the works of Popper and Albert[34]. Critical rationalism tackles in particular the problems of dogmatism, and the value and ideology problems. The method of the critical test is based on the fact that all thinking and acting is subject to the possibility of error. The best way of approaching the truth consists of subjecting hypotheses to the possibility of failure and of making problem-solving procedures and results available for critical discussion. The problem of the determination of mental processes by physical reality[35] can be overcome with this procedure also: Despite the value base of science - consisting of the total socio-cultural background - a rational decision for certain hypotheses is possible, i. e. on the basis of the fact that they proved themselves in reality. Even those decisions are temporary and open for criticism, however. On the other hand, the decision in favor of rationality is a moral decision. But even this "meta"decision can be rationalized by

weighing the consequences. The "value-freeness" of social science hypothesis systems does not imply neutrality of the science as a whole: in the
social sciences the interaction between researcher and research object
is particularly great.

Recent attempts at establishing a unity of the empirical sciences rest on
the conception that processes in the physical, organic, and societal area can
be understood as information and communication processes within more
or less complex systems. This emphatically interdisciplinary orientation
refers to itself as "General Systems Theory"[36]. It assumes that all complex dynamic systems have similar properties, in particular that within
each system there are control and feedback processes guaranteeing the
continuous existence of a system.

Social science system theories

The conception of society as a dynamic, self-regulating system with
cybernetic structures appears more and more often in recent sociological
theory construction. As a result of the extensive specialization of science
the desire appeared for restoration of the unity of the sciences and lead
to a search for theories of general validity - a validity which would go
beyond individual domains of reality. These theories would be formulated
as precisely as possible and would contribute to interdisciplinary communication.

However, the systems concept is not new to sociology. Even in the beginnings of this science society is seen in analogy to biological organisms:
In the writings of Spencer[37] the elements of the societal system appear
just as functional for the whole of the system as the individual parts of
an organism. The analogy becomes problematical if the "goal" of the
biological organism, survival, is carried over to the social system.
Durkheim poses the specific question of how a social system differentiated
according to the requirements of the division of labor would maintain
social order. He finds that the normal functioning of a social organism
is based on the solidarity of its parts; the corresponding collective senti-
ment of individuals develops as a result of social norms, justice, and
morality[38].

Probably the most influential sociological systems theory is due to
Parsons[39]. He uses a new, more general systems concept. The system
now becomes the totality of interdependent parts; it maintains its identity
in a changing environment by regulating itself, integrating reluctant elements, and differentiating itself from its environment. By "social system"
Parsons means the persons involved, their actions, the social roles, the
institutions, and the social relationships. He distinguishes four systems
which interact in the social sphere:
1. the organic-physical system
2. the cultural system of values and norms
3. the social system as the behavior (on the basis of common interaction patterns) of individual social actors
4. the personality system molded by society.

The structure of the societal system appears as a relatively stable relational pattern among the system units, expressed e. g. by regular behavioral patterns or by role behavior. The maintainance of such a structure, i. e. the relative stability of a social system, can only be explained
by a combination of social mechanisms such as role differentiation and
social control, internalized socialized norms and sentiments. Thus each
system has to fulfill certain functional requirements in order to maintain
itself:
1. "pattern maintenance" in order to maintain its fundamental structure by controlling external perturbations
2. "adaptation" to a changing environment
3. "goal attainment" by setting and realizing values
4. "system integration" of the individual by socialization and social
   control.

In this structural-functional theory based on a systems view, Parsons
focusses on the properties of the total system and thus sets up a useful
counterpole with respect to the theories of analytical anatomism and
extreme individualism.

An important additional aspect of social action is introduced by Merton
who - on the basis of functional analysis of social systems for the explanation of social processes - considers not merely purposeful behavior, but
makes a distinction between the "manifest" and "latent" functions of behavior. Manifest functions are the consequences of behavior intended by
the members of a societal system, while latent functions consist of secondary consequences of behavior which are neither intended nor observed[40].

In the theory of Parsons social conflicts appear merely as perturbing
elements. The system functioning "normally" always brings itself back
to equilibrium and changes only very gradually[41]. This aspect is seen
by many sociologists as too one-sided. They view the stability of a social
system as an exception, and construct models of society based on social
conflict and social change. Dahrendorf for example sees society as a
dynamic power system in which the dichotomy of power roles leads to the
formation of interest groups which confront each other in constant conflict over the maintainance resp. change of the status quo[42].

Lewis Coser even turns Parsons' theory around: For him the social conflicts are by no means dysfunctional but - on the contrary - the major
reasons for the continuance of the social system. Only on the basis of conflicts can society renew its energies, search for "better solutions" for
its problems, achieve progress, avoid decadence and rigidity[43].

The theory of overall societal control of Etzioni introduces a further aspect: the conscious control of social change by the central authority of the
system which applies information and power in order to produce consensus and stability. This control capacity is the characteristic of an "active
society"[44].

Cybernetics has also found a direct entrance to political science. Karl W. Deutsch[45]-who describes the political system as a cybernetic process - does not address himself to a specific problem to begin with; he attempts to recover the elements of a self-regulating mechanism in the political system. Here also the system goal is the survival of the system in its essential structures; all social phenomena are processes of communication. A constantly changing information input - for example societal needs, or demands by the environment - requires control capacity with whose assistance the needs are satisfied, the system survives, and the dynamic control process is maintained. The required power which such a control authority must have at its disposal, is located in particular within the government of the political system which maintains a monopoly of lawful power application and value realization activity. The output, i.e. the response of the political system to internal and external demands, affects the input by a feedback process: decisions of the system also have an integrative function for the individuals and groups of the societal system, whose needs and values however are not permitted to significantly impair the realization of the overall goal. For this reason the control authority of the political system must possess the ability to control the social structure and the social learning behavior, to establish a common value background for society. In order to minimize blunders, the system must have the ability to store information and to learn new modes of behavior.

Likewise on a systems-theoretical base, David Easton[46] intends to find the fundamental dimensions of all political systems. Not only does he attempt to describe the political process with the aid of cybernetic concepts, he also wants to explain the behavior of members of the political system in these terms. Following Max Weber[47], Easton sees the power of the state as the major characteristic of politics; a power which finds its expression in the societal range of the decisions of the state, in its capability for imposing sanctions, and in the relevance of the goods whose distribution it controls authoritatively. The basic question concerning the reasons for survival, stability, and order of a political system in an unstable environment leads Easton to two necessary conditions essential to the existence of a social system: The political system must be able to distribute existing goods in such a fashion that the members of the system are satisfied to a certain degree. At the same time it has to produce mechanisms which will cause the members of the system to accept the decisions concerning distribution.

Using his cybernetic functional model Easton shows how the political system solves its tasks. Desires, aspirations, and demands of its members and of the environment act as inputs; they necessitate authoritative decisions of the system-immanent control authority. On the other hand, the input also contains support generated by the members for their system. Preconditions of support for the system are legitimacy and value consensus. The system now has to ensure that "demands" and "support" remain within an adequate ratio: the demands should not surpass a certain maxi-

mum (which must be determined empirically for a given system), since
otherwise the state will not be able to take care of them through its distribution decisions; on the other hand, the support by the members of the
system always must be large enough for the authoritative decisions to be
accepted. The output consists of the distribution measures of the state
which serve to satisfy the demands and to maintain the willingness to support the system. Feedback processes take place predominantly on the
basis of information acquisition and processing. The system needs information concerning the existing desires and demands, the supporting measures, and the state of the system, in order to react, to decide, and to
anticipate potential problems.

The theoretical approaches put forward thus far are of a relatively abstract character. The cybernetic description of society initially lead to
merely a novel frame of orientation for social science analysis. Still
missing is the specification of hypotheses formulated and empirically
validated on the basis of a system model; hypotheses which could then be
used to explain the phenomena taking place in the domain of social systems. The systems theories presented do not at all suffice as a base for
the simulation of social systems.

Theories of social psychology

It seems important at this point to discuss two more problems specific
to the social sciences. In the domain of human behavior there are only
very limited possibilities for experiments. In particular in larger social
units, e. g. large groups, masses, or entire nations it is hardly possible
to carry out specific and systematic experiments. On the other hand the
number of combinatorial possibilities and, accordingly, the "uniqueness"
of historical situations increases with the multiplicity of factors. Accordingly the possibilities of comparing such situations with each other are
limited. Apart from the comparison of historical data already collected,
the planning of studies of intercultural comparison is problematical. Not
only is it necessary to consider language barriers; in addition there are
in particular differing indicators for one and the same variable[48]. These
difficulties have lead to the fact that so far mainly "quasi theories"[49] have
been developed in the social sciences which are valid only for certain
space-time domains limited to given historic-cultural contexts. For obvious reasons, experiments are performed especially in social psychology,
mostly with small groups and individuals. For this reason "individualistic"
theories are better developed than others[50]. By contrast, other approaches
dealing with larger aggregates[51] can hardly be classified as theories; i.e.
consistent and comprehensive systems of hypotheses which could compete
with each other in the sense of the paradigm do not exist here[52]. A second
problem is connected to this aspect: the so-called reduction problem.

Many writers doubt whether theories which apply to individuals are
equally applicable to entities such as groups, organizations, states. In

this connection it is maintained that social entities have characteristics
which cannot be determined on the basis of analysis of the characteristics of individuals. On the other hand, the physical relationships of solid
bodies can be identified and analyzed without considering the structure
of the bodies to the smallest detail. In general it is considered to be
problematical to transfer these conceptions to the social domain. However, there is much to be said for a wider application of the theories
(mostly psychological) available today. Naturally even an "individualistic"
theory considers relational characteristics; the individual is not put into
empty space. In addition, the principles used in an explanation could well
be of a psychological nature, while the constraints represent social conditions. One merely needs for this rules linking sociological and psychological concepts. Several social theoreticians have shown that such linkage
rules can be determined[53]. In this manner it seems possible to achieve
scientific progress by testing a general theory by deduction of a wide range
of hypotheses in all domains of the social sciences[54]. The proper definition and measurement of the collective characteristics however (e. g. of
the behavior or attitudes of a group or a nation) remain problematical[55].

As a result of the development of systems analysis and computer technology, one gradually begins today to alleviate the shortage of possibilities
for experimentation as well as the lack of precision of social science theories. Connected with the reformulation of verbal theories and hypotheses
into a formal language such as mathematics is the compulsion for precision and logical consistency of the hypotheses. It is possible to experiment
with the aid of computer simulation and to obtain results which could
hardly ever be achieved by the traditional methods of empirical social
research: questionnaires, observation, laboratory and field experiments,
etc.[56].

The wide-spread opposition against this "systems method" can be partially
explained as a result of the conception that social science theories cannot
be quantified because they contain concepts such as "value", "emotion",
"social expectation", etc. This is a misinterpretation of mathematics.
Abstract mathematical relationships do not have to be of a quantitative
nature[57]. The numerical description of social facts depends in particular on the measurement instrument used. Another reason is the fact that
the traditional system theories of Parsons, Easton, Deutsch and others
are extremely abstract and are mainly of heuristic value; they are far
from representing models which could be used for simulations.

Balance and dissonance theories, which are already well-confirmed in
social psychology, basically also derive from a systems concept. Here
the system consists of the perception field of a person; its elements are
other persons or objects as perceived by the person. Gestalt-psychology[58]
on which these balance-theoretical approaches are based, is a widespread
concept in social psychology. One proceeds from the assumption that an
individual recognizes in his perception the environment as being orga-

nized in patterns which may be experienced as either pleasant or unpleasant. Pleasant patterns are simple, rounded, and subjectively satisfying. The individual searches for pleasant patterns and directs his actions to change unpleasant situations into pleasant ones. According to the balance theories of Heider[59] and Newcomb[60], a system is well-balanced in the perception of a person when there exists a positive relationship between positively valued elements, resp. a negative relationship between negatively valued elements. In the case of two persons and an object, a well-balanced system would appear as follows

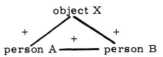

If person A believes that person B values object X negatively, the system is unbalanced, and person A will attempt to change the relationship in order to obtain an equilibrium:

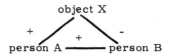

Person A has the following possibilities: Object X is henceforth valued negatively, or person B is valued negatively, or person B is persuaded to change its opinion with respect to object X[61].

In reality the net of relationships between elements of perception is naturally significantly more complex. Each element belongs to a multitude of systems; if one valuation is changed, other systems may become unbalanced. A corresponding generalization of the balancing concept has been worked out by Cartwright and Harary[62] on the basis of linear graph theory.

Of all social-psychological balance theories, Festinger's theory of cognitive dissonance[63] has the greatest importance. It has already been tested in numerous empirical studies, and has been validated in many cases.

According to the theory of cognitive dissonance either an irrelevant or a relevant relationship may exist between cognitive elements. An irrelevant relationship exists whenever there is no connection between the elements. A relevant relationship may be consonant or dissonant. Consonance exists whenever one element logically follows from another. Dissonance exists whenever the contrary of one element follows from the other. The set of all cognitions of a subject establish his "life space". Cognitive dissonance may appear in three different situations: Following a decision, following behavior based on coercion or reward which contradicts the subject's attitudes, or following desired, forced, or accidental receipt of new information which is incompatible with previous cognitions. The resulting dissonance causes a pressure to remove the dissonance and to avoid further dissonance. A reduction of this dissonance may result from a change of one or several cognitions; generally a change in attitudes results. However, reduction of dissonance is also made possible by a reduction of the significance of dissonant elements or by addition of new cognitions.

Following a choice between positive alternatives there is always dissonance. In the cognitive process taking place during and after the decision, the actor considers the positive and negative aspects of the decision; in order to maintain, or obtain a subjective equilibrium he has to revalue the positive aspects upward, and the negative aspects downward. The magnitude of the dissonance, and simultaneously the degree of subsequent change in attitudes depend on the importance of the decision, on the attraction of the alternative rejected, and on the similarity of the alternatives available for selection. A decision situation exists even for forced compliance, as coercion also implies a decision for the more favorable alternative. In cases of forced compliance the following rules applies: the smaller the coercion, the larger the dissonance. As long as there is no consent, dissonance increases with increasing coercion. The maximum dissonance occurs whenever the pressure just suffices to cause a behavior contrary to one's own attitude. The larger the pressure was, the smaller the dissonance is following consent, since the behavior can now more readily be justified[64]. Dissonance as a consequence of new information results from anticipation of the resulting unpleasant state of stress. Following a decision, one searches for consonant information and ignores dissonant information.

Of the numerous attempts to reformulate the theory of cognitive dissonance[65], the theory of cognitive hypotheses of Irle appears of particular relevance for the simulation of social systems[66]. Irle assumes the existence of subjective hypotheses concerning the relationships between cognitive elements; these hypotheses explain the joint appearance of these elements. This theoretical approach is concerned with a broadening of the theory of cognitive dissonance from behavioral decisions to decisions concerning elements of knowledge. Cognitive consonance exists whenever the appearance of two cognitions at a fixed point in space and time can be explained by a subjective hypothesis. By contrast, cognitive dissonance exists whenever the joint appearance of two elements cannot be explained by a hypothesis, or whenever an event contradicts an existing hypothesis. Usually the cognition appears in more than one hypothesis; the change of one hypothesis thus requires changes in other hypotheses. The same is true for the resistance of a hypothesis to change, since a hypothesis usually is related to several other hypotheses in a cognitive relationship, i.e. in a "theory"[67].

Likewise, a large portion of the theories of social perception - which explain information distortion - can be reduced to gestalt-psychological concepts in general, and to the hypothesis approach in particular. The subjective tendency for the balance of cognitions results in a defense of existing hypotheses against discrepant information. Thus the hypotheses influence the type and extent of perceptions, while the perceptions in turn determine the hypotheses[68].

Finally, brief mention will be made of two important aspects of social psychology which must by all means be taken into account in simulations of human behavior: learning behavior on the one hand, and the sociali- zation process on the other.

The social-psychological learning theories intend to explain behavior on the basis of previous experience, where behavior is understood as a res- ponse to certain stimuli. In the theory of "classical conditioning"[69] innate stimulus-response sequences are assumed. Learning merely consists in the coupling of a new stimulus to an existing one, which will now also evoke the original response. Thus a new stimulus-response association is obtained, which however is less durable than the unconditional innate sequence. Conditioning theory describes pure reflex behavior not coupled to any cognitive processes[70]. This behavioral point of view is also held by Skinner and Hull in their reinforcement theory which is of great signi- ficance to recent sociological behavioral research[71]. According to this theory of "instrumental conditioning", the frequency of a response, resp. the probability of its occurence depends on whether the response is followed by reward or punishment. By trial and error in the sense of reward and punishment, learning takes place as a gradual adaptation to "successful" behavior. The theory also explains the emergence of wants which - as neutral stimuli - are associated with a rewarded response, and of "gene- ralized reinforcers" which - again as stimuli - are coupled to a multitude of different rewards.

A gestalt-psychological point of view has been the starting point of theories explaining learning on the basis of cognitive processes such as understand- ing of relationships. Following Miller and Dolland as well as Bandura and Walters, learning by way of imitation and observation requires the avail- ability of a model, and the cognitive storage of behavioral modes about which the learner has been informed. As in other learning theories, learn- ing is here seen as being controlled by the comparison of expectations and achieved results: successes operate as positive, failures as negative reinforcements. In cognitive learning theories, learning however does not merely find expression in behavior, but also in attitude changes[72].

Closely connected to the aspect of learning is socialization as integration of the individual into society, and adaptation to its norms and behavioral patterns. However, in this area so far only isolated hypotheses have been put forth; consistent theoretical systems are still lacking. It is definitely possible to accommodate socialization as a special process of social learn- ing into the general approaches of learning theory[73].

Sociological behavioral theories

Based on social-psychological and especially learning-theoretical approaches, interaction theories[74] develop a model of social behavior as exchange. Following Homans[74], exchange obeys the economic principle of profit maximization: The occurence of a certain behavior becomes probable only if the benefit resulting from the behavior is greater than the cost. Rewards and punishments are handed out by other individuals or by the collectivity.

As plausible as this theory appears, it does have several deficiencies: The object of Homans' studies is the behavior of individuals in direct contact with each other. In addition, merely small groups with closed system relationships are studied.

Blau in his macrosociological exchange theory[75] attempts to explain social power and standardization processes with the help of the interaction approach: Each individual does indeed expect rewards for his actions, however, neither their appearance nor their magnitude are precisely determinable. This uncertainty is reduced by social standardization, by a process of generalization of the reward expectations of certain actions. An additional social stabilization results from the fact that a certain imbalance of the distribution of resources leads to an inequality in the distribution of rewards. However, not always does the individual commanding the greater amount of resources receive the higher rewards; rather, these individuals in particular are in a position to pass out more rewards than they themselves receive. By this process they acquire esteem, high rank, and power. Such responses, which could be termed social recognition or approval, are rewarding as well[76].

Conflict research

A central category in sociology is the concept of social role. Human behavior is regulated by social norms which relate to the individual as occupant of a certain social position. Connected with the expectations the social environment has of a certain role, is a certain assurance with respect to the sequence of actions and responses; at the same time these expectations represent the "annoying fact of society"[77] by forcing the individual to adapt to the social norms and role expectations. The important problem accompanying such a role assignment is the role conflict arising whenever a person is subjected to contradictory expectations on account of his occupying several roles simultaneously. So far a specific role theory does not exist in sociology; approaches to date are concerned with descriptions and typifications[78].

Sociological conflict research in addition is concerned with two different forms of conflict: class struggle and international conflict. Since Marx published his theories[79], attempts have been made to explain societal

conflict by differences of ownership. These differences are explained by
the class of capital owners exploiting the unpropertied classes, which can
only sell their labor on the capitalistic market. In view of the fact that
political conflict exists as well in non-capitalist societies, this theory as
an exclusive explanation of social conflicts cannot be maintained. Dahrendorf has formulated a theory of conflict which starts from the assumption
that authority is the source of social conflict[80]. The holders of power
positions establish norms, distribute sanctions and goods, and in this way
generate a social structure to which the governed are forced to adapt.
The resulting structural and adaptation problems lead to conflicts resulting in constant social change in turn.

The study of international conflict focusses, in addition to the sociology
of authority, also on the points of view of interest group politics. Recent
critical peace and conflict research[81] moves the control and avoidance
of conflict to the foreground. To this end the dynamic processes of
armament, of threats, of the application of force, of the international
economic interconnections, and of the problems of the Third World are
studied in particular. This research area uses the results of social-
psychological aggression and participation research. Its declared goal
is the accomplishment of a constructive contribution with respect to
strategies for the peaceful solution of conflict.

Research on pluralism and elites

Approaches to a theory of interest groups are based on a pluralistic conception of society: One stresses the group structure of a political system
- political decisions are seen as the results of negotiations between competing social groups having different interests[82]. Such interest groups
have in modern complex societies become essential components of the
political infrastructure as a result of the differentiation of power and of
the functions of the state. With the exception of a general theory of political group behavior[83], and a functional coalition theory[84], both of which
are formulated on a very abstract level, there are merely a multitude of
empirical case studies on individual phenomena within this wide field[85].
So far it has been possible to identify individual factors which are important for the influence of interest groups on political decisions such as:
type of goals, group size, degree of organization, internal power structure, and fiscal politics. However, a theory of interest groups in the
sense of a system of coherent and consistent hypotheses has so far not
been developed.

Many sociologists and political scientists do not share the view that the
political and societal process is the result of group struggles. These
researchers rather are of the opinion that history is shaped by elites.
Some of their theories of elites maintain the existence of a single power
elite composed of the influential persons of all areas of societal relevance; this elite is characterized by common interests such as the

acquisition and maintenance of power[86]. Other theoreticians of elites
speak of competing elites with differing value systems[87], in particular
in the context of recent discussions of the theory of democracy. This concept today finds more support as well as more empirical evidence. Most
of the more recent studies of elites are concerned with the description
and typification of influential persons; they attempt to determine the origins of their socialization, attitudes, and recruitment, and to study the
common aspects and the relationships between different elites within a
system, as well as differences between democratic and totalitarian states,
and between industrially highly developed and less developed states.

Organization sociology

Organization theory is to be mentioned as a further contribution of sociology to the simulation of societal systems. It has been developed within
the past two decades in particular in American social research. Organization means the cooperation of numerous individuals who aspire to a
common goal. The sociology of organization considers the structure of
social entities, the societal processes, the conscious, "organized", and
unconscious actions. In this area one concentrates on the construction of
typologies and on the classification of organizations according to the purpose and structure. As a whole, the approach of organization theory rests
almost exclusively on the method of systems analysis, while focussing on
problems of self-preservation, of functional proficiency, and of the efficiency of organizations[88].

Social indicators and the quality of life

In the course of the implementation of the simulation of social systems
on the basis of sociological and social-psychological theories and theoretical approaches a further problem presents itself: i.e. the problem of
operationalization. There exist refined measurement techniques in the
natural sciences; the possibility of experimentation in the object domain
of the natural sciences furthermore allows an intensive verification of
measurement instruments and extensive validation of the results. By contrast, the object domain of the social sciences is much less accessible to
measurements.

In the societal domain measurements are concentrated in the economic
area. As a result there exist excellent economic statistics, which however usually represent the social area unidimensionally by measuring e.
g. prosperity in terms of the gross national product. However, for the
simulation of societal behavior the use of merely econometric data does
not suffice. Major motives of socio-political action are the goal and
value conceptions of individual citizens as well as of the political decision-
makers. Aspiration levels develop for all societal concerns; these aspiration levels are constantly compared to the actual system state. It is
the task of political decision-makers to solve the existing political and
social problems. To this end the proper means have to be determined

in order to obtain a more or less optimal solution which takes into account all socially relevant goals as far as possible. Such a procedure requires a knowledge of the relationships between the different social areas.

A significant contribution to the solution of the measurement problems is due to a more recent development in social research: social indicator research. More and more the "quality of life" is no longer measured in terms of prosperity, but rather in terms of several dimensions. Social indicator systems are set up for this purpose; they are collected in the form of social reports containing extensive information concerning the state of a given society from a social point of view[89]. Social indicators not only serve to describe social facts, they also facilitate the assessment of the current system state by cost-benefit analysis, i. e. by presenting a "social account" in analogy to national economic accounts. The setting-up of indicator time series permits the registration of development trends and of social change. In this way the instrument of the social indicator may assist in foreseeing crises and in tackling societal problems already in early states of development.

Social indicators cannot be limited to public statistics, but should also include the subjective opinions of the population, of decision-makers, and of groups of social relevance (professions, unions, age groups, etc.), concerning their standard of living, their satisfaction, their needs and desires, their goals and aspirations, the supply of public goods and social services, and many other aspects. More and more the view prevails that the concept of "quality of life" should not merely contain aspects measurable by official statistics, but must also contain subjective assessments. This implies the necessity for survey results covering the area of "social satisfaction", which would also allow the setting up of time series in order to cover the whole spectrum of tasks of social indicators research[90].

Social indicators research is still in its infancy. Results so far have produced valuable experiences concerning the measurement of national goals, and of individual values and the possibilities of state analysis in the social domain. These data are urgently required for the simulation of social systems in order to realize the application of existing theoretical approaches.

Systems theory

The framework for the simulation of societal systems must be an applicable systems theory whose structural elements correspond to those of social reality. Starting with von Bertalanffy, Ashby, von Neumann, Wiener[91], an extensive amount of literature has been generated under the general headings of 'systems theory', 'systems science', 'cybernetics', etc. To a large part this literature is characterized by a high degree of abstractness, a complex verbal description which cannot be translated into operational terms (and therefore cannot be tested), and generally only a limited applicability (if any) to problems of the real world. Following N. Müller[92] we divide the systems literature roughly into three categories, whose respective boundaries are naturally fuzzy: "metascientific" systems theory, "functionalist" systems theory, and "formalized" systems theory (the labels are ours). As representatives of the first category we may list the proponents of "General Systems Theory", in particular von Bertalanffy, Ashby, Klir, and Rapoport[93]. Under the second category we may count writers like Parsons, Deutsch, Luhmann, Narr and Naschold[94], all of whom have studied social processes within a systems-theoretical framework. With regard to the ability of being translated into operational terms, the third category is of particular interest to us. It is characterized by the aspect of analysis in state space (see e. g. Zadeh and Mesarovic[95]). This particular research category has significantly enlarged the base for the scientific analysis of technical systems by making full use of mathematical tools as well as the digital computer. The concepts of state space analysis are fully transferable to nontechnical systems as well; they will certainly play a constantly increasing role in the analysis of societal systems.

A societal system consists of a very large number of state variables, whose number and interconnections in addition undergo constant change. The state variables may be deterministic, probabilistic or stochastic, continuous or discrete, exact or fuzzy, numerical or symbolic. The state variables of the causal system and of the system environment are (except for the symbolic environment) mainly of a quantitative-numerical nature, while the state variables of the cognitive processes taking place in the decision stratum and the normative stratum are mainly of a symbolic and nonnumerical nature. For this reason there are considerable differences between the causal system and the cognitive system with regard to the systems-theoretical approach, the mathematical description, and the simulation methods to be applied.

Mathematics

There is hardly an area of mathematics which has not found - or could not find - application to the description of societal systems. An impression can be gained from the relevant literature[96]. We cannot go into details here, but would merely like to point out the fact that the mathematical tools are in certain regards not sufficiently well developed to map certain structures appearing in reality. This is the case in particular in the area of cognitive processes. Zadeh was the first to point to this deficiency and to originate "fuzzy systems theory" in response. Since its inception, several hundred publications have appeared in this new field[97]. Important in this connection are also some new developments of mathematical linguistics[98] and the approaches of the statement and predicate calculus and of normative and deontic logic[99]. All of these approaches are concerned with the processing of fuzzy numerical, linguistic, or symbolic information of the kind appearing in cognitive processes. Im-

portant applications are problem-solving processes and decision-making:
compare e. g. mental processes required for a decision concerning the
question "Sould I take an umbrella today, or shouldn't I? ". We will return
to these questions when we discuss the simulation of cognitive processes;
at this point we merely wish to present a brief outline of the approach to
fuzzy analysis, as it will most certainly gain considerable importance in
the future.

A key feature of fuzzy analysis is the membership function, i. e. the degree of membership of a certain object in a given set. While classical
mathematical analysis recognizes exclusively the true or false, the either-
or, apples or oranges, i. e. memberships of either 0 or 1, fuzzy analysis
allows for all intermediate values in addition. As an example, the membership in a set "young" of a two-year old is perhaps 1. 0, that of a thirty-
year old 0. 6, and that of an eighty-year old 0. 0. Qualifiers such as "very"$_{100}$
or "not very" may increase resp. decrease this membership. Zadeh^{100}
is particularly interested in the representation of fuzzy algorithms which
can be used for the definition of complex fuzzy concepts (as e. g. "oval",
"recession"); for the transmittal of instruction (e. g. to direct a blind
person safely across a room filled with obstacles); or for problem-solving (e. g. the behavior of a driver at an intersection). It is obvious that
these approaches are of considerable relevance to the simulation of the
behavior of individual or social actors.

Simulation approaches

We keep our earlier distinction of environment, causal stratum, decision
stratum, and normative stratum, but will now combine - on account of the
close relationship of the simulation tasks involved - the first two (with the
exception of the symbolic environment) under the heading "material processes", the latter two under the heading "cognitive processes" (we include here also the symbolic environment). The simulation of material
processes then implies in particular the simulation of - in principle -
directly observable and objectively quantifiable processes. By contrast,
cognitive processes consist of mostly only indirectly observable and
usually - at best - only subjectively quantifiable processes; often these
processes consist exclusively of symbol or concept processing. Accordingly, the simulation approaches differ widely.

In our opinion the successful simulation of societal processes requires the
integrated description of the material a n d of the cognitive processes
within and around the (idealized) actor involved. The description of causal
system and environment to the neglect of cognitive processes - so far almost exclusively practiced - is just as incomplete as the representation
of cognitive processes without reference to the dynamics of the material
system. Although the necessity of this integration is increasingly recog-
nized^{101} there are at present hardly any attempts of an integrated approach.
The realization of integrated approaches is being hampered by insufficient

knowledge of the cognitive processes of problem-solving, decision, and normative change. By contrast, there are fewer open questions concerning the simulation of material systems. We will deal with these first.

The simulation approaches must correspond to the diversity of material systems and simulation tasks: there cannot be a single standard approach. Compilations of simulation projects[102] demonstrate the exceedingly broad spectrum of possible approaches. The technological, biological, ecological, economic, organizational, geographical, infrastructural etc. components of societal systems have so far been modelled in deterministic, probabilistic and stochastic, continuous and discrete, quantitative and qualitative approaches. It seems to make little sense to introduce a classification according to these characteristics: in order to accomplish their task, larger models often have to be a combination of submodels each representing a very different simulation approach. The systems analyst advocating a standard approach is out of place in social systems analysis.

Less broad is the spectrum of possible simulation approaches for the representation of cognitive processes. In this case one deals in particular, as already mentioned, with processes of perception, of changes in memory content, of problem-solving, of assessment, of decision, of deduction and induction. Numerical and nonnumerical symbolic information is analyzed, combined, aggregated, changed, stored, recalled, forgotten, concatenated in a free manner or in a goal-oriented fashion, deduced, filtered, selectively reinforced or attenuated, etc.

In distinguishing three major groups of simulation approaches we follow the classification of Harbordt[103]:

    I - Aggregative microanalytic models
    II - Macroanalytic models
    III - Qualitative models.

Models of material systems generally fall under categories I and II, while models of cognitive systems usually belong to category III. In order to illustrate the differences between the three model types we here cite their characteristics and mention some characteristic simulation examples.

Characteristics of aggregative microanalytic models[104]:

"(1) The system to be simulated is decomposed into elements of one or several classes. The state of the elements is described by constants and variables ("state variables").

  (2) On the basis of empirical knowledge or hypothetical assumptions, rules are formulated for the behavior of the elements. These may be in the form of deterministic functions, probability functions, or they may be expressed directly in the form of logic and arithmetic statements relating the constants and state variables of the elements. These rules constitute the core of the model.

48

(3) The ordering of the rules defines one or several processes which the elements undergo individually. In the process, their state variables change as functions of the state of other elements, their own individual state, as well as perhaps the state of exogeneous variables.
(4) The simulation run is characterized by the computer working through the elements in sequence: A test is applied to each element in order to determine whether according to the rules, state changes take place. These changes are determined, and the new state is stored for the next computational pass. The pass is completed as soon as all elements have been processed. In this quasi "atomistic" fashion the evolving state of the total system is projected by way of a series of cyclical repetitions of the passes.
(5) The output variables are aggregated quantities: For certain element state variables of interest, statistical measures such as sum or average over all elements of a given class are computed."

Examples of this approach are simulations of the geographical spread of agricultural innovations[105], restructuring of urban settlements[106], changes in population structure[107], socialization[108], and influence on voting behavior through communication[109]. Further examples are found in e. g. Harbordt[110].

Characteristics of macroanalytical models[111]:

"(1) The system to be simulated is decomposed into aggregated variables. These are not related to the individual system elements - as are the variables of the first type - but they rather describe a characteristic of the total system. One can differentiate between (flow) rate and level variables, i.e. their values are given with reference to certain points in time, resp. time periods.
(2) Generally the variables are related to each other through equations, or perhaps inequalities representing the interconnections between them.
(3) The core of the model is represented by the concatenation of these equations; it represents - more or less approximately - the structure of the real systems or processes.
(4) The simulation sequence results from successive computation of the equations following the input of the required initial values for the endogenous variables as well as the current values of the exogeneous variables. A model pass (simulation cycle) is completed whenever all equations and consequently the values of all endogenous variables, have been computed. A new cycle follows, based on the computed values and on the exogeneous values. The succession of cycles is interpreted as progression along the time axis; consequently in this type of simulation the system state is also projected over time. The repeated solution of the system of equations constituting the model represents the time path of system development.

(5) The model output consists of time series for certain variables which
have been selected as "output variables" during the model construction, or in response to the requirements of the simulation task."

Typical examples of this approach are the world models of Forrester,
Meadows, and Mesarovic and Pestel[112], econometric models[113], models
of production and sales[114], or models of the behavior of industrial enter-
prises[115], managers[116], or students[117].

Characteristics of qualitative models[118]:

"(1) By contrast to the two other types these models represent their subject in a nonnumerical fashion. The variables describe the real process, resp. the real system, not in terms of quantities, but rather
in qualitative categories. These are expressed using categorial
scales, and partially also ordinal scales.
(2) Since there are no quantities, there is no computation. Instead, the
qualitative variables are arranged in a hierarchy of lists, and their
processing consists of changes in the assignment to the different
lists, resp. in changes of rank-ordering on a list. This is accomplished by subroutines for sorting, ordering, storage, recall, comparison, and selection of qualitative information.
(3) The simulation run consists of an interlocking sequence of such subroutines.
(4) The output is composed neither of aggregated variables nor of time
series, but rather of the content of certain lists, i.e. of information
belonging to the same class on account of certain characteristics."

Interesting examples of this approach are e.g. the simulation of selective information processing in a crisis[119], of problem-solving behavior[120],
or of paranoid behavior[121]. This model category finds application in
particular for the simulation of cognitive processes.

The broad spectrum of simulation tasks in the area of societal systems
makes equally broad demands on the simulation languages; often these
demands are best met by special languages.

Simulation languages and user adaptation

The quantitative (numerical) and qualitative (nonnumerical, list-type)
data processing required by the different simulation approaches poses
differing demands on the programming language. Only broad-based general purpose languages such as ALGOL, PL/1, or (with certain restrictions) FORTRAN can cope with both tasks of numerical and list processing.

Today the model builder can almost always choose between several applicable languages which differ in the degree of their specialization. As a
general rule one may state that the more specialized a programming

language is, the more user convenience it will offer, at the expense of
flexibility of application. Highly specialized simulation languages may
permit the construction of more or less valid simulation models even
without much previous knowledge about modelling; however, they also
compel the user to force his model into a certain mold which will usually
not leave any margin for a more problem-adequate divergent description.
This problem is alleviated if the special programming language is fitted
with a "window" for a general purpose language, in order to allow the
insertion of subroutines better suited for the accomplishment of the given
task. Many of the special languages today are provided with this feature.
We shall here give only a brief survey of the most important languages
suited for simulation purposes.

General purpose languages are: ALGOL, FORTRAN, BASIC and PL/1.
The first two have the advantage that they can be used on practically all
existing small and large computers and are standardized to the point
where they are practically machine-independent[122].

Popular simulation languages for continuous systems are in particular
CSMP[123] and DYNAMO[124]; for both of these, versions exist offering
FORTRAN windows, resp. interactive operation (man-machine dialogue).
For the simulation of discrete systems the languages GPSS[125],
SIMSCRIPT[126], and SIMULA[127] are available, in particular. The first
two are based on FORTRAN, the latter one on ALGOL. As list-proces-
sing languages, different versions of LISP[128] enjoy considerable popu-
larity.

In some more recent developments attempts have been made to relieve
the model builder of routine tasks of the programming work in order to
enable him to concentrate fully on the construction of the model core
proper. The resulting special programming languages are really meta-
programs: programs which can generate certain types of programs. For
example, the meta-program MODEL BUILDER[129] employed by the
Mesarovic-Pestel system groups requires merely a listing of model core
equations in FORTRAN, the input of initial values, parameters, and time
series, and the specification of output variables. This approach reduces
the programming effort and attendant programming errors, and testing
and debugging times drastically, while providing the specified set of output variables in a form (numerical and graphical presentation) suitable
for technical reports. Another meta-program, GUIDE[130], produces a
completely interactive program given a model core in FORTRAN, and
information concerning the initial values, standard scenarios, and the
search hierarchies required for user access to input and output variables. GUIDE has been developed in particular in order to allow the in-
telligent use of simulation models by nonexperts. Another interesting
development representative of this trend is the model construction program GRIPS[131] which makes extensive use of the interactive graphic
facilities (light pen) of a minicomputer. In this approach the structure of

the system to be simulated is drawn on the display screen, the type of elements and of functional connections between the elements are selected using the light pen, initial values and exogeneous inputs are specified, and the program produces, after internally generating the proper model core equations and setting up the necessary simulation program, graphical displays of the results as well as a brief documentation on the printer.

These developments meet many of the demands formulated above; i.e. that methods must be developed which reduce the danger of technocratic misuse of simulation studies. The user should be able to work with methods with which he is familiar, using natural language and graphical represent- ation, in order to be able to concentrate on constructing the model proper. All routine programming should be taken over by the model builder program. In this manner the intervention of programming specialists can be avoided - provided the model construction programs are sufficiently well developed. Simulation can then be used as a tool for reflection, analysis, planning, and decision-making directly by the planner, the decision-maker, or other parties concerned.

The development of interactive model construction programs is aided by the fact that - independent of the simulation subject or the simulation ap- proach - the process of model construction always must proceed in the same standard sequence:
- determination of the quantities involved
- structural interconnection of the quantities
- distinction between variables, parameters, exogeneous and endogenous quantities, etc.
- determination of the relations between the quantities
- data input
- test runs, debugging, changes, validation
- experiments and solution of the given task.

Economics

The first attempts at a formalized description of a component area of societal systems - national economics - were made already several de- cades ago in economic science. An extensive arsenal of methods of sta-[132] tistical analysis and parameter estimation has been applied in this area. Nevertheless, the medium and longer range validity of conventional eco- nometric models is quite unsatisfactory. At best, one could describe some of the national econometric models[133] used for short term economic pro- jections as moderately successful. However, these models have to be brought up to date every three to six months by new parameter estimations.

The only relatively modest successes of the systems description in econo- mics can be partially adduced to the facts that (1) here one has almost exclusively concentrated on precise parameter estimation while main- taining an inadequate model structure, and that (2) little attention was focussed on the cybernetic character of the economic system, and on the cognitive processes determining its response. Early suggestions to this effect[134] went practically unheeded. A survey of the development and a view of possibilities of improvement of econometric methods of analysis through application of the methods of classical control science is given by Pfeiffer[135]. We would however suggest going beyond these somewhat antiquated tools and employing the instruments of mathematical systems theory and modern control theory[136], which are better suited to the computerization of the analysis of large systems.

We shall briefly deal here with three approaches of economic science which have some importance for the analysis of societal systems: production function, behavioral equations, and input/output analysis.

The production function of macroeconomic analysis explains the gross national product as a function of production factors such as capital, labor, technical progress. On the basis of United States data between the years 1899 to 1922 Cobb and Douglas[137] determined a relationship between the gross national product Y, and the availability of labor L and capital K:

$$Y = c \, L^{3/4} \, K^{1/4}$$

Today this simple relationship no longer holds, and it has been necessary to introduce as an additional production factor a poorly defined "technical progress" (innovations, increases of productivity, knowhow, organization, technical improvements, etc.), which today is required to explain a considerable portion of the gross national product in this relationship[138]. More recently Gaspari and Millendorfer[139] have formulated a "general production function" and have validated it empirically for countries at very different stages of development. In contrast to the usual formulation as f (labor, capital, technical progress) this production function contains a structural factor (accounting for the efficiency of application of capital and education); a material factor (active capital stock per capita, determined by indicators of energy use); an immaterial factor (educational level, in terms of educated persons in the different categories relative to the total population; a time lag of 13 years is introduced in addition); and an index of mineral resources (resources mined per capita).

The behavioral equations of economics are meant to describe consumer behavior, investment behavior etc. on a macroeconomic level. The approach is identical to that used in the determination of production functions: variables having a possible influence are postulated first, and are connected to each other by addition or multiplication, using initially unspecified parameters; these parameters are then determined from available statistical time series. If a postulated influence is found not to be statistically significant, it is dropped from the equation. Examples may be found in Pfeiffer[140]; thus we find in this reference a relationship for private consumption C_t in the Federal Republic of Germany:

$$C_t = 8.272 + 0.803 \, YV_t + 0.0344 \, C_{t-1} \quad \text{(in millions of DM)}$$

where YV_t is the currently available income of private households, while C_{t-1} represents the level of consumption in the previous (6 month) period.

In contrast to these macroeconomic approaches input/output analysis[141] penetrates on a microeconomic level more deeply to the realities of the given system; it therefore is able to provide more detailed information, in particular with respect to structural change of the economic system. For a given year the coefficients a_{ij} of the input/output matrix indicate which amount of the production of economic sector i (in monetary units) moves into economic sector j as production input or into the final consumption sector j for consumption. The input/output matrix therefore represents - with a lower or higher degree of aggregation (depending on the task, the economic system is split into from 10 to several hundred sectors) - the interconnections and flows of products and services in the economic system. Evidently this is a structural representation of the system.

In view of the increasing importance of aspects of energy, resource, environmental protection, and employment policies, the representation of the economic system in terms of monetary flows alone is found to be deficient for the purposes of economic policy planning and decision-making. For this reason the Leontief approach has recently been applied by himself and other research groups[142] to other production factors such as energy, resources, and labor. Out of such studies one obtains the factor input for a given product or service category as a function of the given conditions of production. Consequences of energy or resource limitations or of structural change in the different sectors of the economy thus can be more easily determined by use of these "technological" models.

Decision theory

The simulation of societal systems requires knowledge about the mechanisms of the processes taking place within the systems. A description by behavioral functions "statistically validated" by use of historical data, as it is practiced in econometrics, is not sufficient; this merely represents an extrapolation of historical behavior. Often, however, minor quantitative differences in the initial situation lead to qualitatively different decisions and to corresponding behavior.

In the course of a decision the actor is required to choose between at least two, often several alternatives. A precondition for the choice is a comparison of the alternatives. This requires (1) an assessment of the consequences of each alternative, i.e. of the probable alternative system states following the occurrence of the alternative; (2) a comparison of these alternative probable system states; (3) a comparative evaluation of the alternative system states, which should at least permit the establishment of a rank-order. Decision theory deals with these issues[143]. In its terminology the decision process translates into (1) the determination of the

possible alternative system states resulting from a decision, and the
probability of their occurrence, by investigations using a formalized or
intuitive internal model of the actor and application of (often subjective)
probabilities; (2) mapping of the alternative system states on identical
sets of relevant decision criteria with usually differing criterion weights
(e. g. cost, security, feasibility) and comparison of the degree of satisfaction of each criterion; (3) mapping of the degree of satisfaction of each
criterion dimension on a common utility dimension in order to finally allow the comparison of alternatives by means of their respective utilities.
In the case where more than one decision criterion has to be considered
one speaks of multiple criterion decision-making.

We will deal here briefly with the concepts: internal model, risk, uncertainty, subjective probability, decision criterion, weighting, and utility.
All of these concepts have subjective elements: models are subject to the
problems of subjectivity caused by the reduction of complexity; risks,
uncertainties, and subjective probabilities can only be given in a subjective fashion on account of our lack of knowledge of the future (even their
substantiation by extensive series of empirical data requires the subjective conclusion that the same circumstances will apply in the future); the
choice of decision criteria and of their relative weights is of a subjective
nature; utilities can only be determined subjectively. "Objective" decision-making is a fiction; at best one may be able to agree intersubjective-
ly on the application of identical criteria - as happens all the time in the
course of human interaction.

The internal model of the actor is his intuitive or formalized representation and interpretation of reality as it enters into the decision-making
process. As a consequence, the actor belongs to the classe of systems
with internal model[144]. The quality of the decision obviously depends to
a great degree on the validity of the internal model.

In decision theory a distinction is made between decisions under certainty,
decisions under risk (in this case the probability distributions of the states
are known), and decisions under uncertainty (in this case the probability
distributions are unknown). The methods for decision under certainty are
relatively well developed. We may mention branch-and-bound methods,
search algorithms, and heuristic optimization[145]. In each case the task
is the minimization of an objective function. In multistage decisions
Bellman's dynamic programming is the most common method.

Important components of the theory of decision under risk are Bayes'
decision criterion and Bayes' method for the improvement of poorly
known probabilities. Bayes' decision criterion[146] requires the selection
- from a set of given strategies - of the strategy minimizing the expected
risk. The application of the strategy requires a knowledge of the probability distributions of the state parameters. However, these are rarely
known completely. With the help of Bayes' method[147], distributions which

are initially only incompletely known or even estimated can be subsequently improved by information becoming available as the decision process evolves. It may be necessary to use subjective probabilities exclusively. There are also other possibilities[148]

In decisions under uncertainty the probability distributions are unknown; the process has to make do without them. A number of decision rules have been formulated for this situation; all roughly according to the maxim: "The less you know about a situation, the more careful you should be!"[149] The best known - although the most pessimistic and unrealistic (the state of knowledge of the decision-maker is not considered) - of these rules is the minimax rule due to Wald[150] which may be formulated as follows: "The decision-maker should act as if that state of the world most unfavorable to him were the true state of the world (min). He then should try to make the best of this unfavorable state (max)."[151]

These decision rules presuppose neutrality of the world vis-a-vis the decision-maker. The conditions change when there are one or more additional decision-makers who may influence the outcome. This entirely different situation is the subject of game theory[152].

The outcome of a decision is to a significant degree a function of the decision criteria which were applied, and of their respective weights. The set of decision criteria permits an assessment of the likely system state with respect to those variables (or derived quantities) which are of particular importance to the decision-maker. Often several criteria have to be considered simultaneously in a decision (e.g. cost, security, resource availability, time spent, etc.). In order to facilitate a decision, the relative weights of the decision criteria have to be known in a multiple criteria decision process; more on this below. The dominant decision criteria of a system derive from the requirement of securing its ability to function properly. As a result, an actor has to orient his decisions in particular with reference to dimensions such as "physical needs", "security", "freedom of action", "adaptivity", and "efficiency of control"[153].

In order to be able to compare alternatives in a multiple criteria decision process, it is necessary to map the degree of satisfaction of the different criteria onto a common dimension ("utility" or "disutility"; "satisfaction" or "dissatisfaction"[154], or similar concepts). Only in this way does it become possible to compare for example a lowering of a pollutant emission with the cost of the pollution control equipment. Still, the application in a real situation is hardly ever straightforward: as soon as different interest groups or social actors are affected we run into difficult and unresolved problems of social choice[155].

The functional dependence between the physical level of a criteria dimension and the associated utility is the "utility function". Modern utility theory had its origins in the work of von Neumann and Morgenstern[156].

Utility functions can only be determined subjectively. Several procedures
have been developed for their determination which are based either on
interview techniques with direct or indirect questioning, or on the analysis of actions undertaken by the decision-maker[157]. Recently interactive
programs for the determination of utility functions find application[158].
Empirical studies have shown that decision-makers in general have remarkably smooth, consistent, and reproducible functions[159]. As soon
as the utility functions for all criteria dimensions are available, the utilities of different decision alternatives can be compared, and a preference
ordering can be established for the alternatives.

A survey of the different methods of multiple criteria decision analysis is
given by MacCrimmon[160]. He distinguishes in particular four approaches:
Weighting methods, elimination methods, methods of mathematical programming, and methods of spatial neighborhood. Weighting methods (to
which utility analysis belongs) use numerical preference calculations of
the criteria values and weightings of the criteria; the weighted preferences are combined to a single measure which then serves as a basis for
comparison with other alternatives. Elimination methods compare the
degree of criterion satisfaction of the different alternatives with respect
to each criterion. Alternatives which do not meet given standards are
eliminated. This approach is often found in natural decision processes;
a special case is Simon's "satisficing"[161] which is found also in biological
processes. Methods of mathematical programming use the apparatus of
linear programming or goal programming; recently also interactive methods are applied, in which the decision-maker iteratively approaches a
quasi-optimal solution by the trial-and-error specification of trade-offs[162].
The methods of spatial-neighborhood finally compare the geometric representation of the alternatives in state space with the representation of
the ideal state; the distance between the alternatives and the ideal is quantified by an appropriate measure. The alternative having the smaller measure of distance is preferred.

Decision theory assumes in general that the alternatives have been developed and merely require comparison and evaluation (exception: methods
of mathematical programming, where the optimal alternative is found
via the objective functions). Generally the development of viable alternatives differing from the status quo is in itself a cognitive accomplishment requiring a complex problem-solving process. In addition, the
change or (re)derivation of decision-relevant behavioral norms requires
a qualitatively different cognitive achievement, whose simulation requires
different tools. The study of problem-solving behavior, and related to it,
of artificial intelligence, has become a scientific area in itself.

Cognitive processes and system adaptation

Actors in societal systems are characterized by the fact that their behavior may change qualitatively if required by a given situation: a platoon
of soldiers encountering a raging river will not continue its march, but

will rather build a bridge; where a dictatorship becomes unbearable, even a "silent majority" will eventually produce revolutionaries. In a simulation, such qualitative changes can be preprogrammed by conditional statements. However, this approaches requires a consideration of all possible eventualities, allowing for all possible relevant influences and possible system states. This assumes a knowledge about the system which the model builder cannot have; at the time of the model construction it will normally not even be available within the system to be simulated. Merely the - in principle infinite - number of possible futures characterizes this approach as an absurdity. There remains as the sole alternative the possibility of deriving new behavioral rules appropriate to a given situation from the available knowledge, and from applicable more general behavioral rules ("norms"), analogous to the procedure employed by the real actor. This approach replaces preprogrammed rigidity by flexibility and the capability for adaptation, it reduces the storage requirements even for simple cases, but it also requires the development of programs which are able to perform cognitive tasks (state pattern recognition, deduction, induction, problem solving).

Of particular importance to the simulation of societal systems appear to be state perception, problem-solving, and the deduction of new behavioral norms. Significant groundwork has been performed in the scientific areas of pattern recognition, the description of cognitive processes, and artificial intelligence.

Actors have the ability to construct an "image" of a situation from a diffuse and constantly changing supply of information concerning state variables, and to recognize the state of their own system, of other systems, and of the environment (albeit through a subjective filter). This enables them to respond sensibly and efficiently to new requirements. The process requires: (1) that relevant indicator variables of the system and the environment (e. g. the "social indicators" of the social sciences) can be observed; (2) that the significance of each variable is known to the system; and (3) that the indicator state can be aggregated and abstracted, and mapped on important functional dimensions of the system (such as the dimensions listed earlier: physical support, security, freedom of action, adaptivity, and efficiency of control). Research with respect to such global functional dimensions appears to be particularly urgent. The concepts of "stability" or "robustness" belong to this class. They are defined in terms of the global system behavior, not in terms of individual variables.

State recognition does not differ in principle from pattern recognition whose major concepts we will now briefly touch upon[163]. It is the task of pattern recognition to extract recognizable patterns from a given information set (deciphering a scribbly handwriting, understanding a non-familiar dialect, recognition of an economic situation as "recession", etc.). The different available approaches to pattern recognition may be divided into two large categories: (1) the decision-theoretic approach

(discriminant approach), and (2) the syntactic (or structural) approach[164].
A further possibility could conceivably be (3) the semantic approach[165].
In the decision-theoretic approach a set of characteristic features is ex-
tracted from the given information; pattern recognition follows from a
partitioning of feature space. Each feature constellation can then be classified according to the partitions. Often the hierarchical construction of
complex patterns from simpler subpatterns is a sensible procedure. In
the syntactic approach, the pattern is represented in terms of a pattern
recognition language consisting of a set of basic patterns which are as-
sembled into a pattern by reference to a picture grammar. The process
of recognition then consists of a determination of the basic patterns and
of a syntactic analysis ("parsing") of their interconnections. The semantic approach attempts in addition to obtain the meaning of a pattern by the
inclusion of "world knowledge" (relevant general information stored in
the computer). This approach, which is of considerable significance for
programs of language translation and question answering systems, will
also have to be applied to problems of state perception in societal systems
resp. actors[166].

In a problem-solving process, means and methods have to be found for
transforming a given initial state into a prescribed final state while observing given boundary conditions and constraints and using only permitted
transformation processes. An example is the construction of a mathematical proof by reference to allowed combination rules. The task is "operationally defined" if all preconditions for a solution are met. In practice
this is rarely the case - usually it is necessary first to clarify what the
problem is all about. Studies of this aspect hardly exist[167]; simulation
studies apparently exist only for operationally defined problems. Successful general problem-solver programs have existed for many years[168]:
In 1962 already, an early representative, the General Problem Solver of
Newell, Shaw, and Simon, was able to solve 70 percent of the first 50
proof problems of the Principia Mathematica by Russell and Whitehead,
some of them more elegantly than the original authors[169]. We will discuss this program briefly.

The development of the General Problem Solver was based on a large
number of transcripts of "think-aloud" problem-solving sessions. The
objective of the program is the simulation of actual cognitive processes
corresponding roughly to the following problem definition: "Assume as
given the description of an initial state (object), the description of a set
of transformation processes (operators), and the description of a certain
final state: Find a sequence of operators which will transform the initial
state into the described final state"[170]. The General Problem Solver
has at its disposal two heuristic procedures for this purpose which may
be applied in a recursive and hierarchical manner: means-ends analysis
and planning. Means-ends analysis permits the determination of those
operators which will lead to a reduction of the difference between the
current object state and the target object state, while planning establishes

the (preliminary) global strategy of the problem-solving process. The original problem is decomposed into a sequence of component problems with the corresponding intermediate transformation goals. In this manner the degree of difficulty of the problem is reduced by orders of magnitude. The General Problem Solver is programmed in the list-processing language IPL-V. It has successfully demonstrated that complex problem-solving processes concerning very specific problems can be carried out by programs which have been developed without reference to any specific problem. The significance for the simulation of societal processes lies in the fact that the construction of simulation models e.g. of political problem-solving processes appears possible in principle without reference to concrete and specific circumstances (which would never be adequately captured in all their diversity anyway).

Related to problem-solving processes is the deduction of new statements from a set of available statements. For this task several programs have been developed which operate in the predicate calculus and are mostly implemented in list-processing languages[171]. These programs use predicates defined over objects or object sets (e.g. D(k, r) = "Karen is Rika's daughter"), connectives ("and", "or", "when ... then ...", "not", etc.), truth values ("true", "false"), as well as other extensions which permit the representation of most statements of natural language. More recent developments[172] also make use of semantic information in order to avoid the limitations of purely syntactic analysis. In connection with the simulation of societal processes, programs of deduction have special significance in the following context: given a certain value system of the actor (formalized in appropriate normative statements) and a concrete situation at time t, differing from that at time t-1: what change of the operational norms concerning a certain action space area can be expected considering the existing value system and the given new situation?[173] Similarly, on a higher hierarchical level of the normative system, changes in the value system are to be determined by reference to the concrete situation and the functional requirements of the system.

It is worth mentioning that successful programs for the induction process have also been developed[174][175], despite statements by representatives of the philosophy of science claiming the impossibility of accomplishing this task. Meltzer has further shown that any program of deduction can be used for induction if certain transformations are observed[176]. This opens up the possibility of simulating even innovative processes in societal systems.

The representation of cognitive processes enlarges the potential of the simulation of societal processes considerably; however, it is not essential for the description of adaptive behavior. This may also be achieved by way of a purely numerical description, e.g. on the basis of the theory of learning systems[177] or of self-organizing systems[178]. In the first case behavior is adapted to new and changing conditions while keeping a given system structure. In the second case the system may change its structure by increasing differentiation, resp. by differentiated construction, destruction, reconstruction and expansion of component structures. These changes will be made by reference to the basic functional requirements of the system. In societal systems the constant structural change of component systems is of particular relevance (e. g. the structural changes in societies following industrialization). We must briefly consider this aspect.

In his excellent survey of computer simulation in the social sciences Harbordt writes[179]: "Historic changes of system structures and qualitative changes of system variables are - in contrast to verbal theory - not representable by simulation models because the model structure is invariant (resp. because the models cannot change their structure spontaneously). The possibility of preprogrammed exchange of some relationships between variables or the application of metamodels controlling structural changes on a lower model level do not change this in principle: the metamodels in turn would be invariant and could only be changed by the model builder."

Like Harbordt, we would not consider the "preprogrammed exchange of some relationships between variables" resp. of entire structural components as constituting simulation of structural change; neither the use of metamodels for preprogrammed structural change. However, the situation is different where component programs are able to generate structural change in a goal-oriented and n o t preprogrammed fashion by a problem-solving process employing aspects of pattern recognition, problem-solving, deduction and perhaps induction. This goal-oriented problem-solving process would take the concrete system situation into account and would be oriented by reference to the more or less invariant functional requirements of the system. This possibility does exist[180] (see the discussion above); it is being applied in different contexts. In principle, simulation can do just as well as a "verbal theory". This means, however, that even the simulation of historic change processes of societal systems is possible.

There are grave and fundamental limitations to this, however. They are due mainly to the stochastics of the cognitive processes of individuals (inventions, discoveries, non-rational decisions of great consequence by individuals wielding power, etc.). No simulation model will ever be able to produce these stochastics correctly. At best it will be able to produce projective simulations of the most likely developments, given the material and cognitive constraints of the actors involved, and the state of their systems and of the common environment. In the simulation of historical processes of change it will therefore be necessary to introduce certain events exogeneously (e. g. the invention of the steam engine and of the electric motor, political constellations, outbreaks of wars). Following the specification of these and similar events it should be possible, on the basis of

what was said, to produce valid simulations of structural change resulting from such events (e. g. the industrialization of Germany). A model
capable of this achievement does not exist today; it would have to combine most of the elements discussed earlier. We note in passing that the
quantitative data base for such simulation studies is hardly available in
the traditional historical sciences. A useful attempt of collecting and
presenting historical data in the form required for simulations has been
undertaken e. g. by Henning[181].

4   RESEARCH GAPS

It will have become evident in the course of our discussion that at present the simulation of societal systems is far from representing an instrument that can be applied routinely and without problems. On the contrary: Missing or poorly validated foundations today cast doubts over
many simulation approaches in this field. Considerable research is yet
required in order to forge simulation into a reliable tool which can be
used routinely e. g. in national policy analysis. At the end of this contribution we now summarize those research problems whose solution appears
to us to be of particular urgency. The list is strongly influenced by our
own research experience; we do not claim completeness. We hope, however, that it will provide some useful suggestions.

Sociological theories

General, well-confirmed theories of social behavior are required for the
simulation of social systems:
- theories valid for larger social groups which are not restricted
  to individuals
- extension of existing theories (e. g. cognitive dissonance theories)
  which so far apply only to certain specific situations
- application of individualistic theories to collectivities
- formalization of sociological and social-psychological theories
  in order to facilitate verification on the one hand, and application
  in computer simulations on the other
- improvement of the experimental situation in the social domain;
  examination of the possibility of large-scale experiments.

Systems theory in the social sciences

A significant amount of basic research will have to be done in this field,
in particular with respect to the following areas:
- applicability of formalized systems theory in the social sciences
  and development of valid systems models
- development of operationalizable systems concepts in subareas,
  which can be inserted into a coherent overall concept
- integration of the material and cognitive components of societal
  systems

- inclusion of influences of affect and emotions
- inclusion of culturally determined, not strictly rational value orientations
- role of cognitive dissonance, and of satisfaction resp. dissatisfaction as factors determining behavior
- delimitation and description of "actor" systems
- theories of normative change and of the change of aspiration levels
- mapping of (social) indicators on (social) orientors (major orienting dimensions)
- simulation of conflict, and of power relationships

Empirical studies in the social sciences

In order to improve the preconditions for valid models of societal systems, empirical studies are required in particular in the following areas:
- exploration of the connections between individual social indicators
- determination of social indicators outside of official statistics: survey results, statements of individual groups etc., in order to study the value orientations of society and social groups
- data series for a complete set of comparable social indicators in as many countries and cultures as possible
- studies about value systems, and of their change (values and their weights), as well as about subjective future weighting functions
- studies on the change of aspiration levels as a function of system state
- determination of the dimensions of the quality of life and of their weights as functions of system type and system state
- studies on the perceived "Is" and "Ought" states of the quality of life orientors
- determination of the collective characteristics of actors, in particular characteristics of their cognition systems
- determination of representative and relevant normative sets of actors, and international comparison
- studies concerning differing problem-solving behavior of different actors, and intercultural comparison
- representation of historic events in a form suitable for systems-analytical studies and simulation.

Decision processes

Decisions in societal systems are almost always multiple criteria decisions. Of particular importance appear to be
- determination of the relevant criteria (for a given decision situation), and of their weights, as functions of the system state
- studies of methods of multiple criteria decision-making
- (interactive) determination of the subjective functions of future weightings (horizon functions)

- (interactive) determination of subjective utility functions, and (related to this) of the functions mapping indicators on the relevant orientors
- determination of the role of subjective probabilities and risks.

Simulation of cognitive processes

Up to now cognitive aspects have been neglected in the simulation of societal processes, even though they substantially determine perception, state analysis, policy synthesis, problem-solving, and decision behavior, normative change and structural change. Of particular importance appear to be studies of the following processes:
- state, problem, and concept recognition; cognitions and cognition patterns
- structure and change of internal models
- cognitive processes of concept manipulation, of psycho-logic, deduction, and induction
- ad hoc generation of normative statements from information about the system state, world knowledge, and basic norms
- problem-solving processes; heuristiscs of problem-solving
- learning from reality and from the internal model; synthesis of behavioral programs; storage and recall by way of classifiers
- self-organization, in particular change of the causal structure as a result of new cognitions.

Fuzzy and nonnumerical analysis

The methods of precise, resp. numerical mathematics are not sufficient for the description of cognitive processes which determine the behavior of societal systems to a great extent. There is a lack in particular of
- methods and programs for the practical application of fuzzy analysis
- studies of the possibilities and limitations of nonnumerical qualitative simulation.

Global indexes

The assessment of the global system state of a complex system requires global indexes which aggregate relevant state variables with respect to the operational requirements of the system (e. g. the dimensions: physical support, security, freedom of action, adaptivity, efficiency of control). In this connection the following items gain importance:
- determination of the basic dimensions
- determination of performance indexes representing the global system state with respect to these basic dimensions
- procedures for the selection of relevant state variables as state indicators
- mapping of state indicators on global indexes

- determination of the relationship between global indexes and basic
  normative orienting dimensions ("orientors")
- topology of the "Is" and the "Ought" in orientor space;measures of
  distance of "Is" from "Ought"
- perturbation approaches for the determination of the shifting of
  the "Is" surface in orientor space in response to changes of the
  system and environmental state.

User adaptation

In order to avoid the very real danger of technocratic misuse, simulation
programs for policy analysis should allow application, verification, and
possibly even construction and modification by nonexperts. This requires
e. g.

- development of interactive model construction programs
- use of natural language and graphics in man-machine communication
- "transparent" programs
- free choice of input and output sets (scenarios and indicator sets)
- automated sensitivity analysis
- reliable validity tests
- algorithms for the restriction of search space for given preferences
- introduction of the approaches of systems analysis into general
  education.

FOOTNOTES

1) FORRESTER 1971, MEADOWS 1972, MESAROVIC and PESTEL 1974 b.
2) DUTTON and STARBUCK 1971, p. 9 - 30.
3) cf. bibliography in DUTTON and STARBUCK 1971, p. 31 - 102.
4) DUTTON and STARBUCK 1971; GUETZKOW, KOTLER and SCHULTZ
   1972; HARBORDT 1974; HOLLAND and GILLESPIE 1963.
5) cf. HARBORDT 1974, p. 233 ff.
6) cf. HARBORDT 1974, DUTTON and STARBUCK 1971; GUETZKOW, KOT-
   LER and SCHULTZ 1972, FORRESTER 1961.
7) This problem was investigated in a study by DATA RESOURCES and
   ABT ASSOCIATES 1975 on the basis of more than 600 simulation models
   developed under government sponsorship.
8) HARBORDT 1974, p. 282 - 258.
9) cf. HARBORDT 1974, p. 242 - 298.
10) e. g. POPPER 1973.
11) HARBORDT 1974, p. 156 - 160.
12) HARBORDT 1974, p. 156 - 206; also GUETZKOW, KOTLER and SCHULTZ
    1972, p. 695 ff; DUTTON and STARBUCK 1971, p. 589 ff; EMSHOFF and
    SISSON 1971, p. 204 - 206.
13) KIRSCH 1970/71/71.

14) cf. MESAROVIC and PESTEL 1972, also: MESAROVIC and PESTEL 1974 a.
15) cf. BOSSEL 1976, p. 423 - 272.
16) cf. FESTINGER 1957, IRLE 1975, KMIECIAK 1974.
17) more detail in KIRSCH 1970/71/71; STACHOWIAK 1969; BOSSEL 1976, p. 423 - 472.
18) KIRSCH 1970/71/71; also: ALEXIS and WILSON 1967, KLIX 1971.
19) In the following the term "social sciences" refers to sociology, political science, psychology, and social psychology.
20) POPPER 1973, ALBERT 1964, HEMPEL/OPPENHEIM 1948.
21) Generalizations can be causal or stochastic laws. See BUNGE 1955, p. 18 ff.
22) ALBERT 1964, p. 61 ff.
23) POPPER 1973, p. 47 ff.
24) For a critical review of the main objections see POPPER 1957 and ALBERT 1964.
25) STAMMLER 1906; for critical remarks see WEBER 1968, p. 42 ff., p. 291 ff.
26) see GILL 1971.
27) This discussion is widely known as "Methoden-Streit".
28) At best there may be different interest in nature and human behavior. See WINDELBAND 1904.
29) WEBER 1968, p. 95 ff.
30) WEBER 1968, p. 146 - 214.
31) see ALBERT/TOPITSCH (eds.) 1971.
32) ALBERT 1968, p. 181 - 210.
33) Some political philosophers like ROUSSEAU 1968 and KANT 1956 showed that normative science can also be justified. But normative and empirical propositions may not be mixed.
34) POPPER 1973, ALBERT 1969.
35) MANNHEIM 1952.
36) see BUCKLEY (ed.) 1968.
37) SPENCER 1876.
38) DURKHEIM 1895, p. 176 ff.
39) PARSONS 1951. For a critical review see BERGMANN 1967.
40) MERTON 1957, p. 49 - 84.
41) PARSONS 1969, p. 35 ff.
42) DAHRENDORF 1969, p. 108 ff., DAHRENDORF 1967, p. 213 - 276.
43) COSER 1972.
44) ETZIONI 1968.
45) DEUTSCH 1963.
46) EASTON 1964, EASTON 1965.
47) WEBER 1964, p. 157 ff.
48) These problems become obvious in a Five Nations Study: ALMOND 1963; ALMOND and VERBA 1965.
49) ALBERT 1964, p. 40.
50) HOMANS 1968, FESTINGER 1957, SKINNER 1938, HULL 1943.
51) e.g. organizations research, role theory, interest group research.

52) KUHN 1962.
53) HUMMELL / OPP 1971.
54) MALEWSKI 1967.
55) HOMANS 1969.
56) The refinement of a model should not result in the neglect of the model validations. See ALBERT 1964, p. 29 ff.
57) HARBORDT 1974.
58) WERTHEIMER 1923, KOEHLER 1929, KOFFKA 1935, LEWIN 1935.
59) HEIDER 1958.
60) NEWCOMB 1959, p. 384 ff.
61) See also OSGOOD / TANNENBAUM 1955, p. 42 - 55. For a survey and critical review see ABELSON et alii (eds.) 1968; OERTER 1970; IRLE 1975, p. 294 ff.
62) CARTWRIGHT / HARARY 1956, p. 277 - 293.
63) FESTINGER 1957. For critical remarks see OERTER 1970, p. 43 ff., IRLE 1975, p. 310 ff., KMIECIAK 1974, p. 44 ff.
64) There may also be attitude changes in a direction opposite to that intended. The direction of attitude change is a function of the strength with which the attitude is anchored in a more comprehensive value system. Cf. von CRANACH / IRLE / VETTER 1969, p. 343 ff.
65) See also BREHM / COHEN 1962, BREHM 1966, GRABITZ et al. 1973.
66) IRLE 1975, p. 343 ff.
67) See also KMIECIAK 1974, p. 195 ff.
68) ALLPORT 1955. For a survey on perception theories see IRLE 1975, p. 52 ff.
69) This theory goes back to the experiments with dogs and humans by PAVLOV and BECHTEREW at the turn of the century.
70) SKINNER 1938, HULL 1943.
71) E. g. OPP 1972, HOMANS 1968, MALEWSKI 1967.
72) MILLER / DOLLARD 1941, BANDURA / WALTERS 1963.
73) For a survey see ZIGLER / CHILD 1954, p. 655 ff.
74) HOMANS 1968. See also THIBAUT / KELLEY 1959.
75) BLAU 1964.
76) Concerning the reception of exchange theory in political science see SCHUMPETER 1950, DOWNS 1968.
77) DAHRENDORF 1967, p. 131.
78) Research on social deviation and reference group behavior has produced somewhat better developed theories. See SACK / KOENIG 1968, MERTON / KITT 1957, p. 279 ff., MERTON 1957, p. 106 - 120.
79) MARX 1970, p. 148 ff.
80) DAHRENDORF 1957.
81) For a survey see SENGHAAS (ed.) 1971.
82) See NUSCHELER / STEFFANI (eds.) 1972.
83) BENTLEY 1949.
84) ALMOND 1963, p. 397 - 408.
85) NARR / NASCHOLD 1971, p. 204 - 238.
86) MILLS 1956.
87) SCHUMPETER 1950, DAHL 1961, BACHRACH 1970.

88) ETZIONI 1967, MAYNTZ 1963.
89) E. g. Presse- und Informationsamt der Bundesregierung (ed.), Gesellschaftliche Daten, Bonn 1974; Central Statistical Office (ed.), Social
Trend, London 1970 - 1973; Institut National de la Statistique et des
Etudes Economiques (ed.), Données Sociales, Paris 1973; Office of
Management and Budget (ed.), Social Indicators 1973 - Selected Statistics on Social Conditions and Trends in the United States, Washington 1973.
90) CANTRIL 1965. Concerning the measurement of "quality of life" see
DALKEY 1972, ANDREWS 1974, ANDREWS and WITHEY 1974. Most
"quality of life" research is strongly influenced by the work of MASLOW
1954/1970. Related to this field are empirical value surveys, e. g.
ROKEACH 1973. A comprehensive survey of theoretical approaches to
value structures and value change as well as a secondary analysis of survey data for the Federal Republic of Germany is due to KMIECIAK 1976.
91) See e. g. von BERTALANFFY 1945, ASHBY 1952, von NEUMANN 1966,
WIENER 1948.
92) MÜLLER 1976.
93) E. g. von BERTALANFFY 1968, ASHBY 1961, KLIR 1969 and 1972,
RAPOPORT 1966.
94) PARSONS 1951, DEUTSCH 1963, LUHMANN 1967, NARR 1969,
NASCHOLD 1969.
95) E. g. ZADEH and DESOER 1963; ZADEH and POLAK 1969; MESAROVIC
1967; MESAROVIC, MACKO, TAKAHARA 1970; MESAROVIC, TAKAHARA
1975.
96) DUTTON and STARBUCK 1971; also GUETZKOW, KOTLER and SCHULTZ
1972; EMSHOFF and SISSON 1971; GORDON 1969; HARBORDT 1974, p.
318 - 371.
97) A good introduction is given by ZADEH 1973. See also ZADEH 1976,
NEGOITA 1975.
98) See e. g. SCHANK and COLBY 1973, NORMAN and RUMELHART 1975,
ELITHORN and JONES 1973.
99) E. g. STOLL 1963, p. 192 ff., LENK 1974, MELTZER in ELITHORN
and JONES 1973, p. 19 - 33, von KUTSCHERA 1973.
100) Cf. ZADEH 1973 and ZADEH 1976.
101) Explicitly e. g. in MESAROVIC and PESTEL 1974 a.
102) Esp. DUTTON and STARBUCK 1971; GUETZKOW, KOTLER and
SCHULTZ 1972; HARBORDT 1974.
103) HARBORDT 1974, p. 30 - 43.
104) HARBORDT 1974, p. 32.
105) E. g. HÄGERSTRAND 1965.
106) E. g. MORRIL 1965.
107) E. g. ORCUTT et alii 1961.
108) E. g. HANSON and SIMMONS 1968.
109) E. g. Mc PHEE 1963.
110) HARBORDT 1974, p. 318 - 371.
111) HARBORDT 1974, p. 37.
112) FORRESTER 1971; MEADOWS et alii 1972, 1974; MESAROVIC and
PESTEL 1974 a, 1974 b.

113) E. g. DUESENBERRY et alii 1965, LÜDEKE 1969.
114) E. g. FORRESTER 1961.
115) E. g. COHEN et alii in: CYERT and MARCH 1963.
116) E. g. ROBERTSON et alii 1970.
117) E. g. BOSSEL 1974.
118) HARBORDT 1974, p. 41 - 42.
119) E. g. POOL and KESSLER 1965.
120) E. g. NEWELL and SIMON 1971.
121) COLBY 1973.
122) For a comprehensive presentation of most programming languages see: SAMMET 1969. BASIC: see SKELTON 1971.
123) See IBM 1966; IITB 1975.
124) PUGH 1970.
125) E. g. EMSHOFF and SISSON 1971; GORDON 1969; see also pertinent manuals.
126) E. g. EMSHOFF and SISSON 1971; GORDON 1969; see also pertinent manuals.
127) BIRTWISTLE et alii 1973.
128) SAMMET 1969, p. 405 - 416. See also references cited there as well as pertinent manuals.
129) See the contribution by SHOOK in MESAROVIC and PESTEL 1974 a, vol. VI, p. C 283 - C 314; VOGT 1975.
130) See contribution by HUDETZ in BOSSEL (ed.) 1977.
131) See contribution by BOSSEL and STROBEL in BOSSEL (ed.) 1977.
132) SCHÖNFELD 1969/1971.
133) E. g. DUESENBERRY 1965, KRELLE et alii 1969, LÜDEKE 1969.
134) TUSTIN 1951, GEYER and OPPELT 1957.
135) PFEIFFER 1975.
136) E. g. ZADEH and DESOER 1963, ZADEH and POLAK 1969; DeRUSSO et alii 1965.
137) E. g. BROWN 1966.
138) See BROWN 1966.
139) GASPARI and MILLENDORFER 1973.
140) PFEIFFER 1975.
141) LEONTIEF 1966; also CARTER 1974.
142) E. g. REARDON 1972, HERENDEEN 1974, WRIGHT 1974.
143) E. g. MENGES 1969, GÄFGEN 1968, RAIFFA 1970, LIFSON 1972, KIRSCH 1970/71/71.
144) KIRSCH I 1970, p. 76 ff.; von KAENEL 1971, p. 229 - 238.
145) MENGES 1969, p. 242 f.
146) MENGES 1969, p. 180.
147) RAIFFA 1970, p. 17, LIFSON 1972, p. 145.
148) MENGES 1969, p. 191 ff.
149) MENGES 1969, p. 223.
150) WALD 1950.
151) MENGES 1969, p. 214.
152) Cf. MENGES 1969, p. 223 ff.; von NEUMANN and MORGENSTERN 1953. For philosophical aspects, see HÖFFE 1975.

153) See BOSSEL 1976 and related contribution in BOSSEL (ed.) 1977.
154) E.g. MENGES 1969, RAIFFA 1970, LIFSON 1972, BOSSEL and HUGHES 1973.
155) E.g. HÖFFE 1975; ARROW 1951; RAWLS 1972.
156) von NEUMANN and MORGENSTERN 1953; see also discussion in HÖFFE 1975.
157) For a survey see KEENEY 1976. Also: MENGES 1969, RAIFFA 1970, LIFSON 1972.
158) E.g. OKSMAN 1974; BOSSEL and SIMON in BOSSEL (ed.) 1977.
159) See studies cited by KEENEY 1976.
160) Survey article by Mc CRIMMON in COCHRANE and ZELENY 1973; see also DEISSENBERG in BOSSEL (ed.) 1977.
161) SIMON 1955.
162) See DEISSENBERG in BOSSEL (ed.) 1977.
163) FU 1968, FU 1974, NIEMANN 1974.
164) FU 1974.
165) Cf. contribution by SIMMONS in SCHANK and COLBY 1973; also: NORMAN and RUMELHART 1975.
166) E.g. SCHANK and COLBY 1973, NORMAN and RUMELHART 1975, KLACZKO 1976.
167) KIRSCH II 1971, p. 200 - 210.
168) NEWELL and SIMON 1971, NORMAN and RUMELHART 1975, ELITHORN and JONES 1973.
169) KIRSCH II 1971, p. 183.
170) KIRSCH II 1971, p. 170.
171) See in particular MELTZER in ELITHORN and JONES 1973; SCHANK and COLBY 1973; NORMAN and RUMELHART 1975; MÜLLER-REISS-MANN and RECHENMANN in BOSSEL(1977); an introduction to the predicate calculus is given by STOLL 1963.
172) E.g. WINOGRAD 1970; NORMAN and RUMELHART 1975.
173) Cf. contributions by BOSSEL, and MÜLLER-REISSMANN and RECHENMANN in BOSSEL (1977).
174) Cf. contributions by MELTZER and WETHERICK in ELITHORN and JONES 1973.
175) Thus according to POPPER 1959, p. 32, induction always contains an "irrational" element. For MEDAWAR 1967, p. 134, 147, induction is outside of logic and cannot be subjected to the laws of logic (cited in MELTZER in ELITHORN and JONES 1973).
176) MELTZER 1970.
177) ZYPKIN 1972
178) MESAROVIC 1962
179) HARBORDT 1974, p. 314.
180) E.g. WINOGRAD in SCHANK and COLBY 1973, also: NORMAN and RUMELHART 1975.
181) HENNING 1974.

BIBLIOGRAPHY

ABELSON / ARONSON / McGUIRE / NEWCOMB / ROSENBERG / TANNEN
BAUM (eds.) 1968: Theories of Cognitive Consistency. A Sourcebook.
Chicago. Rand McNally.

ALBERT, H. 1964: Probleme der Theoriebildung. Entwicklung, Struktur
und Anwendung sozialwissenschaftlicher Theorien, in: ALBERT (ed.),
Theorie und Realität. Ausgewählte Aufsätze zur Wissenschaftslehre der
Sozialwissenschaften, pp. 3 - 70, Tübingen: Mohr (Siebeck).

ALBERT, H. 1968: Wertfreiheit als methodisches Prinzip. Zur Frage der
Notwendigkeit einer normativen Sozialwissenschaft, in: Topitsch (ed.),
Logik der Sozialwissenschaften, 5th ed., pp. 181 - 210, Köln/Berlin:
Kiepenheuer & Witsch.

ALBERT, H. 1969: Traktat über kritische Vernunft. Tübingen: Mohr (Siebeck).

ALBERT, H.; TOPITSCH, E. (eds.) 1971: Werturteilsstreit. Darmstadt:
Wissenschaftliche Buchgesellschaft.

ALEXIS, M.; WILSON, CH. Z. 1967: Organizational Decision-Making.
Englewood Cliffs, N.J.: Prentice Hall.

ALLPORT, F.H. 1955: Theories of Perception and the Concept of Structure.
New York: Wiley.

ALMOND, G. 1963: A Comparative Study of Interest Groups and the Political
Process, in: Harry Eckstein / David Apter (eds.), Comparative Politics,
pp. 397 - 408, New York.

ALMOND, G.; VERBA, S. 1965: The Civic Culture. Boston: Little, Brown.

ANDREWS, F.M.; WITHEY, S.B. 1974: Developing Measures of Perceived
Life Quality: Results from Several National Surveys. Social Indicators
Research 1, 1 - 26.

ANDREWS, F.M. 1974: Social Indicators of Perceived Life Quality. Social
Indicators Research 1, 279 - 299.

ARROW, K.J. 1951: Social Choice and Individual Values. New York.

ASHBY, W.R. 1952: Design for a Brain. New York: Wiley.

ASHBY, W.R. 1961: General System Theory and the Problem of the Black
Box. In: Regelungsvorgänge lebender Wesen. München: Oldenbourg.

BACHRACH, P. 1970: Die Theorie demokratischer Elitenherrschaft. Frank-
furt/Main: Suhrkamp.

BANDURA, A.; WALTERS, R.H. 1963: Social Learning and Personality
Development. New York: The Ronald Press Company.

BENTLEY, A.F. 1949: The Process of Government. A Study of Social Pressures. New ed. Evanston, Ill.: Principia.

BERGMANN, J.E. 1967: Die Theorie des sozialen Systems von Talcott
Parsons. Frankfurt/Main.

von BERTALANFFY, L. 1945: Zu einer allgemeinen Systemlehre. In:
Blätter für deutsche Philosophie. Vol. 18, No. 3 and 4.

von BERTALANFFY, L. 1968: General Systems Theory. New York:
George Braziller.

BIRTWISTLE, G.M.; DAHL, O.-J.; MYHRHAUG, B.; NYGAARD, K. 1973:
Simula Begin. Philadelphia: Auerbach.

BLAU, P. M. 1964: Exchange and Power in Social Life. New York: Wiley.

BOSSEL, H.; HUGHES, B. 1973: Simulation of Value-Controlled Decision-Making: Approach and Prototype. In M. MESAROVIC, E. PESTEL (eds.): Multilevel Computer Model of World Development System, vol. VI. Vienna: IIASA SP-74-6.

BOSSEL, H. 1974: College Student and Dropout Problem: A Qualitative Dynamic Simulation. In: Instructional Science 3, 23 - 50.

BOSSEL, H. 1976: Information Processing, Cognitive Dissonance, and Basic Needs: The Modelling of Behavior. In: H. BOSSEL, S. KLACZKO, N. MÜLLER: Systems Theory in the Social Sciences. Basel: Birkhäuser.

BOSSEL, H. 1977 (ed.): Concepts and Tools of Computer-Assisted Policy Analysis. Basel: Birkhäuser

BREHM, J. W.; COHEN, A. R. 1962: Exploration in Cognitive Dissonance. New York: Wiley.

BREHM, J. W. 1966: A Theory of Psychological Reactance. New York: Academic Press.

BROWN, M. 1966: On the Theory and Measurement of Technological Change. Cambridge: University Press.

BUCKLEY, W. (ed.) 1968: Modern Systems Research for the Behavioral Scientist. A Sourcebook. Chicago: Aldine.

BUNGE, M. 1955: Causality. The Place of the Causal Principle in Modern Science. Cambridge, Mass.: MIT Press.

BUNGE, M. 1967: Scientific Research. 2 vols., Berlin/Heidelberg/New York: Springer.

CANTRIL, H. 1965: The Pattern of Human Concerns. New Brunswick/New Jersey: Rutgers University Press.

CARTER, A. P. 1974: Applications of Input-Output Analysis to Energy Problems. In: Science, Vol. 184, 19 April, p. 325 - 329.

CARTWRIGHT, D.; HARARY, F. 1956: Structural Balance: A Generation of Heider's Theory, in: Psychological Theory, pp. 277 - 293.

COCHRANE, J. L.; ZELENY, M. (eds.) 1973: Multiple Criteria Decision Making. Columbia, S. C.: University of South Carolina Press.

COLBY, K. M. 1973: Simulations of Belief Systems. In: R. C. SCHANK, K. M. COLBY: Computer Models of Thought and Language. San Francisco: Freeman, pp. 251 - 286.

COSER, L. 1972: Theorie sozialer Konflikte. Neuwied/Berlin: Luchterhand.

von CRANACH, M.; IRLE, M. and VETTER, V. 1969: Zur Analyse des Bumerang-Effektes. Größe und Richtung der Änderung sozialer Einstellungen als Funktion ihrer Verankerung in Wertsystemen. In: Irle, M. (ed.), Texte aus der experimentellen Sozialpsychologie, p. 343 ff. Neuwied/Berlin: Luchterhand.

CYERT, R. M.; MARCH, J. G. 1963: A Behavioral Theory of the Firm. Englewood Cliffs, N. J.: Prentice-Hall.

DAHL, R. A. 1961: Who Governs? Democracy and Power in an American City. New Haven, Conn.: Yale University Press.

DAHRENDORF, R. 1957: Soziale Klassen und Klassenkonflikt in der industriellen Gesellschaft. Stuttgart: Enke.

DAHRENDORF, R. 1967: Pfade aus Utopia. Arbeiten zur Theorie und Methode der Soziologie. München: Piper.

DAHRENDORF, R. 1969: Zu einer Theorie des sozialen Konflikts, in: Wolfgang Zapf (ed.) Theorien des sozialen Wandels. p. 108 ff. Köln/Berlin: Kiepenheuer & Witsch.

DALKEY, N.C. 1972: Studies in the Quality of Life. Delphi and Decision-Making. Lexington/Toronto/London: Heath.

DATA RESOURCES and ABT ASSOCIATES 1975: Federally Supported Mathematical Models: Survey and Analysis. Washington, D.C.: RANN Documentation Center, National Science Foundation.

DERUSSO, P.M.; ROY, R.J.; CLOSE, C.M. 1965: State Variables for Engineers. New York: Wiley.

DEUTSCH, K.W. 1963: The Nerves of Government. Models of Political Communication and Control. New York: Free Press of Glencoe.

DOWNS, A. 1968: Ökonomische Theorien der Demokratie. Tübingen: Mohr (Siebeck)

DUESENBERRY, J.S. (eds.) 1965: The Brookings Quarterly Econometric Model of the United States. Chicago: Rand McNally.

DURKHEIM, E. 1970 (Orig.: 1895): Regeln der soziologischen Methode. 3rd ed. Neuwied/Berlin: Luchterhand.

DUTTON, J.M.; STARBUCK, W.H. 1971: Computer Simulation of Human Behavior. New York: Wiley.

EASTON, D. 1964: The Political System. New York: Wiley.

EASTON, D. 1965: A Systems Analysis of Political Life. New York: Wiley.

ELITHORN, A.; JONES, D. 1973: Artificial and Human Thinking. Amsterdam: Elsevier.

EMSHOFF, J.R.; SISSON, R.L. 1971: Design and Use of Computer Simulation Models. New York: Macmillan.

ETZIONI, A. 1967: Soziologie der Organisationen. München: Juventa.

ETZIONI, A. 1968: The Active Society. A Theory of Societal and Political Processes. New York: Collier-Macmillan.

FESTINGER, L. 1957: A Theory of Cognitive Dissonances. New York: Harper & Row.

FORRESTER, J.W. 1961: Industrial Dynamics. Cambridge, Mass.: MIT Press.

FORRESTER, J.W. 1971: World Dynamics. Cambridge, Mass.: Wright-Allen Press. (Deutsch: J.W. FORRESTER, 1971: Der teuflische Regelkreis. Stuttgart, Deutsche Verlagsanstalt)

FU, K.S. 1968: Sequential Methods in Pattern Recognition and Machine Learning. New York: Academic Press.

FU, K.S. 1974: Syntactic Methods in Pattern Recognition. New York: Academic Press.

GÄFGEN, S. 1968: Theorie der wirtschaftlichen Entscheidung, 2nd ed. Tübingen: Mohr (Siebeck).

GASPARI, C.; MILLENDORFER, H. 1973: Prognosen für Österreich. Wien: Verlag für Geschichte und Politik.

GEYER, H.; OPPELT, W. (eds.) 1957: Volkswirtschaftliche Regelungsvorgänge im Vergleich zu Regelungsvorgängen der Technik. München.

GILL, J. G. 1971: The Definition of Freedom. Ethics (82)

GORDON, G. 1969: System Simulation. Englewood Cliffs, N. J.: Prentice-Hall.

GRABITZ-GNIECH, G.; GRABITZ, H. J. 1973: Der kognitive Prozeß vor Entscheidungen. Theoretische Ansätze und experimentelle Untersuchungen.
In: Psychologische Beiträge, p. 522 ff.

GUETZKOW, H.; KOTLER, Ph.; SCHULTZ, R. L. 1972: Simulation in
Social and Administrative Science. Englewood Cliffs, N. J.: Prentice-Hall.

HÄGERSTRAND, T. 1965: A Monte Carlo Approach to Diffusion. In: Archives
européennes de Sociologie, VI, pp. 43 - 47.

HANSON, R. C.; SIMMONS, O. 1968: The Role Path: A Concept and Procedure
for Studying Communities. In: Human Organization, 27, 152 - 158.

HARBORDT, S. 1974: Computersimulation in den Sozialwissenschaften. Vols.
1 + 2, Reinbek: Rowohlt.

HEIDER, F. 1958: The Psychology of Interpersonal Relations. New York:
Wiley.

HEMPEL, C. G.; OPPENHEIM, P. 1948: Studies in the Logic of Explanations.
Philosophy of Science, 15, p. 135 ff.

HENNING, E. W. 1974: Das vorindustrielle Deutschland 800 bis 1800. Die
Industrialisierung Deutschlands 1800 bis 1914. Das industrialisierte
Deutschland 1914 bis 1972. Paderborn: Schöningh.

HERENDEEN, R. A. 1974: Use of Input-Output Analysis to Determine the
Energy Costs of Goods and Services. In: M. S. Macrakis: Energy:
Demand, Conservation and Institutional Problems. Cambridge, Mass.:
MIT Press.

HÖFFE, O. 1975: Strategien der Humanität - zur Ethik öffentlicher Entscheidungsprozesse. Freiburg: Alber.

HOLLAND, E. P.; GILLESPIE, R. W. 1963: Experiments on a Simulated
Underdeveloped Economy. Cambridge, Mass.: MIT Press.

HOMANS, G. C. 1968: Elementarformen sozialen Verhaltens. Köln/Opladen:
Westdeutscher Verlag.

HOMANS, G. C. 1969: Was ist Sozialwissenschaft? Köln/Opladen: Westdeutscher Verlag.

HULL, C. L. 1943: Principles of Behavior. New York.

HUMMEL, H. J.; OPP, K. -D. 1971: Die Reduzierbarkeit von Soziologie
auf Psychologie. Eine These, ihr Test und ihre theoretische Bedeutung.
Braunschweig: Vieweg.

IBM 1966: Continuous System Modeling Program. IBM Application Description 420-0209-1 New York: IBM.

IITB, 1975: Dialogorientiertes Simulationsprogramm für kontinuierliche
Systeme. Karlsruhe: Institut für Informationsverarbeitung in Technik
und Biologie.

IRLE, M. 1975: Lehrbuch der Sozialpsychologie. Göttingen/Toronto/Zürich:
Hogrefe.

von KAENEL, S. 1971: Einführung in die Kybernetik für Ökonomen. Berlin:
Verlag Die Wirtschaft.

KANT, I. 1956: Die Metaphysik der Sitten. In: Wilhelm Weischedel (ed.)
Kant, Werke, Wiesbaden: Insel.

KEENEY, R. L. 1976: Multiattribute Utility Analysis. - A Brief Survey. In: H. BOSSEL, S. KLACZKO, N. MÜLLER: Systems Theory in the Social Sciences. Basel: Birkhäuser.

KIRSCH, W. 1970/71/71: Entscheidungsprozesse, vols. I, II, III. Wiesbaden: Gabler.

KLACZKO, S. 1976: Pattern Recognition as a Model for Cognitive Processes. In: H. BOSSEL, S. KLACZKO, N. MÜLLER: Systems Theory in the Social Sciences. Basel: Birkhäuser.

KLIR, G. F. 1969: An Approach to General Systems Theory. New York: van Nostrand-Reinhold.

KLIR, G. F. 1972: Trends in General Systems Theory. New York: Wiley-Interscience.

KLIX, G. F. 1971: Information und Verhalten. Bern: Huber.

KMIECIAK, P. 1974: Auf dem Wege zu einer generellen Theorie sozialen Verhaltens. Meisenheim am Glan: Hain.

KMIECIAK, P. 1976: Wertstrukturen und Wertwandel in der Bundesrepublik Deutschland. Göttingen: Schwartz.

KÖHLER, W. 1929: Gestalt Psychology. New York: Liveright.

KOFFKA, K. 1935: Principles of Gestalt Psychology. New York: Harcourt, Brace.

KRELLE, W.; BECKERHOFF, D.; LANGER, H. G.; FUSS, H. 1969: Ein Prognosesystem für die wirtschaftliche Entwicklung der Bundesrepublik Deutschland. Meisenheim am Glan: Hain.

KUHN, T. S. 1962: The Structure of Scientific Revolutions. Chicago: University of Chicago Press.

von KUTSCHERA, F. 1973: Einführung in die Logik der Normen, Werte und Entscheidungen. Freiburg: Alber.

LENK, H. (ed.) 1974: Normenlogik - Grundfragen der deontischen Logik. Pullach: Verlag Dokumentation.

LEONTIEF, W. 1966: Input-Output Economics. Fair Lawn, N. J.: Oxford University Press.

LEWIN, K. 1935: A Dynamic Theory of Personality. New York: McGraw Hill.

LIFSON, M. W. 1972: Decision and Risk Analysis for Practicing Engineers. Boston, Mass.: Cahners.

LÜDEKE, D. 1969: Ein ökonomisches Vierteljahresmodell für die Bundesrepublik Deutschland. Tübingen: Mohr (Siebeck).

LUHMANN, N. 1967: Soziologie als Theorie sozialer Systeme. In: Kölner Zeitschrift für Soziologie und Sozialpsychologie, vol. 29, pp. 615 - 644.

MALEWSKI, A. 1967: Verhalten und Interaktion. Tübingen: Mohr (Siebeck).

MANNHEIM, K. 1952: Ideologie und Utopie. 3rd ed., Frankfurt/Main.

MARX, K. 1970: Das Kapital. Kritik der politischen Ökonomie. Studienausgabe, 2nd ed., Frankfurt/Berlin/Wien: Ullstein.

MASLOW, A. H. 1954/1970: Motivation and Personality. New York.

MAYNTZ, R. 1963: Soziologie der Organisationen. Reinbek: Rowohlt.

McPHEE, W. N. 1963: Formal Theories of Mass Behavior. New York: Free Press.

MEADOWS, D. H.; MEADOWS, D. L.; RANDERS, J.; BEHRENS III, W. W. 1972: The Limits to Growth. New York: Universe Books. (Deutsch:

D. MEADOWS, D. MEADOWS, E. ZAHN, P. MILLING; 1972: Die Grenzen des Wachstums. Stuttgart: Deutsche Verlagsanstalt)

MEADOWS, D. L.; BEHRENS, III, W. W.; MEADOWS, D. H.; NAILL, R. F.; RANDERS, J.; ZAHN, E. K. O. 1974: Dynamics of Growth in a Finite World. Cambridge, Mass.: Wright-Allen Press.

MEDAWAR, P. 1967: The Art of the Soluble. London: Metheun.

MELTZER, B. 1970: The Semantics of Induction and the Possibility of Complete Systems of Inductive Inference. In: Artificial Intelligence 1, pp. 615 - 644.

MENGES, G. 1969: Grundmodelle wirtschaftlicher Entscheidungen. Köln und Opladen: Westdeutscher Verlag.

MERTON, R. K.; KITT, A. S. 1957: Contributions to the Theory of Reference Group Behavior. In: R. K. Merton, Social Theory and Social Structure. 2nd ed. p. 279 ff. Glencoe, Ill.: Free Press.

MERTON, R. K. 1957: Social Theory and Social Structure. 2nd ed. Glencoe, Ill.: Free Press.

MERTON, R. K. 1957: The Role-Set: Problems in Sociological Theory. In: British Journal of Sociology, 8, pp. 106 - 120.

MESAROVIC, M. D. 1962: On Self-Organizing Systems. In: M. C. YOVITS, G. T. JACOBI, G. D. GOLDSTEIN (eds.): Self-Organizing Systems. Washington, D. C.

MESAROVIC, M. D. 1967: General Systems Theory and its Mathematical Foundations. Record of the IEEE Systems Science and Cybernetics Conference, Boston, Mass.

MESAROVIC, M. D.; MACKO, D.; TAKAHARA, Y. 1970: Theory of Hierarchical, Multilevel Systems. New York: Academic Press.

MESAROVIC, M. D.; TAKAHARA, Y. 1975: General Systems Theory: Mathematical Foundations. New York: Academic Press.

MESAROVIC, M. D.; PESTEL, E. 1972: A Goal-Seeking and Regionalized Model for Analysis of Critical World Relationships - The Conceptual Foundation. Kybernetes Journal, Vol. 1.

MESAROVIC, M. D.; PESTEL, E. 1974 a: Multilevel World Model Project, Technical Reports, Vols. 1 - 6. Laxenburg bei Wien: IIASA.

MESAROVIC, M. D.; PESTEL, E. 1974 b: Mankind at the Turning Point, New York: Dutton. (Deutsch: Menschheit am Wendepunkt, Stuttgart: Deutsche Verlagsanstalt.)

MILLER, N. E.; DOLLARD, J. 1941: Social Learning and Imitation. New Haven, Conn.: Yale University Press.

MILLS, R. L. 1965: The Negro Ghetto: Problems and Alternatives. In: The Geographical Review, Vol. 55.

MÜLLER, N. 1976: Systems Theories in the Social Sciences. In: H. BOSSEL, S. KLACZKO, N. MÜLLER: Systems Theory in the Social Sciences. Basel: Birkhäuser.

NARR, W. D. 1969: Theoriebegriffe und Systemtheorie. Stuttgart: Kohlhammer.

NARR, W. D.; NASCHOLD, F. 1971: Einführung in die moderne politische Theorie. Vol. III: Theorie der Demokratie. Stuttgart/Berlin/Köln/Mainz: Kohlhammer.

NASCHOLD, F. 1969: Systemsteuerung. Stuttgart: Kohlhammer.

NEGOITA, C. C.; RALESCU, D. A. 1975: Application of Fuzzy Sets to Systems Analysis. Basel: Birkhäuser.

von NEUMANN, J.; MORGENSTERN, D. 1953: Theory of Games and Economic Behavior, 3rd ed. Princeton University Press.

von NEUMANN, J. 1966: Theory of Self-Reproducing Automata. Urbana, Ill.: Univ. of Illinois Press.

NEWCOMB, T. M. 1959: Individual Systems of Orientation. In: Koch, S (ed.) Psychology. A Study of Science. p. 384 ff. New York: McGraw Hill.

NEWELL, A.; SIMON, H. A. 1971: Simulation of Human Thought. In: J. M. DUTTON, W. H. STARBUCK: Computer Simulation of Human Behavior. New York: Wiley. pp. 150 - 169.

NIEMANN, H. 1974: Methoden der Mustererkennung. Frankfurt: Akad. Verl.

NORMAN, D. A.; RUMELHART, D. E. 1975: Explorations in Cognition. San Francisco: Freeman.

NUSCHELER, F.; STEFFANI, W. (eds.) 1972: Pluralismus. Konzeptionen und Kontroversen. München: Piper.

OERTER, R. 1970: Struktur und Wandlung von Werthaltungen. München: Oldenbourg.

OKSMAN, W. 1974: Markov Decision Processes with Utility Independent Objective Functions. Dissertation Harvard University, Cambridge, Mass.

OPP, K. -D. 1972: Verhaltenstheoretische Soziologie. Eine neue soziologische Forschungsrichtung. Reinbek: Rowohlt.

ORCUTT, G. H.; GREENBERGER, M.; KORBEL, J.; RIVLIN, A. 1961: Microanalysis of Socioeconomic Systems: A Simulation Study. New York: Harper and Row.

OSGOOD, C. E.; TANNENBAUM, P. H. 1955: The Principle of Congruity in the Prediction of Attitude Change, Psychological Review, 62, pp. 42 - 55.

PARSONS, T. 1951: The Social System. London: Routledge and Kegan Paul.

PARSONS, T. 1969: Das Problem des Strukturwandels: eine theoretische Skizze. In: Wolfgang Zapf (ed.) Theorien des sozialen Wandels. Köln/ Berlin: Kiepenheuer & Witsch.

PFEIFFER, R. 1975: Kybernetische Analyse ökonometrischer Makromodelle für die Bundesrepublik Deutschland. Tübingen: Institut für Angewandte Wirtschaftsforschung. (Also: Basel: Birkhäuser 1976)

POOL, I. de SOLA; KESSLER, A. 1965: The Kaiser, The Tsar, and the Computer: Information Processing in a Crisis. In: American Behavioral Scientist, 8, 31 - 38.

POPPER, K. R. 1957: The Poverty of Historicism. London.

POPPER, K. R. 1973: Logik der Forschung, 5th ed. Tübingen: Mohr (Siebeck).

PUGH III, A. L. 1970: D Y N A M O II Users Manual. Cambridge, Mass.: MIT Press.

RAIFFA, H. 1970: Decision Analysis. Reading, Mass.: Addison-Wesley.

RAPOPORT, A. 1966: Mathematical Aspects of General Systems Theory. In: General Systems, Vol. 8, pp. 123 - 128.

RAWLS, J. 1972: A Theory of Justice. Oxford.

REARDON, W. A. 1972: An Input/Output Analysis of Energy Use Changes from 1947 to 1958 and 1958 to 1963. Richland, Wash.: Pacific Northwest Laboratories/Battelle.

ROBERTSON, G. N.; FERNALD, C. G. E.; MYERS, J. G. 1970: Decision Making and Learning: A Simulated Marketing Manager. In: Behavioral Science, 15, 370 - 379.

ROKEACH, M. 1973: The Nature of Human Values. New York: Free Press.

ROUSSEAU, J. J. 1968: Der Gesellschaftsvertrag. Stuttgart: Reclam.

SACK, F.; KÖNIG, R. (eds.) 1968: Kriminalsoziologie. Frankfurt/Main: Akademische Verlagsanstalt.

SAMMET, J. E. 1969: Programming Languages: History and Fundamentals. Englewood Cliffs, N. J.: Prentice-Hall.

SCHANK, R. C.; COLBY, K. M. 1973: Computer Models of Thought and Language. San Francisco: Freeman.

SCHÖNFELD, P. 1969/1971: Methoden der Ökonometrie, Vols. I and II. Berlin und München: Vahlen.

SCHUMPETER, J. A. 1950: Kapitalismus, Sozialismus und Demokratie. München: Francke.

SENGHAAS, D. (ed.) 1971: Kritische Friedensforschung. Frankfurt/Main: Suhrkamp.

SIMON, H. A. 1955: A Behavioral Model of Rational Choice. In: The Quarterly Journal of Economics, Vol. LXIX. Also: M. ALEXIS, CH. Z. WILSON: Organizational Decision Making. Englewood Cliffs, N. J.: Prentice-Hall.

SKELTON, J. E. 1971: An Introduction to the BASIC Language. New York: Holt, Rinehart and Winston.

SKINNER, B. F. 1938: The Behavior of Organisms. New York: Macmillan.

SPENCER, H. 1876 - 1882: The Principles of Sociology. London.

STACHOWIAK, H. 1969: Denken und Erkennen im kybernetischen Modell. Wien: Springer.

STAMMLER, R. 1924: Wirtschaft und Recht nach der materialistischen Geschichtsauffassung. 5th ed., Berlin and Leipzig.

STOLL, R. 1961: Introduction to Set Theory and Logic. San Francisco: Freeman.

THIBAUT, J. W.; KELLEY, H. H. 1959: The Social Psychology of Group. New York: Wiley.

TUSTIN, A. 1951: An Engineer's View of the Problem of Economic Stability and Economic Regulation. In: The Review of Economic Studies, Vol. 19, pp. 85 - 89.

VOGT, H. 1975: Beschreibung des Programmpakets MODEL BUILDER. Hannover: Institut für Systemanalyse und Prognose.

WALD, A. 1950: Statistical Decision Functions. New York - London.

WEBER, M. 1964: Wirtschaft und Gesellschaft, Grundriß der verstehenden Soziologie. Studienausgabe (eds. Johannes Winkelmann) Köln/Berlin: Kiepenheuer & Witsch.

WEBER, M. 1968: Gesammelte Aufsätze zur Wissenschaftslehre. (eds. Johannes Winkelmann) Tübingen, 3rd ed.: Mohr (Siebeck).

WERTHEIMER, M. 1923: Untersuchungen zur Lehre von der Gestalt. Psychologische Forschung 4, pp. 301 - 315.

WIENER, N. 1948 (1961): Cybernetics. Cambridge, Mass.: MIT Press.

WINDELBAND, W. 1904: Geschichte und Naturwissenschaft. 3rd. ed. Straßburg.

WINOGRAD, T. 1970: Procedures as a representation for data in a computer program for understanding natural language. Dissertation, MIT, Cambridge, Mass.

WRIGHT, D.J. 1974: Goods and Services: An Input-Output Analysis. In: Energy Policy, Vol. 2, No. 4. (Dec.).

ZADEH, L.A.; DESOER, C.A. 1963: Linear System Theory. New York: McGraw-Hill.

ZADEH, L.A.; POLAK, E. (eds.) 1969: System Theory. New York: McGraw-Hill.

ZADEH, L.A. 1973: Outline of a New Approach to the Analysis of Complex Systems and Decision Processes. In: IEEE Transactions on Systems, Man and Cybernetics, Vol. SMC-3, No. 1, January, pp. 28 - 44.

ZADEH, L.A. 1976: A Fuzzy Algorithmic Approach to the Definition of Complex or Imprecise Concepts. In: H. BOSSEL, S. KLACZKO, N. MÜLLER (eds.): Systems Theory in the Social Sciences. Basel: Birkhäuser.

ZIGLER, E.F.; CHILD, I.L. 1963: Socialization. In: G. Lindzey; E. Aronson (eds.) Handbook of Social Psychology, Vol. 3, p. 655 ff. Reading, Mass.: Addison - Wesley.

ZYPKIN, J.S. 1972: Grundlagen der Theorie lernender Systeme. Berlin: Verlag Technik.

2

CYBERNETICS IN GOVERNMENT: EXPERIENCE WITH NEW TOOLS FOR MANAGEMENT IN CHILE 1971 - 1973

Hermann Schwember

INTRODUCTION: CYBERNETICS AND SYNERGY

This paper describes Project CYBERSYN as it was developed in Chile between November 1971 and September 1973.

Throughout this work, every effort will be made to focus the analysis on the philosophy and the praxis of the project, insofar as they may provide some useful criteria for other models and decision-making simulations which are of interest for new applications.

The central point of view of CYBERSYN is summarized in its name, a concentration of CYBERNETICS and SYNERGY. From cybernetics it takes the emphasis in respecting the totality of a system: its structure; its dynamics; and the relationship between control, information, planning and decision-making. The concept of synergy is stressed because efficiency and performance should be related to the multiplying effect of proper collaborating links between different elements, rather than to abstract formal regulations imposed on the system from the outside.

The first discussion of the project was carried out in November, 1971 but its actual existence began in March, 1972. It was never associated with a rigid schedule or program, as that rigidity would have contradicted the basic ideas that inspired the project, but it contemplated instead a flexible time horizon of five years for its full implementation. It lasted however until September 11, 1973, when the legal Chilean government was ousted and all its projects immediately cancelled.

During its life of approximately 18 months, the project advanced much more than the most optimistic original forecast. This possibility of very fast progress, seems to be intrinsic in the basic approach of CYBERSYN which links research, development, planning and execution in a unique process in which every activity is merely one aspect of the dynamics of the system and there is a steady feedback from each activity to every other one. Fast progress was reflected in many facts, the main ones being: definition of the configuration of the system and effective operation contact of the group of experts with most of the units of the system within the period of one year; development of the whole scheme of information flow required for decision with appropriate computer programs for its analysis, filtration and integration for different levels of decision-making; implementation of such programs and establishment of the routine flows of information; substantial progress in the development of programs for long-range planning and simulation; ample discussion of the project at all levels of the system and programs for training of high and medium range executives and workers.

CYBERSYN was specifically developed for that sector of the Chilean industry that was nationalized between 1971 and 1973. From the beginning, it was agreed that the design should be flexible enough to permit application to other sectors of the economy, such as mining, energy, transportation, agriculture and housing. Moreover, as the project evolved in connection with some very fast political developments, it became clear that its tools should not be designed only for the use of specialized agencies of government, but also for those making decisions at the highest policy levels. For this reason, the president of Chile and his ministers in portfolios directly related to the economy of the country were kept informed of the project and periodically briefed on its progress. At the same time efforts were made to include major policy factors such as employment, inflation and production levels in some of the models. These efforts, however, were still too embryonic to provide practical tools by the time the project was destroyed.

Those who participated in the project agree about the advantages of the approach tried in CYBERSYN, namely, the velocity with which practical implementation can be started from the very beginning of activities; the elimination or at least, minimization of boundaries between the people in charge of the study and development of the design and the users of the tools; the extreme adaptability of the approach which allows the design to evolve in response to and interacting with the changes in the system itself; the capacity for self-correction of most of the important algorithms which do not depend on the existence of huge data banks or on the precision of the information; the convenience of using computers and other technological tools in a strongly interactive scheme with men because both, men and computers are using their own "abilities" to best advantage.

The main shortcoming that should be mentioned is the fact that the project was killed too early to allow firmer or more definite conclusions in several areas.

I disagree with some members of the project team with respect to one question: attention paid to economic, and particularly to monetary policies. Although such policies were exogenous to the industrial system, their neglect prevented, in my opinion, better decisions in the areas of sales, production, stocking and salary policies of many sub-systems, particularly during the last stages of the project.

I   THE ORIGINAL IDEAS AND THE STATEMENT OF THE PROBLEM

Some information about the institutional net that provided the project with a structural frame of reference is pertinent in order to understand its development.

Chile is a Third World country with ten million people, sixty per cent of which are urban dwellers. The average annual per capita income lies between

US 550 and US 700 (§). Industry is responsible for roughly 25% of the GNP. Mining and agriculture are the other two important productive sectors.

Since the decade of the thirties, the state has had a very important role as promoter, both technically and financially, of the industrial development of the country. This has been mainly carried out through a state corporation, CORFO, directly dependent of the Ministry of Economics. Historically, this corporation has developed state-owned companies, such as those devoted to power generation, oil and gas exploitation and steel production. CORFO has also assisted private business through financing, technical counseling and international marketing.

In 1971, when the program of nationalization began, CORFO was invested with the responsibility of supervising and managing the newly acquired units. First priority was given to the development of management tools that should be practical in a very short period and also adequate for the absolutely new conditions that were being faced with the new policies.

In order to get some independent advise, a British consultant (§§) was invited in November, 1971,to discuss the actual situation of industry at that moment and the prospectives for the development of new management capabilities, suitable for the new conditions. The consultant was then retained for the duration of the project and was actually appointed its Scientific Director and vested with the pertinent executive power and responsibilities.

The problems as discussed in November, 1971, can now be summarized as follows:

"Given a complex system called nationalized industry, subject to very fast changes (size, product design, price policies, etc.), inserted in a broader system (the national economy, inserted in turn in the whole of the national socio-political life), and subject to very specific political boundary conditions, it is required to develop its structure and information flow in order that decision-making, planning and actual operations respond satisfactorily to a program of external demands and the system remain viably."

This statement requires some elaboration.

"Fast change". By now, it is a truism that all material systems of practical interest are dynamic, i.e., that the time is an essential independent variable

---

(§) The historical very high rates of inflation plus the rates of exchange fixed on a base different from that of the socalled free-market, make it difficult to give a more precise figure. These variations reflect often in international statistical reports on the Chilean economy.

(§§) Professor Stafford Beer, from the University of Manchester.

for behavior description. But here "fast" means that essential perturbations to the system are more frequent than the time required for the system to absorb them and return to some stable condition (§). Typical perturbations were for instance, incorporation of new productive units to the system (occasionally more than one per day), sudden total discontinuation of an imported input, urgent demand of an out-of-schedule line of products, etc.

"Insertion of the system in a broader system". Fig. 1 is a crude scheme of the situation at the end of 1971. Up to that moment, the productive units had been almost completely autonomous. This means that they had evolved as a response of private business to profit expectations, given a certain level of stimuli for investment. From nationalization onwards, they were supposed to evolve according to levels of demands required to satisfy needs of consumption and of capital goods. The word need is underlined to stress the concept of effective needs (biological, psychological, cultural, etc.) rather than the spectrum of demands determined solely by income distribution. This norm meant that industrial production should be coupled to and regulated in accordance with the behavior of the whole system, i.e., of the national society at large. This contrasts with the simple and, in a certain restricted sense, effective regulation provided by supply and demand. Consequently, any hope to control and regulate the industrial system would require knowledge about the system structure and management of the information patterns. In other words, appropriate structural and behavioral models were required.

It will be shown below that in the approach that was chosen, every structure is modelled on the basis of different niveaus (§§) of recursion (or hierarchies of complexity), every component of which is isomorphic to the basic "viable" model. The patterns of information flow partake also of this property of recursion.

"Political boundary conditions" means here that there were particular norms or value criteria that had to be compatible with the design and implementation to follow. In addition to the already mentioned norm of "producing to satisfy real needs", it was specified that the system to be implemented should accept a high degree of relevant information for all the workers in the system, from top executives to production-line workers. Moreover, the design for information management should be such that relevant and effective participation of the workers in the decision-making process at the different niveaus of recursion should be a practical possibility.

(§) See for instance Beer "Laws of Anarchy", The Irvine Memorial Lect. Univ. of St. Andrews (1975) for a discussion of the time dimension of an organization.

(§§) The word "niveau" has been chosen in order to avoid confusion with the particular concept of "level" inside a given niveau.

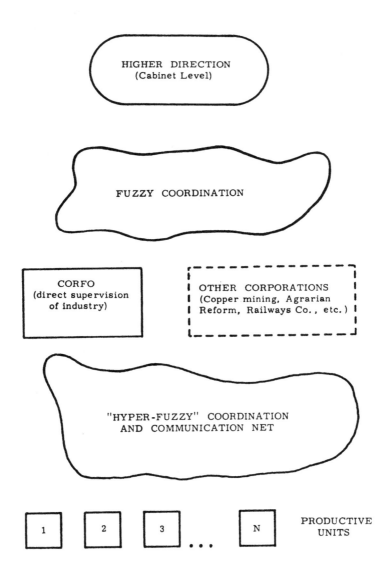

Fig. 1 - SCHEME OF THE SITUATION BEFORE CYBERSYN

Additionally, the system should be able to explore constantly its future prospectives not on the basis of a rigid, mechanical plan or an algorithm for deterministic predictions, but rather through development of scientific tools that would allow the study of different alternatives, given different time horizons, boundary conditions and policy priorities at the various niveaus of recursion.

The concept of viability was accepted as the cybernetic expression of the "health" of the system rather than the more traditional ideal of optimum.

Viability is associated with the overall ability of the system to survive and evolve harmonically in a dynamic environment, while optimality requires for a very complex system that it be permanently cornered into compatible extreme values of some coordinates with the frequent risk of all kinds of oscillations in other identifiable and non-identifiable coordinates.

II THE STRUCTURAL MODEL

A detailed presentation of the model can be found in Beer's The Brain of the Firm (1972). A very dense résumé, hopefully sufficient to render this presentation coherent, is given here.

Two ideas are postulated:

-   The essential criterion for structural design of a complex system is that it be viable, i.e., that it can survive (§). This means that it can adapt sufficiently fast to a changing environment (learning or self-adapting), and that it be vested with homeostatic control (§§); in other words, that its regulating sub-structure is sufficiently rich to keep its essential critical variables within narrow limits, in spite of gross variations of the environment.

-   A complex, viable system is made up of sub-systems, which in themselves must be viable.

(§) At the time of the project, and as part of their own research, the Chilean biologists H. Maturana and F. Varely developed the concept of "autopoietic system" to characterize living organisms. An autopoietic system is one that has its own organizational structure as its homeostatic variable. This rather complex concept lead to very enlightened discussions inside the CYBERSYN team but no operational advantages for it in the particular context of CYBERSYN were found. (See references at the end.)

(§§) In the sense elaborated by R.W. Ashby in Design for a Brain (1952).

These two structural properties - viability and recursion - are sufficiently demanding to determine all the essential characteristics of the structural model.

Fig. 2 shows the nested set of viable systems which represent the Chilean structure in which CYBERSYN was inserted. There are 12 niveaus of recursion (or of resolution), which determine 12 hierarchies of homologous systems If attention is focused on any given niveau, the systems in it are made up of viable subsystems and are inserted in a given "metasystem". Actually, CYBERSYN experience dealt mainly with niveaus 1 to 9 and even more particularly with 6 to 9.

The representation of the figure should not be viewed as implying any centralized, mechanistic determination of the behavior of any system at any niveau.

Actually, a strongly pressed point during the whole development was the effort to discard as an irrelevant category of analysis the dichotomy between centralization and de-centralization. No viable system can be rigidly and completely controlled from a central unit, on the one extreme. No viable system can, on the other extreme, prescind of some form of central control in order to monitor the system performance and the environment evolution and consequently, to direct dynamic adjustments of the system so as to keep homeostatic variables within "physiological limits".

Rather than centralization or de-centralization, the model emphazises a dynamic equilibrium involving: (a) sufficient autonomy of the system with respect to its metasystem, in order to cope with its relevant environment without trivial overloading to and interfering from the metasystem; (b) sufficient linkage to the metasystem, so that a higher-order control is accessible whenever the environment or other iso-hierarchic systems perturb the system beyond its own capacity; (c) sufficient control over its own sub-systems, as to insure that its broad goals will not be hampered by the lower-order, eventually conflicting goals of the sub-systems; and (d) sufficient complexity in its own sub-systems as to vest them with enough autonomy to deal with their own relevant environments insofar as these are "opaque" or trivial for the main system.

This central concept of the balance between autonomy and dependence is expressed in this specific application through the additional, following properties:

1 - The internal structure of any system at any niveau models isomorphically onto the viable "prototype" (see Fig. 3 and its explanation).

2 - Monitoring of the system behavior by the metasystem is compensated by feed-back from the system to the metasystem.

86

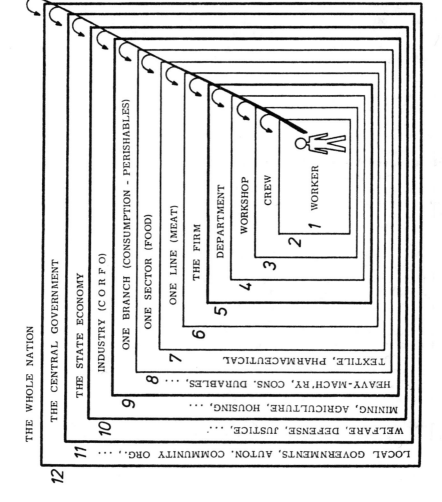

THE WHOLE NATION

THE CENTRAL GOVERNMENT

THE STATE ECONOMY

INDUSTRY (C O R F O)

ONE BRANCH (CONSUMPTION - PERISHABLES)

ONE SECTOR (FOOD)

ONE LINE (MEAT)

THE FIRM

DEPARTMENT

WORKSHOP

CREW

WORKER

1

2

3

4

5

6

7 TEXTILE, PHARMACEUTICAL

8 HEAVY-MACH'RY, CONS. DURABLES, ...

9 MINING, AGRICULTURE, HOUSING, ...

10 WELFARE, DEFENSE, JUSTICE, ...

11 LOCAL GOVERNMENTS, AUTON, COMMUNITY ORG., ...

12

Fig. 2 - - NESTED SET OF VIABLE SYSTEMS

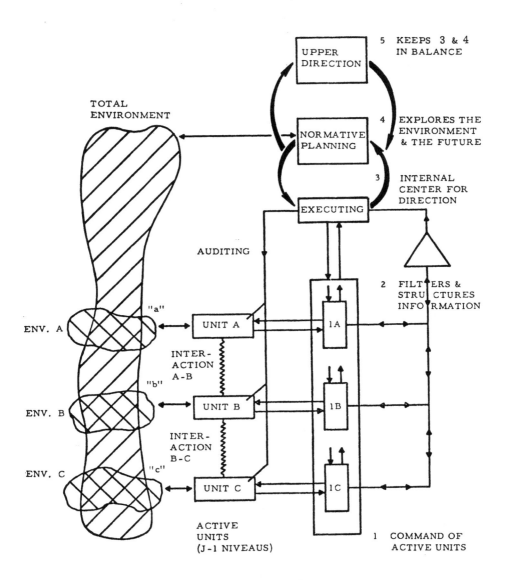

Fig. 3 - THE VIABLE STRUCTURAL PROTOTYPE
WITH ITS FIVE LEVELS (THE WHOLE
REPRESENTS NIVEAU 3)

3 - The relevant environment of a given system at a given hierarchy inter-
sects with the relevant environment of its metasystem but a) is not
wholly contained in it, and b) it resolves much more thinly than the
"meta-environment". Some examples will make this point plain. His
personal hobby - stamps, say - might be very relevant for the worker
(niveau 1) but it will be totally irrelevant for all the upper niveaus. The
firm soccer team will be relevant, maybe, to all niveaus from the firm
down and will be irrelevant from it upwards. Design of packing labels
will be a problem that will not normally interest higher niveaus than the
firm. Customer satisfaction should be measured in great detail by the
firm, but in more and more aggregate forms as one goes up to superior
niveaus.

4 - The individual should have effective and organic feed-back channels to
all niveaus of the system, if the participational postulate is going to become true and if effective satisfaction of needs is going to be the performance indicator of the whole system behavior.

The CYBERSYN experience and the aborted Chilean experiment at large,
cannot be invoked as a conclusive proof that this last property can become
steadily and generally valid inside a given society. On the other hand, both
experiments were extremely suggestive of new, effective forms of individual
participation that can be actually developed.

The viable structural prototype

The detailed presentation of this model makes up the core of "The Brain of
the Firm". Making a relevant summary of it would be not only redundant but
probably also unfair to the elegant development of Beer. Therefore, some of
its most essential characteristics will be just pointed out. (See Fig. 3)

1 - If one is interested in the model of a viable system at any niveau of recursion, one should better look at those structural elements which are
absolutely necessary for the survival of the system in a given environment, rather than at particular functions or organs which are the
"morphological" expressions of such elements.

2 - If the survival of the system requires a certain topological structure
and a certain net of information channels, it will be advantageous if
both are simultaneously present in the same model.

3 - The above arguments eliminate from consideration any traditional
static models like the usual organization charts with their irrelevant
lines of formal communications, their rigid vertical controls and their
negligence for the environment.

4 - If any human organization is actually recursive, its final elements will
be individuals. Now, individuals are, beyond any doubt, extremely

viable systems. Then, the cybernetic analysis of the human being should provide the most thoroughly tested prototype of a viable model. (See chapter 6, "The Anatomy of Management" in S. Beer "Brain of the Firm".)

5 - Since the hierarchical structure is recursive, the prototype obtained from such analysis must be adequate to model all the other niveaus.

This is essentially what "The Brain of the Firm" attempted to do, invoking a good deal of neurophysiological and cybernetic arguments.

If one accepts this structural model, then the criteria for information handling and decision-making will be greatly simplified.

A short description of Fig. 3 is now pertinent. It is important to remember Beer's claim that the model contains the necessary description of any viable system, for instance, of any of the 12 niveaus of Fig. 2.

For a better understanding of the property of recursion, if one assumes that Fig. 3 represents a system of hierarchical niveau j, the boxes labelled A, B and C are the sub-systems of order j-1. If the attention is fixed on the metasystem of order j+1, then the whole structure represented in Fig. 3 would collapse into one of the small boxes. This shows that the model represents both the information flow at a given hierarchical niveau and the information flow between a system and its sub-systems.

Level 1   It represents the centers of command of the "active units" by means of which the system carries out or "executes" the activities required for its survival. Depending on the nature of the system, the active units may be different, as illustrated in the following examples:

- the human being has legs to walk, arms to grasp, lungs to breathe and so on;

- the industrial firm may have several divisions with a similar role: production, maintenance, sales, procurements, etc.;

- a branch such as those shown in Figure 2, contains several sectors: food industry, textile industry, pharmaceutical industry, etc.

Every one of these systems contains of course a great deal of complexity but the stable behavior of the whole system requires only a relatively small amount of information about each subsystem. This filtration and handling of information is carried out by means of three kinds of links that resemble the central command through the spinal cord in the vertebrates, the paravertebral sympathetic trunks and the parasympathetic system. Level 1 is strictly the axis of command between level 3 and the active units: it transmits orders and reports reactions, handling simultaneously the appropriate language for system 3 and the peripheral units. The boxes marked 1A, 1B and

1C represent the "division managers".

This is apparently very similar to the traditional hierarchical model of the organization chart, except that that model is bound to be wrong because it leaves out the information required by the whole system and which does not go through the chain of command. That is, the organization chart does not show the sympathetic and parasympathetic systems.

Level 2 The divisional managers (or spinal cord centers) are inundated with information from the units; some of this, they forward to the direction for operations (level 3) but the rest is not suppressed: it is sent to system 2, where all the information coming from the different units is processed and checked for compatibilities or for potential difficulties. Some results, carefully elaborated may go to level 3 and some warnings may return to the units in level 1. The "sympathetic system" is doing the work of "tactical planning". Every subsystem is producing and demanding information in its "own language". Now, flows must be compatible and this compatibilization is the job of level 2. For instance, most of the information coming from level 1 can be ignored by level 3, provided there is a discriminating filter at 2 to block information, unless it is important for the upper systems. On the other hand, general instructions coming from 3, whose specific role is to command systemic goals or tasks, need to be detailed for the various subsystems in their own language. Then, 2 is a filter for the information coming from level 1, a codifier for the remaining information in the meta-language, an amplifier for information coming from level 3 and a codifier for such amplified information in the language of the lower level.

At the same time, level 2 is a center of exchange of information between the different elements of level 1.

These concepts, so extremely simplified, provide the central philosophy for manipulation of information required by level 3 to make decisions that will keep the whole system stable and responsive to the environment.

It should be clear that level 2 is not executive, in the sense that it does not make decisions, but rather handles information upwards and horizontally so that the process of decision-making and decision-implementing is effective.

Beer explains in detail how the role of level 2 is played in the human being by the spinal cord. Any elementary description of the function of the spinal cord will convince the reader that it actually works as a compensator between autonomy of the level 1 organs, and centralized control coming from the brain, specifically from the medulla oblongata and cerebellum.

It is also easily understood why this balance between autonomy and central control is so poor in many social organizations. Conventional design of instructions pays little attention, if any, to providing effective channels, filters and amplifiers between levels 3 and 1. The level for the Direction of Operations

is usually overloaded with information and demands for decisions, while the
productive units are either too timid to use their autonomy or they press for
total autonomy.

Level 3   The internal direction of operation. This level is in charge of the
           whole "present" of the system. It gives orders for activities which
in turn are split into many tasks for the different sub-systems of level 1 organs.

The command "run now" means in the individual certain rhythms of respiration,
of heartbeats, certain movements of legs and arms, etc. Details of those orders
and of their feed-backs are kept at the reflex level of the spinal cord but
perturbations are transmitted up and down (muscles overstressed, breathless,
etc.).

At the niveau of the firm, the command "increase production of model X by
2%" means changes in purchases, in machine-tool loads, storage allocations,
sales efforts, etc. If all of these things are specified in detail by level 3,
then its people should be transferred to a lower level.

There is one aspect though, in which 3 should have direct contact with 1 and
that is what could be called "Auditing and Emergency Action", at the niveau
of the firm, or parasympathetic control at the niveau of the individual. Under
"auditing" one tries to express the need of 3 to check if messages coming
from 2 are not leaving out something important in the meta-language of the
upper direction. Typical symptoms to look after are: people's dissatisfaction,
financial abuses, excessive waste, customers complaints and so on. Typical
orders to go through this channel are: develop emergency plans to meet urgent demands, settle the dispute on working conditions overruling the standard
practice, deplete the stocks in order to satisfy special demands, transfer
manpower to another unit undergoing temporary crisis, etc.

Level 3 has nothing to do with the external environment, except through
level 4 and levels 2 and 1. On the other hand, level 3 is in turn the source
of routine reports to the next higher niveau (not level) and of reception of
the corresponding feed-back from that niveau.

It is obvious then that level 3 is simultaneously a very active center of
decisions and a very critical node of information. Since level 3 is far from
the environment, it is obsessed with intense performance of the system but
is very reluctant to change. Any decisions for change coming from the level
of higher direction, or from the upper niveau forces level 3 to an important
effort of adjustment.

Level 4   The function of this level is the exploration of the environment
           and of the future. The human nervous system is connected to the
environment through the different senses. Perceptions through the senses
are carried to the inner part of the brain (region of the corpus callosus and
the third ventricle).

In strict analogy to this function, any viable system must perform the activity of exploring the environment and the future if it intends to remain viable in spite of the external changes.

At the niveau of the firm, niveau used here as an easy reference, activities such as marketing, research and development, and planning are typical of this level 4. There is very little concern here for the routine activities of the system, except to keep level 3 informed of relevant changes in the environment. This level is occupied with change or adjustment to conditions that will appear in the future. The people working at level 4 want to change the product lines, to invest in new facilities, to explore new markets, etc.

Planning and simulation are the main tools at this level. Specifications about the information pattern must be adequate for this task. What information and how frequently should it be obtained from the environment? What information and under which codification language should it be delivered to levels 4 and 5? Which principles should regulate the internal manipulation of information?

Level 5   After the description of the previous four levels, it is not obvious that an additional one should be needed. After all, it is apparent that productive activities are taken care of by sub-systems at level 1; that short range survival and reporting to the upper niveau is the task of level 3, and the environment and the future are monitored by level 4.

The task of level 5, higher direction, is nevertheless absolutely essential. The system so far defined has no ability to make the big options: emphasis on the future or on the present, lines of evolution, risky decisions that may hamper the future survival of the system, etc. In other words, level 5 synthetizes the conservative pulls of level 3 and the progressive pushes of level 4 and moreover, looks for the unexpected or the unpredictable, i.e., it is the cortex of the brain or the conscience of the system. Beer says "that it keeps the homeostat 3 - 4 under control".

CYBERSYN developed a bold method for information handling of level 5, the key decision-making spot of the system.

With this condensed review of the prototype structure of the system one is in the position of making a coherent analysis of the tools developed by CYBERSYN, and that task will be the object of the following sections.

Before doing that, however, some practical principles resulting from the above analysis will be stated as conclusions of this section.

1 - The cybernetic approach requires that the system structure, with its pertinent niveaus, be recognized together with the relevant paths of information.

2 - Different structural niveaus associate with different relevant environments. These should also be clearly identified.

3 - The "present life" of the system (level 3 for the direction of operations)
is not separable of the exploration of the future (level 4). If "planning
and simulation" is isolated of the daily life of the system, there is a
strong risk that the work of the planners will stay in the future forever.
In that case, level 5 will work only with level 3. Actually, it will almost
certainly coalesce with it and level 4 might become an outside "group
of consultants", i.e., part of the environment. The system will become
blind and deaf.

4 - What is happening today in level 1 must, after proper filtration at 2 and
3, reach level 4. Otherwise, simulations refer to a system which existed
long time ago.

5 - The structural model does not tell how participation of the individuals,
that is, the ultimate social control, can be achieved. Whatever progress
was made in this direction, was developed through the history of CYBERSYN
in interaction with the political dynamics of the surrounding environment.
The curly arrow in Fig. 2 was not contained in the original model. To
which extent this arrow became existent and effective, is part of the
story that follows.

III CYBERSYN AND THE DEVELOPMENT OF NEW STRUCTURES

Section I has shown what structural elements were available at the beginning
of the project (see Fig. 1). Section II has shown the basic theory of the
structural model. This was the situation after the first period of discussions
in November, 1971.

The developments that followed were not only (and even not mainly)the result
of CYBERSYN work. Otherwise, the whole description of the model would be
baseless.

One must remember, though, that in those days the socio-political environment in Chile was extremely dynamic. No group of experts would have been
given the monopoly of design of the new structure. The people at large,
through political parties, worker unions and federations were exerting their
pressure and making their voices heard. The CYBERSYN team understood
from the beginning that it had to advise and help inside these sometimes
oscillating, sometimes chaotic dynamics. The experts had to find their way
to key executives, leaders and politicians. Otherwise their ideas, no matter
how good the theory, would have been pushed aside. Loosely speaking, level
4 found its place in the body of the system.

In a few months, the existing structure was adapted to the new purposes, to the extent at least, to fill the vacuum between CORFO (niveau 9 in Fig. 2) and the productive units (niveau 5). The niveaus called Lines (6) were created using mainly human resources of the firms themselves. The Sectors (7) and the Branches (8) were structured by relocating a high percentage of the working force of CORFO that had previously been a strongly centralized bureaucracy.

CORFO itself adopted a viable structure. For this, it identified the executive vicepresident and a very small staff with the role of level 5; it created units for over-all planning investment control and the central team of CYBERSYN, which configurated level 4; it established a general manager position to act as head of level 3; an office was created for coordination of information, which was at the same time the central office of a new Telex net. Level 2 was thus recognized. Four "Branches" were established which became "level 1 units" inside CORFO. Their areas are given as an illustration of the kind of division possible: Branch 1 for industries devoted to perishable products for consumption; Branch 2 for durable consumption products; Branch 3 for heavy industry such as steel mills and oil refinement; and Branch 4 for machinery and finished capital goods.

This detailed enumeration is given to show two important characteristics:

1 - The five levels are not associated with internal hierarchies or bureaucratic status. For instance, the lower level 1 was headed by highly qualified full managers, with great autonomy; whereas level 2 was a technical office headed by a competent member of CYBERSYN with no authority over level 1; the head of level 3, the general manager, was the second highest-ranking officer of the corporation, while units in level 4 were headed by the best available specialists with no authority over level 3 and with a lower status than the general manager.

2 - The branching responded to a logic associated with normative criteria that did not depend on internal affinities, as for instance, similar technologies of professional expertise but rather depended on value criteria meaningful for the meta-system. The top performance criterion of the whole economy was one of satisfaction of needs. Basic individual needs are satisfied through consumption goods but capital goods are also directly related to the future ability to satisfy basic needs.

The performance of any given Branch was immediately indicative of the level of satisfaction of a certain type of needs or of some strategic prospectives.

For instance, Branch 1 grouped food, textile and pharmaceutical industry. It is obvious that the Branch management was forced to think in terms of levels of satisfaction and could not have the know-how or the specialized staff to meddle in the specific business of the individual lines, not to speak of the individual firms.

At the same time that CORFO acquired its new structure, the Branch units were organized in accordance with the same model, although they needed a rather modest staff. No exact figures are now available but it is believed that no Branch was using more than 30 people by the middle of 1973. By this time people had generally got convinced that the importance of a given unit had little to do with the size of the payroll.

I served a short time as head of the Sector for Food Industry. Since Sectors were directly responsible for the actual performance of the productive units, it might be helpful to show a typical sector organization, see Fig. 4.

One must remember that at that time the process of acquisition of new units was a very dynamic one, that there was a situation of permanent emergency and that the end of such instabilities was hard to determine or even to guess. The 35 companies that made up the productivity capacity of the whole sector were grouped in 7 different lines according to the nature of the products, the type of processes and the required materials. Typical lines were: meat and poultry, canned vegetables and fruits, soft drinks and beer, wine and spirits, sugar and edible oil, etc. The performance of each line was supervised and coordinated by a line manager, whose main concern was troubleshooting in connection with logistic support related to raw materials, transportation, warehousing and distribution. Besides these executive duties, focused on solving emergencies, the managers were helping the information unit (level 2) to organize the rational flow and co-ordination of information in accordance with the schemes of the CYBERSYN group (see Sec. VI below).

The set of line managers reported to the head of the Operations Division, who in turn had three additional supporting groups. The information group that was also performing the tactical planning for day-to-day operations; the team of Financial Auditing that had direct access to the productive units; and the group for Labour Relations, that was in charge of promoting worker participation and regulating wage policies and monetary stimuli.

Informational structure responded again to the same three key issues: routine information for daily management (levels 1 - 3); environmental information for planning; and symptomatic information for decision-making at levels 3 - 4 - 5.

Although, as it should be expected, level 3 is the center of routine information for the upper niveau (in this case, the Branch), level 5 is responsible for reflecting the "meta-policies" inside the system. This means that its basic responsibility is to keep abreast of national economic and industrial policies, of new regulations, of crisis in other Sectors that might in turn reflect in the Sector performance. In addition, level 5 was responsible for translating these facts into Sector policies and implementing them through the activities of levels 4 and 3.

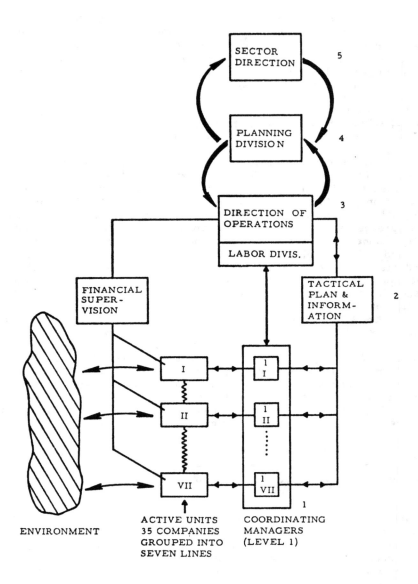

Fig. 4 - FOOD SECTOR STRUCTURE

IV   SOME IDEAS ABOUT INFORMATION MANAGEMENT

Although the principles of information theory can be presented in several
alternative ways with different degrees of mathematical sophistication, it
seems sufficient here to use Beer's presentation based on Ashby's concept
of VARIETY:

"VARIETY is the measure of complexity in a system, defined as the number
  of its possible states."

The relationship of this concept to the idea of entropy as defined in statistical
mechanics is obvious. The same can be said in relationship with the number
of bits required to store a certain description.

The concept of variety seems more convenient than either entropy or bits,
because it lacks their narrow practical connotations.

The design of information flow is directly related to the complexity of the
system has to be controlled. This is expressed in Ashby's Law - also called
the Law of Requisite Variety - and which can be paraphrased as "only
variety can absorb variety".

This idea is fundamental to the whole philosophy of CYBERSYN but the apparent simplicity of its statement might be misleading.

"If the regulator has less variety than the system to be controlled, then there
  are possible states of the system which are unattainable under the command
  of the regulator."

"If the regulator has more variety than the system to be controlled, there
  will be a waste of regulator capacity."

Since the first statement corresponds to the usual conditions of practical
interest, there is no other solution but to design attenuators and amplifiers
as shown in Fig. 5.

This is exactly the role of level 2 in the structural model discussed in the
previous section.

As computers are mandatory tools in the management of any modern complex system, it is important to verify whether the Law of Requisite Variety
is relevant to their use.

A computer has a high bit capacity and man has a low bit capacity; therefore,
man-computer interaction requires the introduction of attenuators and amplifiers.

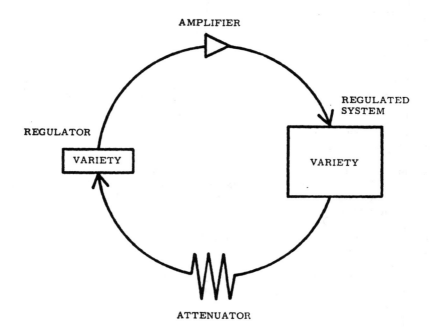

Fig. 5 - THE LAW OF REQUISITE VARIETY

There are however activities, such as judgement, abstraction and inductive logic where man is substantially superior to automata of the near future. Therefore, the best scientific solution should use that combination of man-machine interaction as to take best advantage of the best qualities of the human being and of the machine. (§)

It has already been mentioned that another characteristic of contemporary complex systems is the high frequency of the perturbations compared with a relatively long relaxation time.

This property reinforces the need for computers. If relaxation times are going to be shortened or if perturbations are going to be detected before they have taken the system out of its band of control, relevant information must be processed rapidly. The decision-maker needs to base his judgement on what is happening now and not a year ago. That computers are fast is an understatement. But computer speed does not solve the problem. They must be fed with recent information and their results must reach the decision-maker as soon as possible.

All these ideas show how the quality, quantity and "age" of the information become important for the decision-making process. It is that balance inside the system structure which is important and not the total amount of information or the size of the data bank or the sophistication of the mathematical algorithms.

A heuristic loose principle could be: at every link of the decision-making chain the balance of quality, quantity and age of the information should be adequate for the variety capacity of the link and for the relaxation time of the system.

With the Law of Requisite Variety, with the model for the viable structure, with the practical fact that computers are an almost mandatory requirement to the management of complex systems, and with the principle of recent information, the following "recipelike" statements can be listed:

1 - In a purely human link, whenever there is a relationship many-to-one, an attenuator of variety is mandatory, and conversely an amplifier is mandatory in a relationship one-to-many. Otherwise variety is not balanced.

2 - Lots of data are not information. Information must be meaningful for the receptor, i.e., it must be inside the bounds of variety of the receptor and presented in the language of the receptor. Thus, the usual computer print-out is no information for a man, but only to another computer.

(§) See, for instance, articles by Friedman and Leondes.

3 - Man can take much less information than a computer but he has more access channels than the computer. This means that besides lists of figures or properties, man is able to discern topological patterns, colors, relative size, movement, etc. This means that whatever information is available to man should: (a) be inside his variety bounds, and (b) take full advantage of his access channel capacity.

V   ORGANIZATION OF CYBERSYN TEAM

Resources for the project - both in manpower and in investment funds - were extremely limited during the whole period.

CORFO allocated a group of around ten engineers that could devote full-time to the project. In addition, other companies or state corporations contributed some manpower, usually on a part-time basis and with the hope of eventually getting access to the tools developed. This was completely acceptable as it was considered to be in the national interest that the maximum number of companies should profit from the project.

From the beginning a close contact was established with ENTEL, the communications corporation, in order to implement the telex net; with ECOM, the state data processing corporation, which provided ample computer facilities for the project; and with INTEC, the State Institute for Research and Development, which contributed with manpower, space and facilities for the design and manufacture of visual aids, photographic laboratory, etc.

The central team would concentrate on the development of specific tools, such as computer programs, telex net supervision, design, construction and implementation of the Operation Room. In addition, part of the team would keep in permanent contact with Branches, Sectors and eventually firms, so that these could develop their own working teams for application of the tools, such as flow diagrams, selection of indicators, efforts of internal adjustments to the new model of structural organization, and use of the information as a tool for their own management.

Besides all this, a small seminar group was organized. The group included several of the participants in the project but not all of them, and included also outside experts who were interested in the project. The group would meet every second week and did not have a fixed subject. It did not restrict itself to matters of interest for the project, but would also explore subjects that might eventually relate to it. The group included around 25 people but attendance was usually about 15 and thus was adequate for lively discussions and full participation. Among these participants there were two biologists, one mathematician, one psychologist, one industrial designer, one sociologist, one political scientist, one linguist and the rest were engineers. The consultant, while in Chile, would occasionally attend the seminar. Subjects covered a wide spectrum such as autopoietic systems, principles of industrial design, tests of the "algedonic meter" or measurer of participation (§), the Calculus of Forms as developed by G. S. Brown, several lecturers by Heinz von Foerster who was a temporary guest, etc. The seminar was a very remarkable experience, as motivation to the project, as an interdisciplinary forum and as a test in informal self-education.

Although the team was always overstressed and substantial additional resources should have been granted for better performance, it was a remarkable proof of the possibilities for injecting synergy at low cost into a huge system. As a reference, one should mention that CORFO had approximately five thousand employees of which probably fifteen hundred were engineers.

VI   DEVELOPMENT OF THE PROGRAM IN CHILE

When the team had developed a clear understanding of the ideas about structure and information, as presented above, it was possible to develop a strategy for implementation, according to the following scheme:

1 - Management of the productive units could be effectively handled by CORFO with the structure of niveaus 5 to 9, provided that:

a) A minimum net of up-dated information between the companies and CORFO could be established. A discussion of tools for information handling and for acceptable time-lags in information resulted in the establishment of a telex circuit, covering essentially all the firms, sectors, branches and CORFO itself. A time-lag of one day was fixed as adequate for the routine information between CORFO and the companies. This meant that the particular value of a given indicator measured on day d_o in the production line should reach CORFO no later than $d_o + 1$.

b) The requirement that variety be adequate for the communication channels and the receptors resulted in the decision of developing for each company a limited number of relevant indicators that could be easily understood at the upper levels. If the indicators were to be actually indicative of the company behavior, they should perforce refer to the most essential and concrete activities of the company. This ruled out any complicated, abstract economic measurement referred to aggregated value, productivity or the like. A fortiori, such concoctions as balance sheets, cash-flows reports and other tools of the accountants were banished from the information circuits. It was decided that the

(§) A very simple instrument developed by Stafford and Simon Beer that would allow a speaker or lecturer to have immediate feedback of the reaction of the hearers.

system would start with indicators referring to production and to workers' attitudes.

c) The requirement that the upper levels not be overloaded with information was solved by having the daily values of indicators filtered through very elaborate computer programs. For each indicator, the computer could determine a range of normal behavior. As long as the indicator remained inside the healthy limits, no message was reported, that is, information would be trapped by level 2.

d) The requirement of adequate autonomy was satisfied as follows: the first time that an indicator fell out of its normal band, the fact was reported back only to the unit of origin. If the abnormal behavior was corrected, no message upwards would follow. If the deviation persisted, a warning upwards would be given by the computer itself.

2 - The tools developed for management of the routine operations, i.e., telex net, method of indicators tied to the chart-flows and computer programs, were developed with the intention that they should be equally applicable inside a given company (niveaus 1 to 4) or at higher policy levels (niveaus 9 to 11).

3 - Tools and programs developed for the routine operation and which are ideal for level 3 in the structural prototype are not adequate for the tasks of level 4, that is, for planning and exploration of the future.

For this purpose, two concepts provided the logic foundations to choose the best tools:

a) The idea of flexible planning. This means that planning is not a discrete activity which operates in cycles of 1, 3 or 5 years, but it is rather a continuous activity centered around a dynamic model of the behavior of the system under consideration.

Fig. 6 shows an obvious illustration of the idea. The plan should be continuously adjusted with recent information about the system and with criteria provided by new policies.

It is apparent that several alternative techniques of dynamic modelling are adequate for this purpose.

CYBERSYN chose the methodology of Industrial Dynamics, as developed by Jay Forrester. This method has the advantage of an ample battery of well-tested computer programs and of suitable adaptability for the different niveaus of the model.

b) The strategy of combining the so-called Normative, Strategic and Tactical modes of planning as developed by Beer.

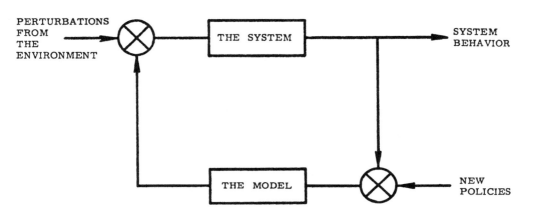

Fig. 6 - REPRESENTATION OF FLEXIBLE PLANNING

Fig. 7 is a convenient scheme to analyze these ideas.

The concepts displayed in the figure have the following meaning:

Assume that a given indicator relevant for the plan has a normative goal of 1.00 (example, a plant that ought to produce 20,000 units per year, in order to comply with a goal of satisfaction of real needs). The indicators are always presented in non-dimensional form, the value 1.00 corresponding to the norm. Then, POTENTIALITY, i.e., the value that should be reached when all improvements and enlargements considered in the Master Program of Goals (determined according to social needs) are achieved, is the reference of the Normative Planning.

CAPABILITY refers to the best value that the indicator can attain given the present conditions of equipment, bottlenecks, availability of materials and so on. In other words, what should happen with the optimum use of existing resources.

ACTUALITY is what should be actually programmed when all the practical limitations of the system are accounted for, such as quality of manpower, failures of maintenance, quality rejects, etc.

The meaning of PRODUCTIVITY, LATENCY and PERFORMANCE are rather obvious. It is interesting, however, that PRODUCTIVITY and LATENCY may have any combination of relatively high and low values (between 0 and 1, of course). A high PRODUCTIVITY reflects the current achievement (level 3 is doing very well). A high LATENCY means that the system has an output capacity which is close to that required to satisfy the anticipated needs.

These quantitative concepts provide a bridge between the planning experts and the operations people. Once an indicator is defined, the daily reports processed through the computer trace the evolution of actual deviations from ACTUALITY: the periodic observations of the facilities, equipment, workers performance, etc., obtained through the up-dating of the simplified chart flows, allows keeping track of the CAPABILITY; the overall evaluation of needs and means of satisfaction, through Normative Planning, yields the POTENTIALITY information.

Fig. 8 shows a typical sketch of the recorded behavior of an indicator.

4 - Additional specific tools for information handling at the upper direction level were prepared. The basic idea in this case was that the task of level 5 is to produce the dynamic synthesis between the efforts of level 3 to improve the behavior of the system without disturbing changes, the pushes of level 4 to adapt very fast to the new possibilities and demands, and the own perceptions of level 5 about higher policies, eventual crises and other impredictable and more subtle "moods" of the environment and of the higher niveaus.

105

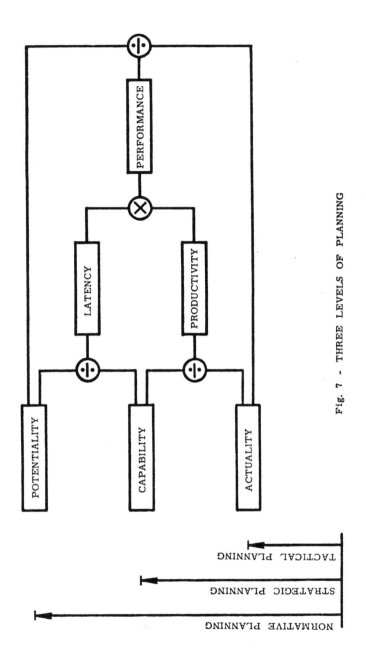

Fig. 7 - THREE LEVELS OF PLANNING

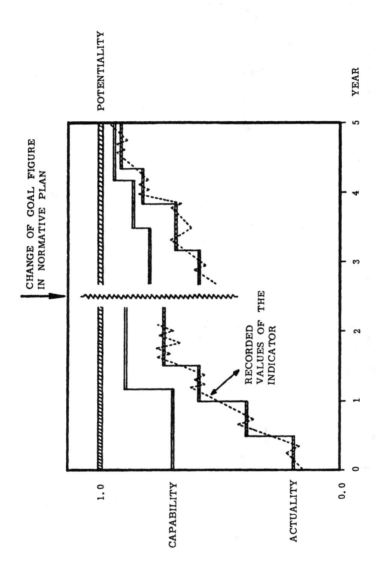

Fig. 8 - GRAPHIC RECORD OF A TYPICAL INDICATOR

In addition to the synthetic nature of the task of level 5, it was decided
that the tools should be adequate for collective rather than individual use.
Higher direction was not supposed to be an autocratic exercise of power
in the hands of an executive-bureaucrat, but rather a collective effort of
discussion and persuasion in which the "boss" acts as a leader of a team,
as a source of strategic information and as a responsible supervisor of
execution of whatever is decided at level 5.

For these reasons, the idea, design and implementation of the so-called
operation rooms was developed. A detailed description of the different
experiences known to me will be given below.

At this point, it is interesting to remark only that several experiences
were made with different levels of sophistication. A complete, advanced
prototype was built to be used by CORFO's upper direction; several local
rooms were developed for lower level niveaus, one of them by myself to
be used in the Food Industry Sector, another was started at a large factory devoted to tire manufacturing; the design of a room intended to be
used by the coordinating group of the Ministries of the Treasure and of
Economy was advanced to the level of layouts and discussion of key indicators. This project was discontinued in April 1973 due to political
difficulties that were already reaching a critical stage.

Some key criteria that resulted from these experiences are:

a) Although the room is intended for collective use, its size should be
   limited to accomodate a group adequate for the decision-making
   process. Seven seems to be an ideal number and probably ten should
   be an absolute upper bound.

b) Information should be presented with strict adherence to laws of er-
   gonomy. Maximum care should be exercised to avoid overloading the
   group with mere data. Use of graph displays should take full advantage of human capacity for pattern recognition, and should make in-
   telligent use of colors and dynamic elements.

c) A sound combination of flexible and rigid tools should be provided, so
   that the environmental conditions effectively lead to decision-making
   rather than to general speculative discussions. For instance, in addition to displays for structural information and gadgets to present the
   dynamic models, a small conventional black-board was provided in
   every room but in such a way that its use was rather discouraged.

d) Although the detailed design of the room is very important, its development should keep pace with its environmental conditions. For
   instance, in the Food Sector where general facilities were good but
   modest, the elements in the room partook of this characteristic. It
   is not the quality of the "gadgetry" that determines the success of

the room but rather its acceptance inside the decision-making process
and the harmonic structure of the systems-information patterns.
Gadgets will help only if the overall concept is sound and the implementation careful.

5 - Efforts to develop workers participation.

The original structural model proposed by the consultant did not consider this aspect explicitly. The requirement of workers participation
was a consequence of the particular political criteria that were an essential part of the Chilean experience. Deep discussions on this question
were necessary in order to find methods and try experimental situations
to test participation. President Allende paid particular attention to this
point and made suggestions and requirements about it and personally
participated in some of such experimental situations. The extremely
positive attitude of the consultant in coming to grips with the problem
and in devising and suggesting new methods and tools deserves full recognition.

Again in this matter it is not possible to draw firm conclusions, but the
kind of experiments carried out were quite encouraging:

a) At the end of 1972, some experiments in workers' education for participation were made. A special team was formed including some
workers with a higher level of education and political understanding.
A small battery of instruction material was assorted, and a factory
was chosen to test the system. A full week of lectures and pannel discussions was held with approximately 30 workers. Lectures with
visual aids were given by members of CYBERSYN, by engineers of
the factory and by one member of the Cabinet. An expert in education
plus a cartoonist attended the seminar in order to use the experience
to prepare further material.

Reception by management of the factory was far from warm, but the
workers attitude was extremely positive. They learned to make the
flow charts by themselves and by the end of the course they could
develop sensible arguments about organization, planning and production improvement. By then, the main operation rooms was almost
finished and one session was held with a group of workers to test their
attitude with respect to advanced techniques.

b) On January 1973, another two-day session was spent in a textile factory with full time participation of President Allende and in this case
no systematic discussion of management tools was made as Allende's
continuous presence kept the meetings at a very high level of excitement. The workers were too eager to discuss the very urgent problems
of lack of raw materials, sabotage of spare parts supplies, economic
unbalances and the like. Although no positive conclusion about the

use of CYBERSYN tools was attained, the meeting showed once again the interest of workers in problems of management and production when they feel that their views are accepted.

c) In the same period several efforts to prepare materials for training were made. Series of cartoons showing the principles of cybernetic management were prepared, some of them made by the workers themselves. The consultant himself prepared some documents ad-hoc. This material, in spite of its high quality, could not be printed before September 1973, and part of it at least has been lost.

d) With the assistance of the consultant, a more ambitious training program was designed, including movies and other visual aids. The program was intended to operate around the year and provide 15-day training sessions to 24 groups of seventy-two workers each. The project could not take off before the September events.

e) Between April and September 1973, a whole program of participation was carried out in most of the productive units. This was launched by the office of the National Plan, independent of CYBERSYN, and by the time of the putsch it was very successfully under way. The program attempted to have the workers discussing the production and investment programs for 1974. It was a sort of determination of the ACTUALITY levels for the coming year. At the Food Industry Sector, this program was given first priority and it was developed in the largest productive units such as the National Brewery Monopoly, the Sugar Line, the Vegetable Oil Line and the largest producers of pasta. Together with this program of discussion and elaboration of the Plan, the programs for workers representation in the boards of the companies and in the consulting boards of the Sector Committees were being implemented.

f) The consultant got extremely interested in exploring possibilities for education provided by the mass media and a very flexible, autonomous work was established by mid-73 to develop some motivation means through folk music. The first song was composed and Beer has reported on it. (§)

g) The problem of continuous survey of the reaction of the workers and the public at large was a source of permanent concern for the CYBERSYN team. No tool exists for this purpose anywhere, besides the usual public opinion polls. The limitations of these methods and the cost of carrying a continuous poll left this possibility out of consideration. Alternatively, it was decided to start some very tentative small scale tests, such as the one using the on-line reaction "measurer". Tests at the level of internal discussions groups in CYBERSYN were made.

(§) See On Heaping our Science Together, in "Platform for Change", Beer (19'

VII   DISCUSSION OF THE KEY TOOLS   (§)

Once the principles of cybernetic, recursive organization are understood and the concepts of information management are inserted, it is necessary to present the actual tools with sufficient details as to make them understandable for new applications.

VII.1   Quantified Flow-Charts

Each niveau, such as the twelve described in Section II is characterized first by "something that happens" at it and by a certain scale of complexity. That "something" has to do with several or all of the following possibilities:

1 -   some people working in it;

2 -   some material substance and/or energy flowing through it;

3 -   some equipment or material infrastructure available at it;

4 -   some money flowing through it;

5 -   some information bei ng processed; and

6 -   some decisions being made.

These six "things" will be found in one form or another in every one of the twelve niveaus shown in Fig. 2. This will be valid at the niveau of the crew (if we leave aside for the time being the physiological and psychological processes of the individual workers), of the firm, of the whole industry or of the nation. It will also be valid if we examine other completely different services such as health services and hospitals, city administrations and transit departments, the Central Bank and international trade, or even the social security services and the pension administration.

(§)   This section should be considered supplementary to Beer's presentation. As such, it will attempt to avoid redundancies and to emphasize rather those aspects which I came to learn and to interpret inside the Chilean environment.

See "Cybernetic Praxis in Government" in S. Beer "Platform for Change" (1975)

In the particular nested set inside industry (niveau 9), material production plays the essential role, and the corresponding processes are identified mainly with productive units or firms. From this fact, the tool of quantified flow-charts evolved. Many kinds of process charts or flow charts have been used for many years as a tool of industrial engineers. The approach used here, however, is essentially different from the traditional ones. In these latter ones, the aim is usually improvement through balancing, elimination or modification of operations and various methods to achieve perfection in details. All this has resulted in techniques such as studies of Time and Motion, industrial layout design, etc. In CYBERSYN, the goal was the opposite: how to describe the process at a given niveau with a minimum of detail in order that the corresponding decision-maker knows how his system is performing. In other words, how to build a filter of variety of the process.

Fig. 9 shows a typical process flow-chart for a canning plant with a level of resolution adequate for its operation manager and for reporting information to the niveau immediately above (the line or sector niveau). The arrow widths are intended to show the relative importance (on a merely qualitative basis) of the respective processes, and the levels inside each box are indicative of the ACTUALITY of the respective unit. The chart has enough detail to understand the basic inputs, processes and outputs, to detect bottle-necks (on the Packing Unit in this case) and to provide a starting point for tactical planning (for instance, increase of can warehousing, cooking and packing facilities, and boiler capacity).

The chart provides the ground on which to build indicators and this is probably the heart of the whole information structure. The variety concept is the guidance for this process. Once a chart has been built the next questions are: where are the most relevant points of this process? Which measurements will unvail the hidden homeostasis of the system? The answer requires some understanding of the philosophy of the whole approach and a lot of experience and insight of the process itself. And consequently, it should be the cooperative work of the systems expert with the plant worker. At the same time, the economy of the whole system requires that indicators be kept at a minimum. Following the chart, a simulation will show how the set of indicators is built:

1 - Which supplies are critical? Is there one that will determine the behavior of the whole system, for instance tin cans or sugar? Are their levels of stock reflected immediately on production or are there significant time-lags? Should we measure incoming values or levels at the warehouse?

2 - Among the processes, is there a critical point relevant for the whole plant behavior? For instance, daily production, or number of batches going through the sterilizing retorts? If there are several relevant points, could one obtain a balanced picture with just very few points? For instance, kilograms of peeled fruit, number of cans to the canning line, vapor consumption? Or is this information merely redundant?

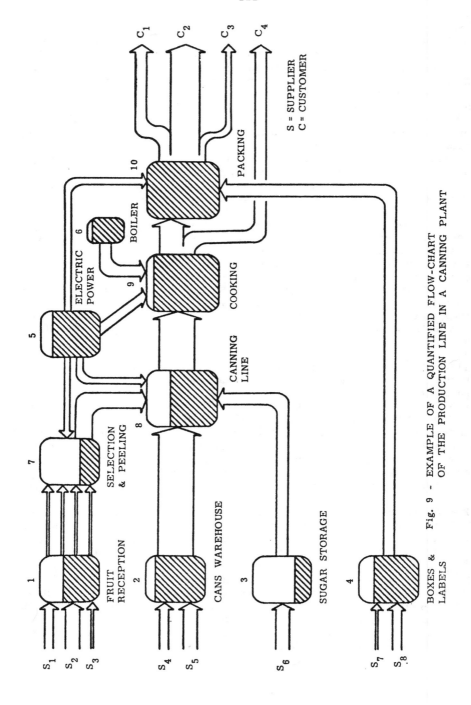

Fig. 9 - EXAMPLE OF A QUANTIFIED FLOW-CHART
OF THE PRODUCTION LINE IN A CANNING PLANT

S = SUPPLIER
C = CUSTOMER

3 - Are there indirect measures of efficiency? For instance, amount of fruit rejected in the selection stage or amount of garbage thrown from the peeling section?

4 - Is there any machine that will by itself provide the indicator, the counter of the sealing unit or the integrating clock of the boiler?

5 - What about the final product? Is there any need to keep overall balances of different products by kind, size, and quality, or is there one or just a few that will provide essentially the same information? Do we need rather to keep track of the deliveries to a particular customer, due to his size or to the importance of his purchase for other relevant production units?

Answering these questions might appear very simple, and this example has been chosen because of its simplicity. There were, however, much more complicated cases as for instance, a company manufacturing copper and brass wires, cables, tubes and sheets with a variety of hundreds of different products. In that case there were "integrating points" such as electric furnaces, scrap storage and power consumption.

At any rate, an empirical rule of thumb could be that less than five indicators is too little and more than twelve is confusing. If more is needed, turn attention to the lower level of recursion; if too few are possible, then integrate at a higher level.

Up to here, and assuming that the proper measuring points have been detected, three questions remain:

1 - What to do with these quantitative measurements?

2 - What about the other factors of production such as manpower or available cash?

3 - What happens at other levels of recursion?

The first question is answered through the concepts of ACTUALITY, CAPABILITY and POTENTIALITY. This means that for every measurement, a non-dimensional indicator will be built in such a manner that its potentiality will be 1.0 exactly; its capability will be a certain value (between 0 and 1), determined as the available capacity if there are no other limitations in the associated line; its actuality is again a number between 0 and 1, determined as the present possible level given the existing conditions. An example will clarify this:

Assume in Fig. 9 that the Normative Plan would require a 20% expansion of the cooking unit (in order to satisfy a certain goal of social needs allocated to this company). This goal plus associated technological improvement plus an improvement in productivity calls for additional boiler capacity up to say 1.500 kg vapor. This compares with an existing capacity of 1000 kg and a present use of 900 kg. Then

Potentiality	(1500 kg)	=	1.0
Capability	(1000 kg)	=	0.67
Actuality	(900 kg)	=	0.60

Obviously, then

Latency	= Cap/Pot	=	0.67
Productivity	= Act/Cap	=	0.90
Performance	= Lat x Prod	=	0.60

Remember that Performance is a relative measure of satisfaction of needs while Productivity is a measure of the level of use of available resources.

Just to show that consistency with these concepts requires sometimes the opposite assignment of numerator and denominator, here is another example. Assume that we measure losses in selection and peeling, and assume that improvements in the quality of fruit production, transportation and storage sets a goal of 25% of waste referred to incoming weight. Assume also that present facilities and procedures if unchanged should yield 30% of waste and that the actual records show a 40% value. Then

Potentiality	(25%)	=	1.0
Capability	(30%)	=	0.833
Actuality	(40%)	=	0.625
Latency	= Cap/Pot	=	0.833
Productivity	= Act/Cap	=	0.75
Performance	= Lat x Prod	=	0.625

A later section will show how the indicators are used in association with computer programs in order that the data become information.

Besides production measurements, which were the central concern of CYBERSYN, some attention was paid to manpower. In this case, a first stage consisted in merely keeping track of absenteeism (or rather, of attendance in order to have a positive measure in which 1.0 is the optimum and 0 is total failure). This apparently limited goal convinced us empirically after a short period of the importance of this indicator. It turned out that, under normal conditions, absenteeism is a very stable figure for each plant, with some impressive changes from plant to plant depending on working conditions, physical strain and, above all, working morale. The fraction of women in the labor force is also reflected in this index although less spectacularly than one would imagine. It turns out that almost invariably even a small variation of 2 to 4% in this indicator reflects an abnormal circumstance. This, however, was often caused by conditions external to the factory, such as sport or political events or by the fact that either the previous or the following day was a special holiday. At any rate, manpower attendance should be always included among indicators, as the most likely signal of the health of the system.

Although CYBERSYN did not attempt to build other indicators of manpower behavior, it is not difficult to develop them. In Chile they did not have first priority because at that period the policy of full employment prevailed - and very properly so - over productivity goals. In a rational social economy, productivity should grow pari-passu with investments while keeping full employment. The CYBERSYN experience suggests the following avenues to keep track of the manpower effort:

- The adaption of dynamic flow charts to assign a certain labor force fraction to every relevant activity shown in the chart. The concepts of Actuality, Capability and Potentiality are an obvious extension in this case.

- The development of indicators of the same type to measure ratios of supervisory force, white collar workers and supporting task people to productive workers on the line.

- Development of indicators measuring the qualifications of manpower in different categories from non-skilled workers up to highly specialized technicians.

There might be people opposing these suggestions on the mistaken grounds that it would be a new application of computers to manipulate people. This would be once more the wrong presentation of the issue. Computers can be always, and are very often, used to manipulate people. This does not depend so much on the social context, political values and participation mechanisms. The realities of the Chilean experience faced many times the issue of efficiency, allocation of resources, critical priorities, qualification of the labor force and so on. This will necessarily happen in any complex system. The difference between the many possible social models is one of the normative values and not of technicalities. Therefore, the issue will be settled at the level of rational and feasible political options and not at one of technicalities. Much less will it be helped by any form of iconoclasm, either from the extreme right or the extreme left.

Moreover, the whole CYBERSYN project was an effort to develop real democratic participation and several parts of this presentation attempt to reflect such efforts.

With respect to money indicators, a whole essay could be written on the subject. Discussions about this issue were plentiful and inconclusive.

As efforts started and concentrated at the niveau of the firm and since production was the key issue, the choice to reflect physical production was an appropriate option. This was reinforced by the fact that Chilean chronic and gigantic inflation makes of every attempt to keep track of money figures a self-defeating task if not a completely misleading effort.

In the late stages of CYBERSYN however, when some studies at sub-cabinet level were attempted, the money issue came up but the government was ousted before reaching any clarification in this respect.

Leaving aside for a moment the problem of money as the proper metric (§), and assuming temporarily that money flows, sinks and sources might reflect important aspects of the behavior of the system at certain niveaus, again some suggestions might be advanced:

1 - Even if the absolute significance of money is subject to argument, there is no doubt that it presents at every niveau some possibilities of reflecting relevant aspects of the relative behavior of the system. Such are for instance the ratios of salaries to total expenditures, gross income to total sales value, investment costs to costs of operation, and so on. Here, the feasibility of exploring ACT - CAP - POT indicators is obvious.

2 - As one goes up in the niveau ladder, it is almost mandatory to keep track of monetary phenomena, particularly when foreign currency, fiscal deficit and the total quantity of available money come into play. The Chilean experience was very deeply affected by loosening the ties between physical measurements and monetary policies. This was not mainly a consequence of the CYBERSYN approach but rather the unavoidable result of political-economical events at the national and international levels which acquired a speed and instability beyond the control of any conceivable technical manipulation.

3 - In a situation of extreme inflation (above 60% per year, say) it is very difficult to assess the worthiness and feasibility of keeping track of money phenomena. In conditions of relative stability (below 15% yearly inflation, say) particular attention should be paid to the relevant frequency of each indicator.

4 - At the higher niveaus of the total system, money indicators might be dangerously misleading if they are divorced of the social "meta-values". The recent world experience with economic indicators of growth becoming an almost impossible guideline for development of feasible, acceptable social policies is a warning in this sense. This is probably the crucial point: how to connect the apparently simple measure of money with other objective goals of the system. For à whole nation some concepts such as quality of life, full employment, care for the very young and the very

(§) See Beer, Platform for Change, "Questions of Metric".

old might find new quantitative expressions. At the level of a productive unit there is even a greater need of finding the equivalent concepts such as effective satisfaction to the public, balance between innovation and production, between participation and accountability, etc. Again here, the corner-stone called "viability" might be the starting point of the answer. Certainly this is an interesting avenue for future inquiries.

5 - Some efforts related to economic analysis per se will be described in the section devoted to policy simulations.

Let us examine now the general situation at the other niveaus of recursion.

It is apparent that the extension of the quantified flow chart to lower niveaus is only a matter of resolution. At the department niveau, inputs might be disaggregated and might refer to outputs from other departments; the same method will apply to working stations, machinery and output. Supporting activities such as sales or maintenance require more effort and testing but in this case the conventional methods of industrial engineering provide a starting guideline.

CYBERSYN left the initiative at these niveaus to the local technical teams, except for the training of supervisors and workers which has been already mentioned.

The real problem appears when one attempts to integrate at higher niveaus. Here there are two phases which overlap and interact until a clear picture emerges. The first one has to do with mere integration; for instance, if one takes the whole line of canned food and related processes, a certain scale of resolution has to be chosen. Inputs may be classified in broad categories such as food materials(which in turn are subdivided into various species: meat, fish, vegetables, fruit, oil, sugar, others); containing materials (subdivided into tin-cans, plastic and glass containers, and so on); packing materials (card boxes, labels); electric power and other energy sources. Processes could again be re-grouped, as it is not difficult to find broad classifications such as cleaning and preparing, cooking, packing, etc. However, such information would be essentially irrelevant for decisions at that level. A black-box called processing would be sufficient except that careful analysis is required in order to obtain an adequate representation of the Actuality - Capability levels. These values will be important in the development of investment programs and production requirements for the whole line of canned food and related processes.

The output of this niveau however, requires often a very different approach. In the food industry for instance, regional re-distribution in a country like Chile with two absolutely different patterns for regional production and local demands, was an essential factor. This in turn reflected in transportation and warehousing problems and in scheduling of operations in different regions. It is this kind of problems which are rather irrelevant for the individual unit but which are essential at the Line or Sector niveau, that provide a real task for such niveaus, and which otherwise might merely become a bureaucratic hindrance to the whole system. (§)

The second phase of the flow-charting at a higher niveau has to do with the compatibilization of the flows added in the first phase. For instance, the Sugar Line will have significant outputs in the national scale which in turn are inputs for canned foods, soft drinks, wine and spirit liquors, and so on. There might appear crossed and feedback flows, such as between the Poultry Line and Pasta industries. (§§) These flows might be important or irrelevant for decision-making and again, it is up to the experience and ability of the analyst to include them or reject them, according to their information content.

As one continues to upper niveaus, the interaction becomes more and more complicated between different industrial sectors; between branches; between industry, agriculture, energy corporations, mining and transportation; between national raw-materials, processing units and consumption on the one hand and the possibilities of exportation and the necessity of paying for imports, etc., on the other.

This process was carried out only to a minor extent in the time available. Basic sectors analyzed and charted at this niveau were Energy, Wood and Pulp, and Tires and its related products. Some progress was under way in the textile sector and in primary processing of copper semi-finished products.

VII. 2   The CYBERSTRIDE Program

The next logical step after the development of the organization structure linked by the telex net, which provided an organic whole (anatomy) and the quantified flow charts which in turn provided the material description of the relevant processes in this organism (physiology), was to construct an effective processor of information (neurology). In other words, data from the measuring points had to be converted into indicators, which in turn should be interpreted as to their real meaning and used to make decisions (when decisions were

_____

(§)   For this reason, the pilot operation room of the Food Sector contained a map of the country that was well elaborated with respect to productive units and flow of materials but that was not a good model of regional demands at the time of the putsch. I personally feel that the "moving slides" developed by CYBERSYN would be an ideal solution for dynamic representations of flows between different regions. Preliminary discussions in that direction were held in connection with the pre-project of the operation room for the whole economy.

(§§) Both relatively very important in Chile. Pasta industries are heavy consumers of eggs and supply by-products to the chicken food mills.

called for, and ignored otherwise). This parenthesis is not irrelevant. One
of the main sources of noise in any complex system is the ample diffusion of
figures or indicators that flow through the system just to collect signatures
that certify that the figures exist and are being read by the whole hierarchy.

It is here that computers were specified as the proper and actually only possible tool. The CYBERSYN battery of programs was developed in England by
a group of consultants. I am familiar with the general strategy of the program
but not with the detailed software handled by the computer people. The core
of this program was the statistical analysis based on the work of Harrison
and Stevens (1971). A very crude specification of the program is shown in
Fig. 10, without concern for some trivial details such as the DO loops, coun-
ters for batches of many data, or the branching with plotting routines.

The object of such analysis was the following: Assume that one has a series
of values of a given indicator which have been obtained during a period sufficiently short as to assume that no essential change has occurred in the conditions or environment around the process "indicated". Then the method
devised will determine a band of normality, that is, a range inside which the
indicator might oscillate due to natural minor perturbations. The method will
also determine whether any new value shows a particular trend to increase
or decrease and will also evaluate the first derivatives of the trend: whether
the trend is steadily upwards or downwards (this is called a change along a
slope), whether there are indications of a steady positive or negative jump
(step change) or whether the change is accidental and could be disregarded
for the time being (transient change).

Prior to the incorporation of a given indicator into the statistical program,
an analysis was required to find the parameters of the indicator. This was
made by means of the socalled CALIBRATION PROGRAM which would take
40 or more measurements at a given point and would analyze them for consistency and steadiness (i. e., would check whether they could belong to a
sample of a single universe); it would determine the band of normality and
the parameters required to evaluate derivatives and determine the trends.

These two programs were fully operative by the end of 1972.

As it is not the detailed software which interests us here, but its applications,
the following remarks are pertinent:

This strategy had two tremendous advantages with respect to any other known
method of modern use of data for information purposes:

1 - Once a value was measured - and this was a very simple task - the com-
    puter could immediately explore its significance, not only for the system
    where the data originated but also for any upper niveau.

2 - The human decision was actually not using past information but "future
    information". In other words, the computer could announce that a cer-

1   READ A FIGURE WITH ITS CODE OF ORIGIN

2   CONVERT IT TO A NON-DIMENSIONAL VALUE

3   APPLY TO IT THE STATISTICAL FILTER

4   CHECK WHETHER IT REMAINS INSIDE BAND OF NORMALITY

5   IF YES, REPORT IT AS NORMAL AND GO TO 13

6   IF NOT, CHECK THE TREND WITH PREVIOUS VALUES

7   IF TREND IS TRANSIENT, REPORT IT AS TRANSIENT AND GO TO 13

8   IF TREND IS SLOPE CHANGE OR STEP CHANGE, CONTINUE

9   REPORT CHANGE AND TREND TO ORIGINAL NIVEAU

10 CHECK IF TIME FOR CORRECTION AT THAT NIVEAU IS EXHAUSTED

11 IF NOT, GO TO 13

12 IF YES, REPORT FACT TO UPPER NIVEAU AND GO TO 10

13 CHECK IF INDICATOR IS USED IN OTHER SUBROUTINES

14 IF NOT, GO TO 16

15 IF YES, CALL SUBROUTINE FOR THAT NIVEAU AND GO TO 2

16 END

Fig. 10 - SCHEME OF COMPUTER STRATEGY FOR INDICATORS

tain trend would prevail unless something was done (for instance, a corrective decision).

The calibration program could be applied to new data as they were coming, in such a way that the quality of available information improves steadily.

The possibility of permanent improvement of the program is a very simple matter. Such improvements may consist of the addition of indicators of any nature. The program is not restricted to figures of production or workers attitude; it could include any measure of economic behavior. The time frequency of indicators can be adjusted for any of them. Evaluation and plotting by the computer of the graphs POT - CAP - ACT is also a natural extension. Incorporation of the data for new niveaus, either with higher resolution or higher aggregation is also possible.

Although the CYBERSTRIDE program was effectively applied at the niveau of individual firms and plants and at that of Line and Sectors, its major advantage is that exactly the same program can be used at the level of the whole nation (to measure things like public satisfaction, international trade situation, inflation rate, cost of living and the like), down to any small compartment (be it a class-room, a hospital ward, a maintenance department or a purely bureaucratic unit). All that is required is a proper quantified flow-chart and a coherent definition of a measurement procedure.

Autonomy and freedom at any niveau can be effectively respected by limiting the reporting subroutines. It goes without saying that information can be manipulated, as it is the case with any scheme of modern information technology. Only that in this case, there is the additional advantage that the simplicity of the method makes it accessible to almost every citizen. One can well imagine that the worker who understands the performance of his work-shop will not have many difficulties understanding the performance of local or central government, if presented in the same language.

VII. 3   Simulations for Planning

The tools presented in sections VII. 1 and VII. 2 cover basically the needs for decision-making and interaction at levels 1, 2 and 3 in every niveau. The situation at level 4 is completely different. In this case daily routine information is usually irrelevant.

Exploration of the future is associated with the activity of planning. This one has developed many specialized tools according to the sector involved: city planning, government planning, private business programs, etc. Whatever the particulars of the system under consideration, the conventional tools partake of the following scheme:

-    a certain description of the system at time $t = t_o$ is available;

- a given time horizon Δt for the plan is postulated;

- a set of (hopefully) compatible, desirable goals for the system at $t_1 = t_o + \Delta t$ is determined;

- a strategy to take the system from t_o to t_1 and achieve the specified goal is recommended;

- a scheme for periodic revisions and adjustments might be provided.

The problem with the approach is that usually it freezes the environment at t_o if it considers it at all.

The actual performance of the system is strongly affected by unforeseen changes in the environment, which might involve major perturbations (for instance, natural catastrophes, changes in international situation such as oil crisis, etc.). The plan has no way to incorporate such perturbations, not even to record the performance of the system on a continuous basis in order to keep track of the degree of compliance with the pre-established goals.

This problem is even worse when the planning scheme is too rigid, that is, when the planning process is mechanically extended from the top to the bottom. This has been an old criticism of central planning schemes in which a set of goals at a higher niveau (production for consumption, for instance) is rigidly disaggregated down to the lowest niveau ("this factory must produce exactly so many thousands of shoes").

This aspect does not constitute an essential objection. Once a clear understanding of the different niveaus is achieved and the structure of the system is properly represented, it is not difficult to conceive a scheme of disaggregation where the goals retain a certain degree of flexibility and they are specified within a range rather than as fixed figures.

The first objection however - inadequate response to perturbations - is much more fundamental. The only way to overcome it is to replace the deterministic approach to planning by some method of dynamic simulation of the system and its environment.

In the Chilean situation there was already a tradition of planning activities using the conventional tools. The central government had a planning unit under the responsibility of an expert with Cabinet status since 1964; every large corporation and state company had also its own planning group. Any effort to impose a radical change of methods, no matter how sound from the theoretical point of view, would have collided with strong institutional resistance and personal mistrust on the part of the professionals. On the other hand, the development of the effective new tools in practical application would have taken several years. In these circumstances it was obvious that poor planning was better than none at all.

Therefore, the decision in CYBERSYN was to develop a method of dynamic simulation without interfering with conventional methods. The intention was to make the new method available by stages, as and when it became effectively operative.

As to the method itself, the specifications were:

- it should be flexible enough to be used at any niveau;

- it should be able to represent realistically the interactions with the environment;

- it should be adequate for computer use with similar characteristics of flexibility, improvements and self-correction as those specified for CYBERSTRIDE;

- its output should be adequate for use and easy understanding by the relevant people at any niveau.

These considerations led to the selection of the latest existing version of the DYNAMO compiler as developed by J. Forrester.

In addition to the above specifications, this method had other advantages:

- there is a great deal of public information about it. In particular, Forrester himself had presented applications at the industrial level, as a tool for city planning and as a tool for exploring the future prospectives of larger systems (§).

- the method involves an adequate, well-known, graphical representation for the structure of the model under consideration. This representation is simple to learn and, independently of the associated computer programs, provides a useful tool for discussions of structural relations. This structural pattern is a very good tool for discussions between planners and other executives and provides a means for exploring changes in the model through discussions with specialists. The fact that one has this "language" is advantageous to overcome resistance on the part of the executives. Once they start grasping the graphic representation, they tend to get over-enthusiastic with it rather than antagonized to it.

- the compiler itself is simple and has been subject to extensive testing.

Although the method has been subject to some criticism, particularly in connection with the results presented in World Dynamics (§§), such criticism does not refer to the method itself but rather to the underlying assumptions

_____

(§) See references

(§§) See references

and the conclusions obtained in particular applications. The more basic objection to the method (and actually to any other simulation approach) is that it often gives results which might appear reasonable even if the structural representation is grossly inadequate. There is no easy answer in this respect. The structural relationships inside a complex system are not yet subject to easy determination like the transfer functions of elementary systems. One can only resort to a posteriori comparison of the actual behavior and the predicted one, and even this is limited by the possibility of undetected perturbations.

The development of a good model remains in this respect still to a large extent more of an art than an exact analysis. It is here that experience of those who know the system is basic and it is also here that the easy access to Forrester's graphics has a definite advantage.

In the Chilean project, the first task was to train a group of engineers in the use of the method and the compiler. This was achieved by sending an engineer to England for several weeks and then using his expertise to organize a team of five or six local professionals, including a psychologist-engineer.

By the middle of 1972, the team was ready and they started a tentative program of applications. Due to the evolution of the local situation, rather than concentrating in simulation of a particular industry, priority was given to the exploration of the behavior of the total economy.

This was a very controversial area to start with. The main problems that the Chilean system was facing had to do with a critical scarcity of resources for investment in several conflicting and essential sectors; with growing inflation and increasing social pressures for new salary and price policies; with unbounded oscillations of resource allocations to agriculture and industry, housing, mining and transportation; with a growing gap between foreign currency obtained through exports and the needs for essential imports, without access to foreign credits or to financial assistance, and the whole picture aggravated by direct embargoes of copper and supplies for the copper mines.

At present there is no access to any record of the work done. The following superficial description is based therefore on personal recollections.

The team was able to produce a model of the basic interaction between production for consumption, production of capital goods, levels of imports and exports and levels of satisfaction of basic needs of the population. This model was in turn tied to a monetary model in which the level of activities and of satisfaction of basic needs was related to the fiscal deficit. One must remember that a large part of the production of goods and services was at this state under direct state control and that consequently, the fiscal deficit was strongly influenced by the level and cost of services provided and goods produced while their prices did not adjust to the demands of the market, but rather to a policy of satisfying minimum levels of consumption.

Policy options were explored in the computer. Various combinations of acceptable deficits, price and salary adjustments and increments in production were tried. For instance, the computer produced the graphs of buying power of salaries when the policy was one of bounded deficit, prices continuously adjusted as required by fiscal budget, and salaries periodically adjusted to repair the loss of buying power. In this case, the model reflected very well the spiraling of prices and the increasing rates of salary deterioration. The model gave a realistic indication of the very limited usefulness of monetary policies in a situation where the state is responsible for production and for improvements in the standard of living and at the same time has very little control of local financial speculation and of international economic policies.

Several local sectors were also simulated with the DYNAMO model. One such model was developed by the planning group of the Copper Corporation, the most important of the state corporations from the point of production of foreign currency. In this case, the model attempted to simulate the copper production of the five largest Chilean mines under various constraints of costs, international price, critical inputs and processes. The phenomenological model was quite advanced by May, 1973 but I have no information concerning the actual computer outputs.

The overall judgement of the application of the methods of Industrial Dynamics in CYBERSYN is inconclusive. On the one hand, the phase of model designing and structural analysis went rather far and proved very useful even as a method of discussion of a given system; on the other, although the computer came to work perfectly well, the number of applications, the continuity of them and the follow-up were too precarious as to draw any firm conclusions.

My personal feelings are mixed. I see a definite methodological improvement in the dynamic simulation procedures as compared to deterministic planning for fixed timespans. On the other hand, they present the danger of becoming a sort of toy in the hands of the experts which are never satisfied with the level of resolution attained. Every simulation can be improved by adjusting the model or by introducing some extra, more realistic details (although the actual computations often show that most models are rather insensitive to changes of lots of parameters and to the addition of local improved resolution).

I feel that until we have more experience with tools of dynamic simulation, the best solution is probably the one that was being tried in Chile: to keep the conventional effort of planning with traditional tools in spite of its shortcomings, while at the same time the exploration with methods of dynamic simulation is intensified.

VII. 4   The Operations Room (§)

The complex process of decision-making can be significantly helped by the
use of appropriate tools but it should not be confounded with the mere use of
tools. As we go higher in the level hierarchy of the system, decisions become
more complex and correspondingly, tools become more of an aid to be used
under the control of, but never as an Ersatz for sound judgement and experience.

The summit of the decision-making process is provided by the complex interaction of levels 3 and 4 under the guidance of level 5.

The first condition should be then that any technical method or devise designed
for this process should be simultaneously available to a group of people.

Moreover, if they are truly respecting the appropriate degrees of autonomy
inside their system, their concern should refer to basic, general interactions
between the system and the environment, and between the present and the
future. For instance, financial prospects might be subject to discussion and
analysis but the technicalities of detailed budget reports will be probably irrelevant, if not misleading for such analysis.

The basic postulate of the socalled operation rooms (§§) is then, to provide
an environment suitable for the decision-making process of the upper direction of a given system.

In this environment there should be enough access to technical tools as may
be required by the kind of decisions taking place in it.

Three experiences of this sort, known to me, will be reviewed.

1)   The CORFO room

      This was completely designed, built and operated by the CYBERSYN
      team in order that CORFO's upper direction could use it for the manage-
      ment of the complete industrial sector.

      It became completely operative by March-April 1973, after a period of
      several months of tests and simulation meetings, some of which were
      attended by president Allende, members of the Cabinet and high officers
      of several departments in government. As usual, the CYBERSYN policy
      was to disseminate the tools under development beyond the boundaries
      of the industrial sector, whenever possible.

(§) See Beer's "Platform for Change", Chapter on Cybernetics in Govern-
     ment.
(§§) I assume that this name might come from similar experiences in the
     military field. "Management Room" or "Upper Direction Room" might
     be more appropriate.

The description that follows is complementary to the one presented by Beer (which includes several colour photographs of the room itself).

The room consisted of an equilateral octogon with a diameter of approximately 10 m. This was inside a small building devoted exclusively to the room as it was impossible in the short period available for construction to make all the remodelling that would have been needed in CORFO's headquarters. The building provided additional space for the man responsible for information updating and maintenance, for a telex terminal and for one secretary.

The center of the room was occupied by seven chairs of special design that could rotate in 270° and from each of which there was easy view and access to every wall. Each chair had a control switchboard on its right arm to operate the slide display.

The walls presented displays of the following:

a) The cybernetic model of a viable system. This was a large screen with back illumination that had the five levels presented in such a way that names of different sub-systems could be attached in pertinent boxes. In the connecting links corresponding to level 2, the ACT - CAP - POT values could be represented and the flow of information was shown through moving arrows. The effect of movement of the arrows was produced by a very clever simple device developed in England, which consists in illuminating through rotating disks of polarized glass. The polarized light is received on the screen in which the arrow paths are made of plastic strips of different color shades. The rotation of the disks causes the effect of movement when the strips are illuminated.

b) All the structural information is contained in another wall with 4 screens (DATAFEED); the top one contains the control slides with the 5 digit binary code to call any of 400 slides contained in each of the three lower screens. Actually, to get access to any slide one uses the 5 digits twice in combination with the control screen (§). The slides, projected from the back and stored in automatic projectors connected to the control units in the chair arms, display information describing the systems such as the quantified flow charts for the system under consideration as well as for other upper and lower niveaus; the graph of historical record of ACT - CAP - POT; and even some physical pictures of plant and facilities.

Since the slide trays are easily removed and replaced, the system can be expanded almost without limit provided that any particular discussion is not using more than 1200 slides and that an adequate logistic effort of updating the DATAFEED is made. Since this is structural information, intended to show what the system is, what is produced, and how it relates to its environment, it is relatively simple to keep

(§) See Beer's article with the graphical examples of the control boards.

it updated by changing very few slides every month.

It is obvious that very simple improvements, like a cathode-ray screen directly linked to a computer, or even a procedure to make slides directly from computer plots on paper, will increase significantly the power of DATAFEED.

The important point is that a simple, cheap method of having immediate access to almost any information characteristic of the system was provided. Moreover, any participant would learn in a few minutes, as the actual tests effectively showed, how to use the control screen and the corresponding panel at his chair. This gave to every member of the meeting direct access to all the relevant information.

c) The evolution of the performance of the system could be followed in the third wall where the output of the computer in terms of indicators could be displayed. Here there were two screens which were usually operated from the back. Making a computer program for them or using a directly linked cathode screen would be a simple matter. Only that the Chilean situation did not allow the time nor the money required to import the corresponding hardware. The important fact again is that the possibility of using the indicators to provide relevant information reported by exception was tested. The other screen had three different levels and colors: green for pending problems that should be solved in their own niveau; yellow for those that had already reached the niveau immediately above the original one; and red for those that required action at a higher niveau.

d) The fourth wall had a magnetic board to which different symbols corresponding to Forrester's code would adhere. The lines representing flow of either materials or information (i. e. , actuating control valves), were built with different flexible modules that could also represent movement by the same trick explained in (a). Only that in this case, polarized light through moving disks came from the roof in the front of the board. In this case, the purpose was to use the board both as a working tool of the DYNAMO experts and as an aid for discussion of the model with the executives.

e) Since there was no direct access to the computer through remote consoles due to the same limitations mentioned in (c) above, two additional screens for back projection were provided so that plots from the computer could be shown. These were used with typical outputs such as those explained in the previous chapter and referring to the price-salary-inflation problems.

f) There was also a conventional blackboard that was included against the initial specifications of the consultant. The period of use of the room proved that the blackboard was not essential but added an extra facility at practically zero cost.

The other two sides of the room provided access doors to the rest of the building.

Both the experimental period from November 1972 to April 1973 and the initial period of actual use of the room from May to August demonstrated the tremendous potential of the room as a tool for decisions. Unfortunately, the period was too short and the prevailing conditions in the country were too chaotic and critical to allow a more systematic follow-up of the use of the room and to obtain firm conclusions with respect to its advantages and shortcomings. I am convinced of the importance of this experiment and of the fact that many improvements are possible with simple additions of hardware.

2)   The room of the Sector for Food Industry

In this case it was impossible to use any gadgetry except the information received by telex from the different plants and from the computer. It was decided not to adapt for this purpose the CORFO room described above, as the permanent crisis that was in full development at the moment forced the executives of the Sector to stay almost permanently in their own headquarters or in troubleshooting missions at the different plants. For these reasons, the conference room adjacent to the manager's office was adapted. The walls were used to display the minimum structural information that consisted of maps showing all the production plants (about 35) and their inter-relationships. A map of regional demands was being prepared at the time of the putsch. In addition, ultrasimplified flow-charts for the various lines were included.

In order to follow the daily performance of the various subsystems, a board equivalent to that described in (c) above, was built to reflect the main problems of the basic lines (sugar, edible oil, canned foods, beverage, meat and poultry, milk and related products, etc.). For each line, indicators concerning supply of raw materials, availability of transportation means, levels of production, workers absenteeism and storage problems were provided. These indicators were tracked by the computer in those cases where the corresponding analysis had already been done, and otherwise, through qualitative information by telex.

Finally, a very simple board to keep track of exceptional problems was also developed. This consisted of a list where items would be added or removed by hand and included information referring to strikes, price conflicts, budget emergency, overstocks that had to be quickly disposed of, and the like.

This development was improvised as an emergency tool. No serious effort was made to keep track of its results and the room was being used for all sort of emergency meetings. These disadvantages resulted however in a very dynamic use of the room that thus provided practically the sole source of information available to the executives. It proved one positive and one negative aspect of "scientific management". The positive one: a minimum of information obeying to the Law of Requisite Variety is more useful than oodles of data. The negative one: any amount of gadgets and of technical support will be useless in an environment of crisis when the system reaches the level of collapse. In the last weeks of August, the upper niveau - the whole country - was out of control, almost paralyzed by sabotage, by lockout of the private transportation firms, by total lack of fuel, by internal political struggles, etc. At that point our information room was showing very clearly that every indicator was falling to zero and all efforts to help the individual subsystems were useless.

3) The third experience was carried out at a higher niveau than any so far considered. In March, 1973 I was asked to explore the possibility of fast development of rational information for the Minister of Finance and the Minister of Economics. (The first one is the equivalent to the Secretary of the Treasure and the second has to do with Industry, Commerce and Supplies.) The problem could be specified as follows: in the last thirty years the structure of government had evolved in a very irrational way with the consequence that there was no possible unified direction of the economy except the one that the president himself provided. The Cabinet members responsible for the Treasure, Industry, Agriculture, Mining, Transportation, Housing and Public Works reported directly to the pre- sident (§) of the nation and would frequently push their individual policies to the point of conflict. The political situation prevented any main effort of reorganizing the structure of the cabinet. Therefore, it was decided that the only means of supplying a practical forum for rational discussion consisted of designing a space of basic common information.

A rapid survey of the methods and means of the most important minis- tries showed the incredible situation that no common policy of inform- ation, not even rational routine (besides volumes of periodic reports full of rubbish) existed anywhere. This was not the result of the existing government; it had always been like that. Many services had their own unit of statistics and there was also a National Office of Statistics. The amount of data being collected was very large, its consistency never questioned, nor its accuracy and the time lag of the information varied between a few months and several years.

A serious application of CYBERSYN methods was out of the question. The period specified to implement the system was only of six weeks

---

(§) This was complicated by the fact that the tradition had sanctioned cabinet status for the head of the National Planning Office and for the Chairman of CORFO, and both would almost always collide with their colleagues of other economic sectors. The irrational mixture of activities of levels 3, 4 and 5 at the government was obvious.

(the time considered necessary to prepare the physical facilities in a large room provided by the Ministry of Economics).

Instead of working out relevant flow-charts, a different approach was chosen: the whole economic system was divided in three subsystems:

- the monetary system;
- the physical system;
- the flows of foreign currency.

A minimum structure was postulated for each one. For instance, the monetary system was identified with a black-box called Central Bank that could report on a weekly basis the very essential data, such as amount of new money; growth of the fiscal deficit split into several categories (deficit created by nationalized industry, deficit created by the fiscal budget of current expenditure, deficit originated in the bank and savings system); imbalances with the copper companies due to artificial rates of exchange, etc.

The physical system was simplified to include basic production figures vs. levels of needs in the following areas: agriculture, energy, mining, industry, housing and transportation. For each area 5 to 10 figures were defined and the feasibility of obtaining recent data on a steady basis was checked.

The flows of foreign currency were to be followed up through figures of exported goods (divided into copper and others); imported goods (divided into food, fuel, essential machinery and parts, and others); new credits and foreign debt levels.

It was also decided that a set of classical indicators should be included as general symptomatic information: consumers price index, industrial production and fuel consumption levels, etc. This set of indicators would hopefully evolve and improve to the point of being eventually processed through the CYBERSYN programs. All the indicators would be initially hand-plotted on removable boards of which 5 to 7 could be displayed simultaneously.

The second tool considered was a large screen for back projection on which geographical patterns could be shown. The peculiar Chilean geography was a frequent source of problems: transportation bottle-necks and sea port saturation; troubles in distribution of fertilizers, foods and basic materials, etc. There existed already good sector information on a geographic basis, concerning for instance, the electric power system, the railroad system and the fuel system.

It was considered that these two tools, indicators plus maps, would provide a zero-order approximation to a dynamic picture of the economic behavior of the country.

It was expected that DYNAMO simulations could be integrated to the system at a later stage and that this would be a significant improvement and could eventually evolve into a coherent solution similar to CORFO's room.

This project advanced to the stage of physical design of the room and selection of the basic indicators with the corresponding institutional sources and frequencies of reporting. Political difficulties aborted this development by the middle of April 1973.

Besides the conclusions advanced by Beer and the comments contained above, the experiences carried out in Chile were definitely convincing as to the needs of providing a functional environment for the process of decision-making at the higher levels. This as opposed to the classical room where the decision-makers are totally isolated and have to depend on written reports, usually based on out-dated information. The members of the board either study the reports in advance (and add their time lags) or they don't. In either case, their contribution to decisions makes very little use of actual information and they have to rely mainly on their general knowledge and experience plus their prejudices and judgements.

VIII   WORKER PARTICIPATION

The technical tools studied, built and tested (to the extent that they could be tested in the available period) have been sufficiently discussed. Their supporting value for the human process of decision-making has been stressed. We are now in the position of discussing participation as suggested at the beginning in Fig. 2.

The emphasis placed on participation was not the result of an arbitrary management decision. It was rather a normative requirement imposed by the general policy of government.

The first problem was that no definition of participation existed which could be acceptable to all political groups involved. The different attitudes varied from those sponsoring a utopian form that should involve everybody in everything to those that would have preferred some minor concessions to workers by accepting some formal representation in some of the boards or committees. The question was never fully solved and, to the best of my knowledge, there is no known easy answer for it.

But a definition of participation requires much more than a mere choice among several possible degrees of involvement. There are some implicit value judgements behind the idea of participation. We may attempt to make those explicit before defining any scheme:

1) - A truly egalitarian society accepts that every individual is basically qualified to judge himself about his own interests and those of the group he is directly involved in.

2) - The relationship of an individual to his work determines his basic pattern of behavior and his connections to the social structure.

3) - In spite of principle 1, modern society with its intrinsic complexity requires knowledge for the management of complex systems. There is no
immanent wisdom vested in workers or in any other group of society
that will automatically privilege them for spontaneous infallibility.

4) - On the other hand, there is no a priori elitarian group that because of
knowledge or other form of power could claim the right to make decisions
for the people.

These conflicting statements, which will not be analyzed in detail here, are
implicit in one form or other in any type of project of an advanced democracy.
How to make them operative?

Let us look at the problem from a different angle. Participation has to do with
decision-making, otherwise it becomes a mockery. Decision-making requires
information (about the nature of the system, its present state and the alternative outcomes for the future). Information however is not enough. The informed participant must have a relevant voice in the choice of a course of
action.

The previous chapters have shown what we learnt and did about the structure
of the systems and the design of information flows. This could be adapted to
spread information in a rational way among many, ideally all, members of
the system. For instance, there is no substantial objection to making all
workers in a given workshop familiar with its relevant structure (identification
of levels and flow-charts) and with the values of the indicators. (Of course
there will be many objections if management and labor are two conflicting
groups). In principle, therefore, the main problem is one of information,
once the general political context is compatible with the principle of participation.

The real problem is how to design effective forms of involvement in the choice
of a course of action. This again requires some further analysis. The model
of the viable system has already shown that there is a big difference between
the choice of the course of action and its implementation. For instance, if
level 3 has decided that the subsystem at level 1 must switch their activities
to adjust to a new production program, it is their task to carry the changes
out, using 2 and 3 for the necessary coordination and support. One of the
big problems with participation is that these two phases are very easily con-
fused because workers who have had a voice in the choice of the action (as
participants) retain involvement in the implementation (as workers).

There is no magic answer to this difficulty, as there is no magic either to
solve the contradiction between democratic rights and the need for specialized
knowledge.

Our incomplete experience has shown at least some possible avenues of exploration.

First, it is feasible to teach in a short period enough about the principles of organization of viable systems and their basic mechanisms to workers, even if their general education is very low. This was tested through the several experiences and seminars made with semi-skilled and specialized workers. They can effectively understand the process of decision-making and the importance of the ancillary tools. They would even become easily confident in strange environments such as the operation room.

Second, once a problem has been presented in ordinary language but keeping proper focus on the relevant questions, they are able to start a learning process of discriminating the basic issues from the technicalities that should be left to the experts. In the few cases where we could develop the process far enough, they came to learn not only to respect the expert advise but also to demand it. They would also learn to pose increasingly better questions and to keep track of the various stages involved in a given problem. One such experience was the discussion with the workers of a tire manufacturing plant to devise a scheme for the starting up and training in a new plant that was falling behind schedule. The meeting involved the Minister of Economics, the top executives of the plant, CYBERSYN people and a group of some 30 workers. In two days the group could propose a program which was implemented with an essential contribution from the workers themselves.

Third, the most difficult aspect is for those workers who participate in certain kinds of decision-making to avoid confusion of their role. They tended rather easily to consider themselves invested with a new power and show a strong bias to meddle in problems at various levels and areas.

The most likely answer to these difficulties consists in viewing participation as a process, deeply rooted in the overall political development. Participation must develop simultaneously the ability to know the system and the decision-making process with the uses of the new capacities. It must be a process fast enough to avoid discouragement and sufficiently slow to avoid chaos. In principle, it should develop at different levels at the same time. For instance, in the Chilean tradition up to 1973 there were tools of increasing participation in the upper levels of national politics, through Parliament, the Unions and the General Federation of Unions. There were also new forms of participation in local government at the neighborhood and city level.

The obvious point to start filling the other boxes was production (niveaus 4 to 6 in Fig. 2). The program of Planning with Participation developed at the beginning of 1973 which has been mentioned in section VI, was a definite proof that this could be carried out very well.

Fig. 11 shows how the ideal of participation could be expressed in the structure of the system. The essential point here is that rational participation seems possible in all niveaus of the viable structure.

The detailed mechanisms of elections or appointments are secondary. In the

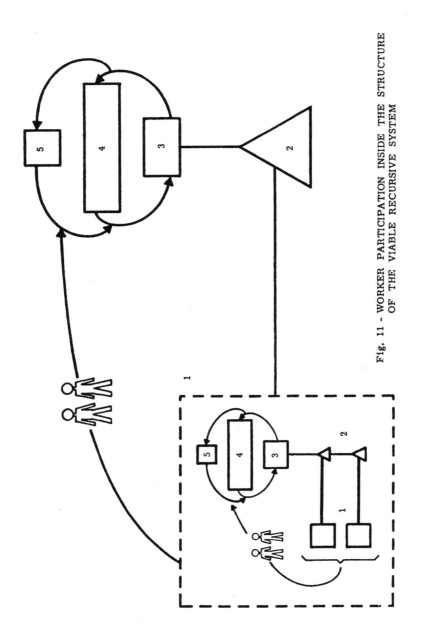

Fig. 11 - WORKER PARTICIPATION INSIDE THE STRUCTURE OF THE VIABLE RECURSIVE SYSTEM

Chilean case, the actual experience came to cover very well niveaus 3, 4 and 5 and progress was being made in niveaus 6 to 9. Niveaus 11 and 12 were taken care of by the conventional political mechanisms.

The above comments should not be understood as implying that everything was perfect. On the contrary, there were many difficulties, problems and misunderstandings. The important point is that the experience showed that effective participation is possible.

Now, at each niveau, participation is an involvement of workers usually at level 1 with the activities of the upper direction (3, 4 and 5). Participation has nothing to do with the process of implementation of the system. Decision-making and executing are two different activities, irrespective of the existence of continuous supervision on the part of the upper direction.

This presentation and the experience of CYBERSYN can therefore be summarized as follows:

1. - The feasibility of any conceivable scheme of participation is strongly dependent on the prevailing ideology. (§) If a substantial fraction of the group does not become convinced of the feasibility and advantages of participation plus its associated responsibilities, the project will be self-defeating. If the society at large puts a larger emphasis on competitive conflicting attitudes rather than on cooperation, it is hard to imagine a successful scheme of real participation.

2. - Participation in decisions is, like democracy, more a process than a set of rules. This process requires a very significant effort of education and training concurrent with the practical, increasing use of participatory mechanisms. It cannot be completely designed from the outside and it has certainly a strong component of trial and error (as every learning mechanism).

3. - The gap between truly democratic forms (i.e., the acceptance that the individual is actually able to know which are his best interests and how they are compatible with those of others), and the need for expert judgement on the part of highly trained scientists and technicians, is an actual one and cannot be ignored. Although we still don't know enough about this problem, the experiences so far known point into a certain direction for solutions: there must be a balance in the society with respect to the know-

---

(§) The pretension so often voiced among some social scientists of the existence of such a thing as pure rational social behavior as opposed to ideological behavior, is considered here only a very crude form of ideology. I don't know of any social organization or theory that does not depend at a deeper level on some accepted values which are not wholly accountable for on rational grounds only.

ledge and understanding of the basic areas of social concern on the part
of all members and the specialized knowledge of the elites. When this
balance is absent, there appear two dangerous alternatives: either an
immanent wisdom is assumed on the part of the people, or forms of mono-
polistic power concentrate in the hands of an elite: scientists, technocrats,
the military, the "priests", depending on the specific forms of social organization. In the past, most of the advanced, stable societies have understood the need to stress and disseminate the social values and the ideology behind their institutions, and they continue to do so, in spite of hypo-
critical claims about abstract rationality.

The process of social organization and development is obviously a political
one. The fact that the existing complexity and velocity of change requires
new expertise, does not eliminate but rather reinforces the need for political
knowledge and consciousness. The dynamic balance between these often conflicting goals becomes more and more the substance of wise government and
wise decision-making.

The fact that the recent Chilean experience ended up as tragically as it did,
is a very serious warning for many, besides being a painful experience for the
Chilean people. That failure itself prevents an easy, cheap endorsement of
the tools discussed in this report. On the other hand, mere tools are never
the cause nor the consequence of either social success or calamity.

The true causes of the Chilean failure are a matter for historical analysis
and argument. Still, those of us that shared the consequences of that failure
share also the faith in the value of the whole experience, including in it the
effort of development of new tools that might help in the solution of problems
of social organization.

ACKNOWLEDGEMENTS

My deepest recognition is due to all those killed, imprisoned or exiled by
tyranny, with whom I had the privilege to work and learn and whose names
must be silenced in the hope of better times; and to Stafford Beer for his
teaching, wisdom, loyalty and friendship.

Adriana has given me her patience, generosity and hard work in our tasks
and has shown her courage and love in adversity.

REFERENCES

ASHBY, W.R. 1956: An Introduction to Cybernetics. Methuen & Co.
ASHBY, W.R. 1960: Design for a Brain. Chapman & Hall.
BEER, S. 1959: Cybernetics and Management. English University Press.
BEER, S. 1966: Decision and Control. John Wiley.
BEER, S. 1972: The Brain of the Firm. Allan Lane.
BEER, S. 1974: Designing Freedom. John Wiley.
BEER, S. 1975: Platform for Change. John Wiley.
BROWN, G.S. 1969: Laws of Form. Allen & Unwin.
FORRESTER, J.W. 1961: Industrial Dynamics. MIT Press.
FORRESTER, J.W. 1969: Urban Dynamics. Wright-Allen.
FORRESTER, J.W. 1971: World Dynamics. Wright-Allen.
FRIEDMAN and LEONDES, C.Z. 1969: Constraint Theory I. IEEE Trans.
    on Syst. and Cybern. SSC 5 Jan. 1969, p. 48 - 56.
HARRISON, P.J. and STEVENS, C.R. 1971: A Bayesian Approach to Short-
    term Forecasting. Oper. Res. Quart. v. 22, No. 4.
MATURANA, H. y VARELA, F. 1973: De Maquinas y Seres Vivos. Editorial
    Universidad de Chile.

3

COMPUTER MODELS FOR POLICY ANALYSIS:
HIERARCHY, GOAL ORIENTATION, SCENARIOS

Hartmut Bossel

0.   INTRODUCTION: ORIENTATION AND PLANNING

Computer models are images of reality: as any other image, they are determined by their object, by point of view, attitude and motivation, by initial
knowledge, ability, tools, and the interest of the model builder concerning
the representation and its purposes. As a result, there exist the counterparts of propaganda pamphlets, caricatures, sketches, abstract and realistic paintings - and maps.

Our interest focusses on the "maps" among the computer models: selected
and structured information concerning a segment of reality, collected and
represented on a certain level of abstractness and aggregation (scale of the
map) for purposes of orientation and planning. Today's computer models
often resemble the world maps of centuries gone by: in addition to well-
surveyed terrain there exist areas for which only fragmented information
is available, and white spots which are often decorated with phantastic crea-
tures in order to round out the total picture.

The map analogy is naturally incomplete, as it does not represent the temporal dynamics of the change of the landscape in the past, present, and
future which is an essential feature of policy analysis. Nevertheless, the
main tasks of maps and computer models as instruments of policy analysis
are one and the same: orientation and planning. In both cases the concrete
application purpose and the initial situation are not known in detail at the
time of construction.

As an instrument of policy analysis the computer model must be oriented
with respect to
    1 - the problematique to be studied;
    2 - the segment of reality which is to be mapped, and the task which
     the model is intended to fulfil;
The choice of the segment is strongly influenced by
    3 - the state of knowledge, point of view, and methodology.
From this follows finally
    4 - the modelling approach.
The interest of the present contribution focusses primarily on instruments
of policy analysis for the study of the long-term development of national
and international socio-technical systems. The task seems to lead more
or less directly to the theoretical framework proposed by Mesarović and Pestel [1]

(which, however, says nothing about the concrete implementation of the approach). Consequently, we are also interested in

    5 - the <u>implementation of the modelling approach.</u>

We shall turn to each of these points separately. As an example of an implementation, the current state of the Mesarovic-Pestel world model project will be briefly described.

1.   THE PROBLEMATIQUE

The term "problematique" will here be used in the sense of its usage by the Club of Rome[2]. "Problematique" therefore means the totality of a long-term societal development whose outcome is uncertain and potentially dangerous, i. e. which contains crisis potential. Examples are the problematique of starvation, of under- and overdevelopment, of unemployment and of war.

As the problematique determines the instrument selected for policy analysis to a significant extent, we first consider the characteristics of typical involved systems. Important characteristics are
- complexity
- dynamics
- decision units
- multidisciplinarity
- openness.

Complexity: The number of system elements of the real system and of their functional connections is extremely high; in addition, the mutual dependencies are generally complex and rarely linear. The total system which has to be considered consists of a multitude of subsystems and decision units, of flows and levels of information, matter, energy and organisms in constantly changing configuration. A description only becomes possible through a radical reduction of complexity which requires the distillation of important components and connections. From this fact follows the unavoidable subjectivity of model construction. The degree of subjectivity increases with a growing degree of complexity.

Dynamics: Changes of the state variables, positive and negative feedbacks, inertias, delays, nonlinearities, stochastics and decisions lead to complex dynamic behavior which can no longer be intuitively grasped and comprehended in the problematiques and systems under study here. In model construction again the difficulty arises of correctly including the major influences on the dynamics of the system.

Decision units: An important characteristic of societal systems is the large number of decision units which are able to influence - independently or in interaction - the behavior of the system. To each unit belongs a more or less developed information processing apparatus with the corresponding programs of perception, assessment, problem solving, learning and response and the corresponding information storage. Each unit orients its behavior with respect to its own norms, values, goals, and weightings of the future. Conflicts between decision units are a necessary consequence; these conflicts are resolved through direct or indirect interaction (via the common environment, as e. g. the exertion of power).

Openness: The stochastics of natural occurrences and of the boundary conditions of the system, and the only partially determined behavior of individual decision units result in a steadily growing bandwidth of the possible future development of individual state variables with increasing temporal distance from the present. The spectrum of possible futures quickly becomes exceedingly broad; a full simulation of all possibilities is out of the question for complex systems. In principle, there remain three possibilities to obtain useful results in spite of this handicap:

1 - Monte-Carlo-Simulation (random variation of the most important uncertain parameters in a large number of runs) and the determination of "river beds" of systems development. For complex systems this requires an extremely large number of simulation runs which can be handled economically only by using analogue or hybrid computers.

2 - The model is "closed" by assumptions of the model builder concerning uncertain events and behavioral modes. This approach is typical for the overwhelming number of simulation models today; it is a basic component of the system dynamics method. The approach is very much open to question, as it suggests to the user - without warning - a certainty of outcomes which is unjustified: in reality, uncertainty has simply been replaced by the questionable assumptions of the model builder. Different scenarios are generated by variation of a relatively small subset of scenario variables.

3 - Only those functional connections and parameters are endogenized about which certainty exists; uncertain events and behavioral modes are not included in the model - it remains "open". Missing parameters and dependencies have to be introduced by the model user; the program itself assists in this input process. The number of input parameters and of the possible scenarios is considerably larger in this approach.

Multidisciplinarity: The system description required for the study of the problematique must be able to cover a multitude of scientific fields in an integrative fashion while still being able to use the often highly developed language and methodology of the individual discipline.

Resulting requirements

From the characteristics of the problematique and of the systems to be studied a first set of requirements for the necessary systems description results:

1 - The approach must allow a reduction of complexity through stepwise decomposition into coupled component system and subsystems.

2 - The component system should be described in a language and method of description suited to the purpose.

3 - The approach should allow for the correct description of the special characteristics of acting and decision-making systems (information processing systems).

4 - A correct representation of the interaction between component systems must be possible, at least in principle.

5 - Due account must be taken of the openness of the future (i. e. of boundary conditions, parameters, and behavioral modes).

2. THE TASK OF THE COMPUTER MODEL

By analogy with a geographical map we here consider computer models whose major tasks are in the areas of orientation and planning. These tasks can be specified more concretely:

- adaption to the language and the state of knowledge of the model user;

- orientation about the current status and about "how we got here";

- orientation about likely developments in the foreseeable future;

- orientation about dynamic behavior and behavioral alternatives; and instrument for the investigation of policy alternatives and for policy synthesis.

User adaptation: The actual or potential crises of the "problematique" affect all to a greater or lesser degree. From this fact derives - within the framework of the value system of many countries - the normative requirement to permit the individual to orient himself and to participate in the problem-solving process. This means that the construction and use of computer models should not be left exclusively to a small group of experts. This postulate is by no means generally accepted; there is the very real danger that computer models will become chiefly the tools of power elites. Fortunately the computer itself and advances in the development of software and peripheral hardware generate increasingly better conditions for the adaptation of computer models to the language and knowledge level of the model user. It is therefore important that computer models for policy analysis and orientation should be designed as teaching programs, should be able to operate on different levels of complexity, should be adaptable to specific questions (and should therefore offer a multitude of branching possibilities), should permit working with the model in natural language or in symbolic language (computer graphics) without requiring the learning of special languages, and should finally be transparent and open to examination with respect to their structure and content.

Orientation about current status and historical development: The computer model should be able to inform the user in a clear and user-adaptive fashion about the current state of the system represented; in addition it should be able to simulate the historical development with some accuracy in order to show why things developed as they did.

Orientation concerning status-quo-continuation and the "standard scenario": In the "standard run" the computer model should be able to project the likely system development (if possible, with uncertainty bands) given the continuation of current trends. This run serves as a reference run for policy analyses.

Orientation about dynamic behavior and behavioral alternatives, and about policy analysis: The most important function of the computer model is as an instrument for the study of alternative futures. Such investigations should be possible on the level of "playing around" with the model as well as on the level of detailed and precise investigation. On the one hand it should be possible for the user to obtain a feeling for the dynamic behavior of the system, on the other he should be able to conduct precise investigations concerning policy alternatives. These modes of model use are completely analogous to the use of a flight simulator.

Resulting requirements

The tasks of orientation and policy analysis thus result in additional fundamental requirements concerning the system description:

6 - Operation of the model should be possible without the knowledge of a special language; the program should adapt itself to the task and to the level of knowledge of the model user.

7 - It should be possible to employ the model as an information system concerning current and past system states.

8 - The model should facilitate the investigation of behavioral alternatives in user-specified scenarios (parameters and boundary conditions); it should assist the user in constructing his own internal model of the corresponding segment of reality.

3. LEVEL OF KNOWLEDGE, POINT OF VIEW, METHODOLOGY

Every model,formalized or not, is subject to restrictions simply as a result of the limited knowledge of the model builder. One should remind oneself occasionally of this trivial conclusion, as it leads to important requirements concerning the modelling approach. We shall here briefly discuss constraints arising from the limitations of
- the level of knowledge
- the point of view
- the methodology.

Level of knowledge: System analyses concerning the "problematique" necessarily involve a multitude of scientific areas with very different levels of knowledge, scientific traditions, and languages. Even a comprehensive systems-analytical methodology cannot fill gaps and uncertainties of individual disciplines; by contrast, it will often only serve to uncover them. There exist enough examples for this, especially in connection with the system-analytical description of the behavior of societal systems. Here the knowledge gaps are particular wide. The system-analytical method may serve as a meta-method to structure holistic investigations in the individual disciplines. By the "system-analytical method" we here mean approaches in the sense of mathematical general systems theory[3].

Point of view: The system analysis of complex systems always requires a reduction of complexity; the selection of relevant elements and relationships is determined by the point of view of the analyst. A different point of view means a different selection, consequently a different description of the system, and different simulation results. Obviously intersubjective agreement concerning the point of view does not imply the nonexistence of different legitimate points of view.

Methodology: The methodology of model construction is today determined by the current methods and tools of analysis of engineering and the computer sciences, of mathematics, physics, and bio-cybernetics. This approach is most certainly too narrow; surely the methodologies of nonnumerical concept manipulation and artificial intelligence and of psychology, and the processes of interaction, conflict, and conflict resolution will eventually have more significance than could be derived from current modelling approaches.

Resulting requirements

From the limitations of the level of knowledge, of the point of view, and of methodology there again follow several requirements concerning the systems description:

9 - The approach should be broad, integrative, and comprehensive without being a priori limited by level of knowledge, point of view, or methodology.

10 - The approach should be open; i. e. it should permit at any time the insertion and application of new and different knowledge, points of view, and methodologies.

4. MODELLING APPROACH

The requirements of the modelling approach resulting from the tasks of orientation and policy analysis are here summarized from the points of view of the overall approach, the system description, and orientation and planning:

Requirements concerning the overall approach:

- C o m p r e h e n s i v e   a p p r o a c h: framework of general validity.

- D e c o m p o s i t i o n: possibility of decomposition into smaller component models.

- O p e n n e s s   o f   t h e   a p p r o a c h: possibility of insertion of different component concepts.

Requirements concerning the system description:

- D e c i s i o n   a n d   a c t i o n   u n i t s: explicit inclusion of decision processes and actions.

- O p e n n e s s   o f   t h e   f u t u r e: Inclusion of the stochastics of boundary conditions, parameters, and behavior.

- I n t e r a c t i o n: Consideration of direct and indirect mutual influence of actor systems.

- O p e n n e s s   o f   l a n g u a g e: Possibility of description by the language best adapted to the purpose.

Requirements concerning the planning instrument:

- A d a p t a t i o n: Adaptation to the language, knowledge, and problem areas of the user; teaching function.

- O r i e n t a t i o n: Design as information source and aid to orientation.

- P o l i c y   a n a l y s i s: Design as a flexible instrument of policy analysis and synthesis; scenario approach.

The Mesarović-Pestel approach

The Mesarović-Pestel approach has been developed in response to the requirements listed; it is therefore of some interest to determine how well
it meets these requirements. However, it is necessary to distinguish between the conceptual a p p r o a c h and its i m p l e m e n t a t i o n
within the framework of the multifaceted and constantly evolving activities
of the Mesarović-Pestel world model project. The current state of implementation will be discussed below. The following discussion is based on the
systems-theoretical foundation of the approach[4], on the description of the
approach for the global model[5], on the approach as it is deducible from par-
ticularities of the implementation[6], on the current state of the implementation[7], and on the approach used by projects coordinated with the Mesarović-
Pestel project[8].

Comprehensive approach: The fundamental approach is that of hierarchical
multilevel systems[9] which grew out of general mathematical systems theory.
On account of the multitude of forms in which it may appear, this approach
cannot be characterized in a brief and compact manner; we only list here its
most significant features[10];

- vertical ordering of subsystems in "levels";
- intervention privileges of the subsystems on higher levels;
- dependence of subsystems on the higher levels on the performance
  of the lower levels.

Mesarović et al. distinguish three types of levels which may partially overlap (the three features listed apply to all of them): "strata" of different
description or different degrees of abstraction of one and the same system;
"layers" of components of different degrees of complexity in decision processes; and "echelons" in organizations with hierarchically ordered deci-
sion-processes.

Examples for strata: Depending on problem definition and purpose, a
biological organism can be represented on different strata: on the atomic,
molecular, or cellular level, on the level of its organs, or on the level of
the total organism. Each of these descriptions is legitimate and is determined by the purpose of the representation. It may be necessary to represent one and the same system simultaneously on different strata, in order
to correctly describe its functioning with respect to the given purpose of
the description. In the Mesarović-Pestel world model this approach is
used in particular in the representation of the economic system: this system
is represented on the lowest level by a technological stratum which describes the physical flows of energies, materials, labor, and products; the
next higher level contains a micro-economic stratum with an input/output
description of the economic system in monetary flows; while the level about
this one contains a macro-economic stratum described in terms of production functions[11]. A characteristic of the strata approach is an increase in

the detail of description as one descends in the hierarchy; by contrast, the
ascent to higher levels is coupled with an increasing comprehension of the
mutual interconnections.

Examples for layers: Complex decision problems are of a hierarchical
structure. As an example, functional and socialized requirements determine
personal values, and, in connection with the characteristics of the real
system, goals. These again are translated into concrete operational norms
to fit the concrete situation and the conditions then prevalent. Similar layers
can be found in natural or artificial problem solving processes[12].

Examples for echelons: The organizational hierarchy of a steel mill is
composed of a large number of echelons reaching from the production process
itself via the different subsystems of process control to the daily processing
schedule and finally to long term planning and the top management of the firm.

The theory of hierarchical multilevel systems permits an adequate description of the system relevant to the problematique under discussion, without
forcing them into a Procrustean bedstead. Naturally the interaction of different hierarchical systems is also included in the approach.

Decomposition: A direct result of the hierarchical multilevel approach is
the necessity of decomposition of the total system into a multitude of subsystems taking over special tasks within the hierarchical structure. These
subsystems are in interaction with other subsystems on the same, or on a
lower or a higher level. This systems structure corresponds exactly to the
structure of the computer programs required for the simulation. For this
reason the individual model parts can be separately developed, verified
and validated as individual subroutines.

Openness of the approach: Another consequence of the hierarchical multilevel approach with its decomposition into subsystems is the possibility
to represent each subsystem in a manner reflecting the task, the point of
view, and the degree of knowledge about it, as long as the compatibility
and ability to interface with other subsystems is guaranteed. This means
in particular that subsystems may be described using the concepts and tools
of the scientific disciplines involved, and that knowledge gaps may initially
be filled by crude approximate models which may be replaced by better ones
in the course of the model development without threatening the modelling
effort from the beginning by the lack of certain information. Finally there
is also the possibility to introduce subsystems of different degrees of
aggregation at the same place in the hierarchy in order to obtain the required
structural detail.

Decision and action units: The explicit inclusion of decision behavior distinguishes the Mesarović-Pestel approach from other approaches having
similar goals. In reality, societal systems continuously adapt to a constantly changing environment. Without changing elementary goals they may

abruptly change their mode of behavior. The routine transformation of a
given stimulus into a corresponding response via a previously known transformation function is not sufficient in this case; the decision unit must have
a number of behavioral modes at its disposal, must be able to conduct a
problem solving process, and must be able to assess the consequences of
behavioral alternatives by reference to normative statements. The structure of even a simple decision unit becomes relatively complex. There are
basically three hierarchical levels to be found in these units: an upper normative level containing normative information and the processes of normative change, a decision level which is able to perform the information processing of situation perception, state analysis, problem solving, assessment
of alternatives and decision-making, and finally a causal level containing
the material subsystem of the decision unit and the effectors through which
decisions effecting the environment are implemented.

Openness of the future: Again in contradistinction to other approaches the
Mesarović-Pestel approach explicitly accounts for the uncertainty of future
boundary conditions, parameters, and decisions by use of the scenario concept. The approach is critical of the often practiced endogenization of uncertain system conditions or of behavior by use of historical information (as in
econometric approaches) or the estimation of plausible response functions
(as practiced in the system dynamics methodology). Instead, assumptions
about the future are left unspecified in the model and must be introduced by
the model user as scenario time series (however, all models provide standard time series in order to permit model runs even if the user does not
provide scenario inputs). In principle models using the Mesarović-Pestel
approach therefore require more exogeneous inputs and can project a wider
behavioral band width via scenarios; they contain relatively fewer subjective assumptions of the model builder than other modelling approaches.
They do require, on the other hand, the active collaboration of the model
user; in order to facilitate his work they therefore have to offer assistance
during the interactive man-machine dialogue.

Interaction: An essential element of the Mesarović-Pestel approach is the
interaction between decision units, between subsystems and between individual modules of the total system. Interaction between decision units are
the result of decision processes; they may consist of direct or indirect control (via the environment) of the flows of information, matter, energy etc.
(exchange, exertion of power, etc.) for the purpose of exerting influence,
obstruction, or cooperation.

Openness of language: While other modelling approaches (e. g. the system
dynamics method) are restricted from the beginning to a certain mode of
systems analysis and systems description and a specific computer language,
the Mesarović-Pestel approach does not suffer any constraints with respect
to the method of description. The method best suited to the task can be used
for each systems component. Within the framework of the approach almost
all types of numerical description (dynamic, static, deterministic, stochastic,

linear, nonlinear, continuous, discrete, etc.) as well as nonnumerical description (predicate calculus), have been used.

Adaptation: The openness of the hierarchical multilevel approach makes it possible to include the user as part of the simulation. This feature is used in particular when the user takes over the function of a decision unit. Adaptation of the model program is a precondition for this mode of model use, as well as for the scenario input, and the use of the model for orientation, policy analysis and synthesis. Considerable development work has been performed by the Mesarović-Pestel groups with regard to this aspect.

Orientation: The hierarchical multilevel approach facilitates the accomplishment of the orientation task by its transparent structure. The different aspects of orientation require a user-adaptive design of the peripheral programs of the computer model. Orientation must be possible with regard to
  - the structure and components of the computer model;
  - the data base used (historical values, initial values of the simulation, assumed parameter time series of future development, etc.);
  - the dynamic response resulting from conditions chosen by the user ("playing around" with the model in order to obtain "a picture" (= internal model) of the dynamic system properties);
  - the future system behavior resulting from "standard" conditions (usually a continuation of the status-quo) and from specific control inputs.
As the quality of the orientation possibilities is decisive for the usefulness of the approach as a planning tool, the Mesarović-Pestel approach devotes considerable attention to these aspects.

Policy analysis: The main task of the Mesarović-Pestel approach is that of providing a reliable, flexible and user-adaptive instrument for policy analysis and policy synthesis. In addition to the task of user-adaptive orientation it must allow the flexible selection of policy parameters (number and quantification), as well as the testing of corresponding strategy scenarios. In the Mesarović-Pestel approach the policy analysis and synthesis can be conducted in a dynamic and iterative fashion: In addition to the boundary conditions and parameter scenarios the user specifies policy scenarios over a time period chosen by him, studies the resulting simulation results and compares them with his objectives. If the results are satisfactory, he repeats the procedure for a new time period. If not, he can return to an earlier point in time, develop a new strategy scenario and test it over the specified time period. This procedure corresponds to the satisficing approach of Simon[13] which is predominant in real decision-making systems. As a result of the great number of policy parameters, the extremely large number of state variables, the openness of the boundary conditions, and of nonspecifiable objective functions, optimization is not applicable and can at best be used to restrict the search space and aid in the preliminary selection of strategies.

A critique of other modelling approaches

It is instructive to compare other modelling approaches for the same problem type in the light of the criteria used here. We here consider those approaches used most often: macro-economic estimation procedures[14], micro-economic input/output methods[15], and the system dynamics method[16]. It should be mentioned that all of these methods may be used - and have been used - to represent certain system levels in the hierarchical multilevel approach (see below). However, they do not represent an adequate framework for the comprehensive study of the problematique - as will be shown in the following.

In macro-economic estimation procedures a given quantity is explained by determination - using historical time series data - of quantities having statistically significant influences. A functional relationship between these quantities is postulated, e. g. for the explantation of consumer behavior. The parameters required for the description are then estimated by matching the functional relationship to the historical time series with a high numerical precision (e. g. by the method of least squares). Several of such relation-ships are then connected in order to obtain a macro-ecomic model[17].

The micro-economic input/output method investigates the distribution of the output (in monetary value) of one economic sector to other sectors and to the end user in a matrix approach. The required data are taken from economic statistics. A special difficulty of this approach is the "dynamization" of the coefficients of the distribution matrix. The mutually coupled changes of these coefficients as a result of structural change within the economic system are not obtainable from historical time series alone. The input/output approach has recently also been applied to the study of different levels of the economic stratum (e. g. energy, materials, labor).

While econometric methods stress in particular the parameter determination and statistical procedures of parameter estimation, the system dynamics methods puts greater emphasis on the correct description of system struc-ture and dynamic behavior. Real systems are represented as systems of coupled nonlinear ordinary differential equations. System dynamics makes a point of including in the systems description those relationships which very likely contribute significantly to the dynamic behavior, but cannot be easily quantified (either because data do not exist, or cannot be easily obtained, or are simply not measurable). These relationships very often concern des-criptions of behavior which the model builder incorporates in the so-called "policies". Much criticism of the method is connected to this approach.

Appropriateness: The methods mentioned do not represent an approach having general validity for the problematique we are concerned with. How-ever, this claim is occasionally made only by the systems dynamics method. It is well to remember that this method describes systems by coupled dif-ferential equations - a mode of description which is not adequate e. g. for the description of cognitive processes in decision-making, and which also does not appear to be appropriate for many other features of systems behavior.

System description: The three approaches are ill-suited in particular for the representation of goal-oriented adaptive behavior: the econometric approaches are restricted to the reproduction of behavior evidenced in the past; the system dynamics methods adds to this the intuition of the model builder concerning possible future behavior. In contrast to the Mesarović-Pestel approach the decision-making process is seen simply as a preprogrammed stimulus-response-transformation; despite the fact that by orientation with respect to elementary normative statements this information process may in reality activate a great number of very different behavioral modes. In connection with this deficiency the openness of the future is not adequately taken into account by a far-reaching endogenization of uncertain behavior as well as uncertain boundary conditions and parameters. These models therefore often exhibit a determinism of system development which simply does not exist in reality. Examples are forecasts of economic development or of energy consumption.

All of the three approaches are severely handicapped by the fact that they require a narrowly prescribed specific mathematical description.

Use as a planning instrument: The user-adaptive employment as a planning instrument depends above all on the quality of peripheral programs, which have little to do with the modelling approach itself. While the programs of the Mesarović-Pestel approach are consciously designed to allow direct use by the decision-maker, the other approaches are mainly designed for indirect model use: the decision-maker specifies his problem to the modelling expert, who then prepares the corresponding model run. The iterative-dynamic mode of model usage for the interactive development of strategy is not allowed for. In particular, the orientation of the model user and the transparence of model use both suffer from restrictions of this mode of model use.

5. IMPLEMENTATION OF THE MODEL CONCEPT

As final part of this account a survey of the current implementation status of the modelling concept of Mesarović and Pestel will be given. One should remember, however, that there is no such thing as t h e Mesarović-Pestel World Model. Instead, there exist a number of component models - some of them at a very advanced stage of development - concerning partial aspects of the global system. For the solution of specific tasks these models are coupled within the framework of the multilevel approach in a problem-specific manner. However, model components are also often used individually for orientation and policy analysis concerning limited systems aspects.

This survey will be grouped according to the emphasis of model development to date:

- Development of models of the demographic-economic stratum, the technology stratum, and the environmental stratum (so-called "causal models", since predominantly causal or pseudo-causal relationships representing events in the material domain are used here);
- Development of models of decision processes, including the simulation of normative change;
- Development of peripheral programs for the interactive use of models in a user-adaptive dialogue between man and computer;
- Coupling of simulation modules for the generation of problem-specific model aggregates;
- Study of systems-analytical aspects of the overall approach.

Regarding a coherent introduction to the world-model-project, we refer to the introductory text on the project[18] and the technical reports[19]. The several model parts were initially developed for a 10-region world; in the meantime a considerable disaggregation on the national scale has been introduced in order to facilitate the study of national policy issues.[20]

Causal models

Corresponding to the overall problematique of the project, the development of causal models has been oriented by the problem aspects population, food, energy resources, environment and structural change (in industrial countries). Models were developed in the following categories:

- population and education
- energy and resources
- economy
- technology (incl. agriculture)
- environment

Population and education: A demographic model consisting of 86 age groups for each sex is used for each of the ten world regional , or subregionalized national models. The corresponding data base is developed from national population statistics[21]. Detailed models of the educational system can be coupled to the demographic models. The education models produce the distribution of educational qualifications for each age group[22].

Energy and resources: The resource base of the economy has been the subject of several studies: energy resources and resources exploitation[23], oil in the global economy[24], and aluminum[25] and copper in the world economy[26]. Other studies concerning the resource base are in preparation (cf. corresponding models under "technology").

Economy: In order to describe the economic systems of the different regions and of individual national economies and their international linkages a number of models have been used so far - most of them based on traditional econometric approaches. On the macro-economic level, production functions[27] of the Cobb-Douglas type were used. Leontief's Input/Output approach has been used to model the micro-economic level[28]. The linkage of national

and regional economies is effected via trade matrices[29]. The current state
of the description of an economic system by an integrated set of models is
reflected in a comprehensive model of the Federal Republic of Germany[30].
This model is again embedded in models of the western European trade part-
ners and of the remaining nine world economic regions.

The economic development is constrained by demand development; studies
of demand development are therefore of special significance. Such studies
were undertaken for energy on the basis of growth assumptions for the regional economies[31]. More recently, more detailed studies (energy, products,
and services) have been made for the Federal Republic of Germany of the
different components of the demand vector by inclusion of saturation analyses[32].

Technology: The performance of the economic stratum is a function of the
characteristics and potential of the technological stratum whose function is
the production of the required goods and services[33]. In a comprehensive approach the sectoral production is presented by the transformation of resources, energy, labor, and capital into products and services. For each
sectoral product, resp. each sectoral service the direct and indirect inputs
of resources (10 categories), energy (6 categories), labor (4 categories),
capital (19 categories) can then be computed and become available for policy analysis and synthesis.

More specific studies focussed on the energy supply system[34] and in particular on the problems of food supply. A large multi-strata model was
developed for this purpose and used for comprehensive policy analysis[35].

Environment: The environmental pollution generated by different energy
policy alternatives was studied by coupling process-specific emissions to
the different processes of energy transformation. Further studies focussed
on the global ecological energy balance and on the regional-ecological water
cycle[36].

Models of decision processes

In the hierarchical multi-level approach central importance is given to
decision units on the different levels. Two separate approaches are taken
in the Mesarović-Pestel world model project to facilitate the inclusion of
decision processes:
1 - The decision process required on a given level is not simulated
    in the model itself, but is taken over by a human interactor who
    interacts with the program during the simulation;
2 - The decision process with its components of state analysis and
    policy synthesis is fully simulated by the model program; in this
    process normative references are required.

Interactive decision process: In this case the decision process is generally
prestructured in multiple layers of a decision hierarchy (general goal layer,

policy layer, strategy layer, implementation layer)[37]. The dialogue between interactor and computer is guided by the program; it leads the interactor from general goals to decisions concerning concrete implementation. The decisions of the interactor represent control inputs determining the further course of the simulation. The method was first applied successfully outside the global modelling project in the context of environmental policy analysis[38]. Within the framework of the world model project it has been applied to the simulation of energy policy decisions[39], to the study of food policy issues[40], in a global oil model[41] and in the analysis of the energy supply system.[42] Special peripheral programs have been developed to handle the interactive mode of operation (see below).

Simulated decision processes: In models of the size of the Mesarović-Pestel world model the representation of decision processes of the different decision units on the different levels of all model sectors and regions by one or more human interactors becomes impossible, if only for organizational reasons. On the other hand, the representation of decision processes by preprogrammed automatic stimulus-response functions is thoroughly questionable. The only remaining alternative is the simulation of the decision process itself. The objective of such simulation attempts can only be to correctly develop the probable decision trends of real decision units; a precise simulation of the decision process and of decision results is not possible and is not attempted.

In an initial successful application, the human interactor in an interactive program for energy policy analysis was replaced by a corresponding simulation program.[43] This program made decisions by reference to a given value system in a heuristic problem-solving process[44]. This initial approach has meanwhile been replaced by a broader conceptual framework. In particular, this approach attempts to describe changes in the normative system[45]. In the world oil model a simulated bidding-allocation scheme has been used successfully to determine the price development of competing energy resources[46].

User-adaptive interactive processing

The Mesarović-Pestel approach requires user-adaptive peripheral programs for model development, interactive processing by the scenario technique as well as the partial takeover of decision-making by the interactor. These programs first had to be developed; the development concentrated on
- programs to simplify the process of model building, data input, and output of results;
- programs for the development of user-adaptive dialogues between the computer and the human interactor.

Model-building programs: Traditionally the development of a computer model requires significant programming effort in a special language. The model itself - often merely a few vector equations - constitutes only a small part of the program. Model-building programs take care of most of the routine programming; the model builder can therefore concentrate his efforts on the conceptualization, verification and validation of the model. Significant changes, even completely new conceptualizations, can be implemented in very little time.

Within the framework of the Mesarovic-Pestel approach the model building program MODEL BUILDER [47] was developed. This program requires merely specification of the model core equations in FORTRAN as well as information concerning input data and the standardized presentation of output data. The possibilities of interactive computer graphics are used in another model building program GRIPS [48]; here the model is developed entirely during a structured dialogue with the computer. The model structure is drawn on the CRT display using the light pen; the program generates the corresponding systems equations and the entire simulation program including graphical and printed output. Functional dependencies and time series are likewise sketched on the display using the light pen. As a consequence, this model builder program is especially well-suited for the model conceptualization state.

The meta-program MODEL BUILDER can also be used for interactive scenario development. In this case the user must learn a few simple commands and parameter names, which he can then use to input the constraint and strategy scenarios he wishes to study during the simulation.

Dialogue construction: The design and development of a s p e c i a l interactive program for user-adaptive policy analysis is extremely labor-intensive. This approach was taken in the development of a program for policy analysis concerning the energy supply system [49]. Since even in very complex interactive programs with multiple branching capability certain elementary steps recur continuously, a meta-program for the construction of interactive dialogue has been developed in the meantime [50]. This program can be used for the construction of dialogues in natural language; it requires merely specification of the query tree and of the query texts. The program is suited for the user-adaptive selective specification of input parameter time series (i.e. for the input of constraint and strategy scenarios)as well as for selective access to the data base for orientation of the user, and finally for the selection of output variables by the user.

Integrated model aggregates

The individual models developed within the Mesarović-Pestel world model project have been used in various combinations adapted to special problems. Of particular interest in this context are the applications to the world food situation [51], to the global oil supply [52], and to policy questions concerning technological policy in the Federal Republic of Germany [53].

Basic systems-theoretical research

The scientific base of the hierarchical multi-level approach has been formulated in two books[54]. In contrast to the abstract-mathematical approach
found in these works most of the studies of the Mesarovic-Pestel project
have addressed themselves to applied problems of model construction.
Several theoretical studies have been made within the framework of the project in order to clear up fundamental questions connected with model development. Mention may be made here of studies concerning error propagation
with time[55], the theory of the modelling approach as a tool of technology
assessment[56] and the statistical foundation for the decomposition into subsystems necessary for model construction[57].

6. CLOSING REMARKS

The systems-analytical tools of computer-assisted policy analysis are still
in an early phase of development. Accomplishments so far are for the most
part products of the first experimental phase; neither are they typical for the
potential achievements of these tools, nor for the manner in which they will
accomplish their tasks in the future. Much depends on the further development of computers, peripheral hardware, programming languages and programs. It is more important, however, to create the conditions for further
development within an open, pluralistic framework allowing for a broad
spectrum of conceptual approaches without losing sight of the major goal:
the development on a solid scientific base of user-adaptive instruments of
orientation and policy analysis for better decision-making concerning the
development of complex socio-technical systems.

A number of requirements concerning the overall approach, the systems
description and the development of an instrument of orientation and policy
analysis were here spelled out as a function of the task definition. These
requirements can be met by the multi-level approach. However, the implementation of the approach requires considerable work for the construction
of modules and peripheral programs. Part of this work has already been
completed within the framework of the Mesarovic-Pestel world model project; this work was here briefly reported. Another part is under development. Finally new development tasks will evolve as a consequence of the
actual use of the instrument and its application to new tasks.

The task of computer-assisted policy analysis cannot be automated decisions
and a totally planned future. By contrast, its major function is that of a map:
an aid to better orientation and policy analysis which helps to avoid catastrophes, points out decision alternatives and their consequences, assists
the analysis process, but leaves the responsibility for decisions to man.

REFERENCES

1) M.D. Mesarovic, E. Pestel: Menschheit am Wendepunkt. Stuttgart, Deutsche Verlags-Anstalt, 1974. Also: Mankind at the Turning Point. New York: Dutton 1974.

2) E.g. A. Pecchei and A. King in Mesarovic and Pestel: Menschheit am Wendepunkt, op. cit. p. 179 - 184.

3) E.g. M. Mesarovic and Y. Takahara: Foundations for the Mathematical Theory of General Systems; New York: Academic Press, 1974.

4) M.D. Mesarovic, Y. Takahara, D. Macko: Theory of Hierarchical Multilevel Systems; New York: Academic Press, 1970. Also: Mesarovic and Takahara: Foundations for the Mathematical Theory of General Systems, op. cit.

5) M. Mesarovic, E. Pestel: A Goal-Seeking and Regionalized Model for Analysis of Critical World Relationships - The Conceptual Foundation. Kybernetes, 1972. Also: E. Pestel: Motivation, Objectives and Conceptual Foundation; and M. Mesarovic: Methodology for Construction and Structure of the Multilevel World System Model; both in M. Mesarovic, E. Pestel (eds.): Multilevel Computer Model of World Development System. Reports SP-74-1 through SP-74-6 (6 vols.), IIASA, Vienna, April 1974.

6) See the individual contributions in IIASA SP-74-1 through 6, op. cit., as well as final documentation on the original world model project: B. Aslani, B. Hughes, J. Richardson: The World Model, vol. I: Model Description, and M. Ghobadi, B. Hughes, M. Mesarovic, B. Partovi, T. Shook: The World Model, vol. II: Model Use. Mesarovic-Pestel World Model Project, Systems Research Center, Case Western Reserve University, Cleveland, Ohio, Sept. 1975.

7) See final report of the project "Anpassung des Mesarovic-Pestel Weltmodells zur Anwendung auf forschungs- und technologierelevante Fragestellungen aus der Sicht der Bundesrepublik Deutschland". (A systems model for research and technology policy analysis for the Federal Republic of Germany) (FRG-Project). Institut für Mechanik, Technische Universität Hannover, 1976.

8) E.g. the contributions by H. Bossel and E. Gruber in H. Bossel, S. Klaczko, N. Müller: Systems Theory for the Social Sciences. Basel; Birkhäuser, 1976.

9) M.D. Mesarovic, Y. Takahara, D. Macko 1970, op. cit.

10) M.D. Mesarovic, Y. Takahara, D. Macko 1970, op. cit. p. 34.

11) See the contributions in IIASA SP-74-2; also: Aslani, Hughes and Richardson, op. cit.; and reports FRG project, op. cit.

12) E.g. A. Newell, H.A. Simon: Simulation of Human Thought. In: J.M. Dutton, W.H. Starbuck: Computer Simulation of Human Behavior. New York: Wiley 1971, p. 150 - 169.

13) E.g. H.A. Simon: A Behavioral Model of Rational Choice. In: The Quarterly Journal of Economics, Vol. LXIX. Also in: M. Alexis, Ch. Z. Wilson: Organizational Decision-Making. Englewood Cliffs, N.J.: Prentice-Hall 1967.

14) E. g. R. Pfeiffer: Kybernetische Analyse ökonometrischer Makromodelle
für die Bundesrepublik Deutschland. Tübingen: Institut für Angewandte
Wirtschaftsforschung, 1975. (Also: Basel: Birkhäuser 1976).

15) E. g. W. Leontief: Input-Output Economics. Fair Lawn, N. J.: Oxford
University Press 1966.

16) E. g. J. W. Forrester: Industrial Dynamics. Cambridge, Mass.: MIT
Press 1961; J. W. Forrester: World Dynamics, Cambridge, Mass.:
Wright-Allen Press 1971; D. H. Meadows et al.: The Limits to Growth.
New York: Universe Books 1972; D. L. Meadows et al.: Dynamics of
Growth in a Finite World. Cambridge, Mass.: Wright-Allen Press 1974.

17) Pfeiffer, op. cit.

18) Mesarovic and Pestel: Mankind at the Turning Point, op. cit.

19) Mesarovic and Pestel: IIASA Report 1974, op. cit.; Aslani et al., op. cit.,
Ghobadi et al., op. cit.

20) See final reports of FRG-project, op. cit.

21) K. H. Oehmen, W. Paul: Construction of Population Submodels; IIASA
SP-74-3. a.a.O., S. B 361 - 480, also H. H. Maier: Bevölkerungs- und
Ausbildungsmodell für die Bundesrepublik Deutschland. Institut für Me-
chanik, Technische Universität Hannover, 1976.

22) H. H. Maier, op. cit.

23) R. Bauerschmidt, R. Denton, H. H. Maier: Energy Reserves and Resources Submodel. In IIASA SP-74-4, op. cit., pp. B 691 - B 771.
Also: N. Chu, B. Hughes: Energy Demand Submodel; in IIASA SP-74-4,
op. cit., pp. B 773 - B 832.

24) B. Hughes: World Oil System Submodel; in IIASA SP-74-4, op. cit.,
pp. B 971 - B 1081.

25) B. Hughes and A. Barsotti: Materials Model - Copper and Aluminum.
Systems Research Center, Case Western Reserve University, Nov. 1975.

26) Hughes and Barsotti, op. cit.

27) M. McCarthy, G. Shuttic: Cobb-Douglas Production Function for the
World Model Project and a One Sector Growth Model Interpretation; in
IIASA SP-74-2, op. cit., pp. B 37 - B 65. Also: A. Erdilek et al.:
Computer Implementation of Macro-Economic World Model; in IIASA
SP-74-2 op. cit., pp. B 67 - B 224. A different macro-economic
approach is found in: W. Ströbele: Untersuchungen zum Wachstum der
Weltwirtschaft mit Hilfe eines regionalisierten Weltmodells. Disserta-
tion Technische Universität Hannover, 1975.

28) T. Shook, W. Ströbele: Computer Implementation of Micro Economic
World Model; in IIASA SP-74-2, op. cit., pp. B 225 - B 360. Also:
final reports of FRG project, op. cit.; in particular W. Oest, W. Ströbele:
Kapitalkoeffizienten in Landwirtschaft, industriellen und Dienstleistungs-
sektoren in der Bundesrepublik Deutschland, Frankreich und Großbritan-
nien.

29) L. Klein, B. Hickman, M. Mesarovic: Specification of Structure for a
Macro-Economic World Model; in IIASA SP-74-2, op. cit. pp. B 5 - B 36.
Also: Dissertation Ströbele, op. cit.

30) P. Möller: Untersuchungen der Entwicklung des Außenhandels von 19
Wirtschaftssektoren der Bundesrepublik Deutschland mit den 13 Weltre-
gionen des Mesarovic-Pestel Modells. P. Möller: Untersuchungen der
Veränderung der Warenstruktur im Handel der Bundesrepublik mit Schwel-
lenstaaten; R. Dayal, P. Möller, W. Ströbele: Welthandelsprognosen mit
verschiedenen Ansätzen, all in final report FRG project, op. cit.

31) s. Chu and Hughes, op. cit.

32) s. P. Möller: Untersuchung über mögliche Sättigungstendenzen des pri-
vaten Konsums für relevante Modellsektoren, Arbeitsbericht BRD-Pro-
jekt, op. cit.

33) R. Bauerschmidt, M. Gottwald: Technologisches Modell der Güter- und
Dienstleistungsproduktion der Bundesrepublik Deutschland. Final report
FRG project, op. cit.

34) H. Bossel: Energy Supply Submodel, IIASA SP-74-4, op. cit., pp.
B 833 through B 970. H. H. Maier: Ein Systemmodell zur Untersuchung
alternativer Energiestrategien, Dissertation, Technische Universität
Hannover, 1975.

35) W. B. Clapham Jr. et al.: Scenario Analysis of the World Food Situation
1975 - 2025; in IIASA SP-74-3, op. cit., pp. B 627 - B 685. Also: W. B.
Clapham, T. Shook, M. W. Warshaw: A Regionalized Food Model for the
Global System; in IIASA SP-74-3, op. cit., pp. B 499 - B 554; M. D.
Mesarovic et al.: The Structural Description and Sensitivity Analysis of
the Food Submodel; in IIASA SP-74-3, op. cit., pp. B 555 - B 625. J. M.
Richardson: Demonstration and Use of the Food Submodel as a Planning
and Decision-Making Tool, in: M. Mesarovic and E. Pestel: Report on
the Demonstration of the Mesarovic-Pestel World Model for Members
of the European Parliament, Institut für Mechanik, Hannover, 24 - 26
Feb. 1975. (European Parliament Report)

36) M. Gottwald, R. Pestel: Environmental Impact Assessment; in IIASA
SP-74-5, op. cit., pp. B 1121 - B 1275. The global ecological energy
balance was studied in: R. P. Heyes, R. A. Jerdonek, A. B. Kuper:
Global Energy Submodel; in IIASA SP-74-5, op. cit., pp. B 1083 - B 1119.
The regional ecological water cycle was modelled by M. A. Cardenas,
J. M. Huerta: Submodel of Global Water Cycle on a Regional Basis; in
IIASA SP-74-5, op. cit., pp. B 1277 - B 1391.

37) Mesarovic and Pestel: Mankind at the Turning Point, op. cit.; P. Gille
et al.: An Interactive Decision Stratum for the Multilevel World Model;
in IIASA SP-74-6, op. cit., pp. C 219 - C 229; F. Rechenmann: Conversational Use of Multi-Layer Decision Models; in IIASA SP-74-6, op.
cit., pp. C 231 - C 246.

38) M. Mesarovic et al.: Multilevel Systems Model for Interactive Mode of
Policy Analysis in Pollution Control. Interim Report 1973 and Final
Report 1974, Systems Research Center. Case Western Reserve Univer-
sity, Cleveland, Ohio.

39) P. Gille et al.: An Interactive Decision Stratum for the Multilevel World
Model; op. cit.

40) W. B. Clapham Jr. et al.: Scenario Analysis of the World Food Situation
1975 - 2025; op. cit.; J. M. Richardson: Demonstration and Use of the
Food Submodel as a Planning and Decision-Making Tool, in European
Parliament Report, op. cit.

41) B. Hughes: World Oil System Submodel; op. cit.; B. Hughes, Scenario Analysis of Problems Involved in the Oil Crisis; and B. Hughes: Introduction to the Structure of the World-Energy Model, in: European Parliament Report, op. cit. Also: M. Mesarovic: An Introduction to the Multilevel, Regionalized World Model and Scenario Analysis for the Assessment of Long-Range Development Policies, in: European Parliament Report, op. cit.

42) H. Bossel, R. V. Denton, P. v. d. Hijden, W. Hudetz, J. Klabbers: Energy Policy Assessment Using an Interactive Model Package. Second UNESCO Seminar on Trends in Mathematical Modelling, Warszawa 1974. See also: H. Bossel (ed.): Concepts and Tools of Computer-Assisted Policy Analysis. Basel: Birkhäuser 1977.

43) P. Gille et al.: An Interactive Decision Stratum for the Multilevel World Model; op. cit.

44) H. Bossel and B. Hughes: Simulation of Value-Controlled Decision-Making: Approach and Prototype; in IIASA SP-74-6, op. cit. pp. C 1 - C 115.

45) H. Bossel: Information Processing, Cognitive Dissonance, and Basic Needs: The Modelling of Behavior. In: H. Bossel, S. Klaczko, N. Müller: Systems Theory in the Social Sciences; Basel: Birkhäuser 1976.

46) B. Hughes: A Cybernetic Energy Model Using a Bidding and Allocation Technique. Systems Research Center, Case Western Reserve University, Cleveland, Ohio, Sept. 1975.

47) T. Shook: The Model Scenario Analysis Package; in IIASA SP-74-6, op. cit., pp. C 283 - C 314; T. Shook: Using the Model Builder, in: Ghobadi et al.: The World Model, vol. II: Model Use, op. cit. Also: H. Vogt: Handbuch für das Model Builder Programmpaket: Institut für Mechanik, Technische Universität Hannover, 1975.

48) W. Hudetz: A Program for the Construction of Dynamic System Models Using Interactive Computer Graphics. In: H. Bossel: Concepts and Tools of Computer-Assisted Policy Analysis, Basel: Birkhäuser 1977.

49) H. Bossel et al.: Energy Policy Assessment Using an Interactive Model Package; op. cit.

50) H. Bossel and M. Strobel: Program for Interactive Input Generation and Output Selection. In: H. Bossel (ed.): Concepts and Tools of Computer-Assisted Policy Analysis, op. cit.

51) W. B. Clapham Jr. et al.: Scenario Analysis of the World Food Situation 1975 - 2025, op. cit.; J. M. Richardson: Demonstration and Use of the Food Submodel as a Planning and Decision-Making Tool, European Parliament Report, op. cit.; also: Pt. 1 and Pt. 4 in Aslani et al.: The World Model, vol. I, Model Description, op. cit.

52) B. Hughes: World Oil System Submodel, op. cit.; Reports by B. Hughes in European Parliament Report, op. cit.; Pt. 3 in Aslani et al.: The World Model, vol. I, Model Description, op. cit.

53) Final report FRG project, op. cit.

54) M. Mesarovic and Y. Takahara: Foundations for the Mathematical Theory of General Systems; New York: Academic Press 1974; M. Mesarovic, D. Macko, Y. Takahara: Theory of Hierarchical, Multilevel Systems. New York: Academic Press 1970. Also: J. Takahara: Coordination Principles for System Interactions; in IIASA SP-74-6, op. cit., pp. D 1 - D 19.

56) R. Pestel: Eine neue, umfassende Methodologie für die technologische
Folgenabschätzung aufgrund der Theorie der hierarchischen Mehrebenen-
systeme. Dissertation TU Hannover 1973. Also: M. Gottwald, R. Pestel:
Environmental Impact Assessment; in IIASA SP-74-5, op. cit.
57) M. Gottwald: Ebenen-Dekomposition hierarchischer Systeme. Dissertation, TU Hannover 1975.

A MODELLING FRAMEWORK FOR SOCIETAL SYSTEMS

Hartmut Bossel

1.   INTRODUCTION: INTERACTION, ORIENTATION, DISSONANCE

The present chapter presents a coherent theoretical framework for modelling individual **and** collective behavior based on the four fundamental hypotheses that

- the composite behavior of societal systems can be properly approximated by the interaction of a few dominant, often abstract, "actor" systems;
- the behavior of an actor system is the result of a complex information processing sequence whose basic structure is identical across actor systems;
- behavior of actor systems is governed by reference to a set of basic orienting dimensions "orientors", whose dimensions are identical across actor systems;
- the processes determining behavior of actor systems are driven mainly by a (generalized) mechanism of dissonance removal.

This conceptual approach forms the backbone of most of the work reported in this book. The approach rests heavily on the ideas of Simon (1957), Festinger (1957), Maslow (1954) and others, much of it presented coherently by Kirsch (1970, 1971a, 1971b). (See also the survey article by Bossel and Gruber in this volume.) More details of the approach are given in Bossel (1975a, b, 1976a). A similar point of view is taken by Kmieciak (1974, 1976), who provides a much fuller discussion of some aspects, such as those of cognitive dissonance and value orientation.

In this contribution, the essential elements of the approach will be summarized in the form of hypotheses, each of which will be exemplified by an "application". The system of interconnected hypotheses is then the basis for the construction of the modelling framework summarized in the form of a systems diagram. For illustrative purposes, the "applications" are mostly taken from the behavior of national actors following the 1973 oil embargo and price increase.

2.   THE ACTOR AS INFORMATION-PROCESSING SYSTEM

Hypotheses concerning actor and interaction

Hypothesis 1: For a given issue, the composite behavior of societal systems can be properly approximated by the interaction of a few dominant a c t o r s y s t e m s. These actors may or may not represent actual individuals, collectivities, organizations, or other entities. Often, an actor will be merely a convenient abstraction.

Application: In 1973, the Organization of Petroleum Exporting Countries (OPEC), whose members supply most of the crude oil used in the industrial nations of the West, roughly tripled the price of their product, thus significantly affecting the economies of their customers. The economic adjustments taking place following the oil price raise represent an issue for analysis. In order to study properly its essential aspects, at least two actors systems must be included in the analysis: (1) the OPEC producer countries, and (2) the consumer countries affected.

Hypothesis 2: The actor system consists of a c a u s a l s y s t e m, including the material system and the perceptors and effectors under the control of the actor, a r e s p o n s e s y s t e m, and a n o r m a t i v e s y s t e m. The actor behaves in an e n v i r o n m e n t on which he depends for support, from which he receives information inputs, and which he can to some extent manipulate directly or indirectly by application of his effectors. The environment may or may not contain other actor systems whose behavior the actor may have to consider in his decisions (Fig. 1).

Application: Consider the industrialized oil consumer countries of the West and the OPEC oil producer countries as two actors as far as a first approximation of the interaction between the two groups of countries is concerned. The consumer country system consists in particular of their aggregated demographic, physical, technological, economic, and ecological systems. Perceptors are the different individuals and organizations in government, industry, and the media, who receive information concerning the state of the material system, and of the relevant environment (here in particular OPEC and other groupings in the world system) as well as other information bearing on the issue. Effectors are those control instruments under the control of the actors: tax measures, sanctions, subsidies, price and wage freezes, research and technology policy, and the like. The response system consists of the (aggregated) apparatus of government, industry, and citizenry which receives information through its perceptors, processes it in order to arrive at a control policy, and refers it for implementation to its effectors. The normative system is the system of norms, standards, laws, conventions, values etc. guiding the synthesis of reponse policy. In addition to the OPEC actor, the actor system "consumer countries" has to consider in its deliberations other actor systems sharing the same environment, such as the group of COMECON countries, and the Third World.

Hypothesis 3: The r e s p o n s e s y s t e m provides behavioral instructions for the effector system under its control on the basis of information received from the environment through its perceptors, from the memories of the processing system, and from the normative system. The basic information-processing components of the response system and their structural interconnection are more or less identical across actor systems and

ACTOR SYSTEM I   ACTOR SYSTEM II

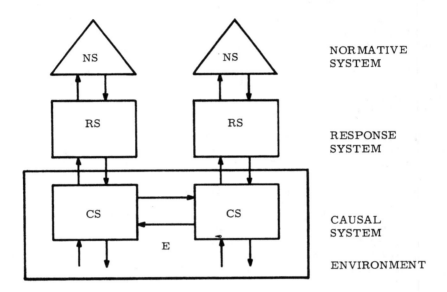

Fig. 1 - Interaction of Two Actor Systems

are determined by the requirements of state analysis and policy synthesis; howeve r, they differ greatly in their actual appearance and in their memory and normative system content. Similarly, the causal systems, effectors, and environmental access of different actor systems may be quite different. As a result, the behavior of actors will generally be quite different.

Application: The policies of control of oil consumption (e. g. restrictions of Sunday driving in many countries) instituted as a first reaction to the oil embargo were arrived at in a process of analysis of the perceived environmental state (price increase and embargo), assessment of possible consequences (especially for economic development), consultation of applicable normative statements (laws, social expectations), search for, and consideration of alternatives in a process of policy synthesis. This information processing sequence had to be followed in all the countries affected; obviously the actual bodies performing these deliberations (parliaments, interest groups, executive officials of the various governments) were just as diverse and different as the causal systems of the nations for whom the policies were developed, and the past experience and normative inputs which had to be considered in the development of policy.

Hypothesis 4: A c t o r s may be a g g r e g a t e d or disaggregated depending on the similarity or dissimilarity (concerning a given issue) of their memory content, their normative system, causal systems, effectors, and environmental access.

Application: In a first approximation to the oil price issue, one must obviously distinguish between countries producing oil and selling it abroad, and countries depending on this oil to maintain their economic system. This distinction requires the disaggregation of the issue system into at least two separate actors, and allows at the same time the aggregation of producer countries and consumer countries into a producer system and a consumer system: the similarities within nations of each of these two systems are much more pronounced than those among nations belonging to the two different actor systems. Obviously, a refined analysis would again have to distinguish among several actors in each of the two systems, e. g. the Arab and non-Arab producers, the United States, Western Europe, and Japan, etc.

Hypothesis 5: The operation of actors having human components is often strongly modified by individual a f f e c t s a n d e m o t i o n s, or their social counterparts. The choice of behavioral modes is a function of the emotional state and affect.

Application: Typical examples are the effects of racial, ethnic, religious, or cultural differences: Northern Ireland, the Lebanese civil war, or the schoolbusing controversies in U. S. cities are examples. The modes of interaction between two ethnic actors given a certain identical situation may range from friendly mutual assistance to violent conflict, depending on the affective feelings one group holds for the other.

Hypothesis 6: The present description of the behavioral response process
applies to all decision-making and behavior and includes the completely
r a t i o n a l   a c t o r   as well as the unsystematic, incoherent, and
i n c o n s i s t e n t   a c t o r. The difference is in the quality of decision
premises and procedures, not in the structure of the response process.

Application: The erratic decisions of some leaders representing national
actors are arrived at after processes of state analysis and policy synthesis, into which "faulty" perceptions and interpretations, together with
"distorted" normative components have entered as input, perhaps with
stochastically changing weights resulting e.g. from abrupt changes of the
environmental state.

Hypotheses concerning the response system
(Note: the term "response" here refers to behavior produced on the basis of
an external or internal stimulus)

Hypothesis 7: The major   c o m p o n e n t s   o f   t h e   r e s p o n s e
s y s t e m   are a supervisor program, different memories, a perception
subsystem, a state analysis subsystem, and a policy synthesis subsystem.
The response system receives information input from the environment and
the normative system: its output controls the effectors of the actor system
to which it belongs.

Application: An active national actor follows more or less formalized
routines of processes of state analysis ("State of the Union" address,
hearings, reports) and policy synthesis (government and parliamentary
deliberations, planning) according to what may abstractly be considered
a supervisor program demanding that certain procedural steps be taken
under given circumstances. The memories of a national actor consist of
the individual memories of individuals contributing to the response process, of files, records, libraries, and statistics. The perception subsystem is mainly composed of individuals (diplomats, journalists, statisticians, scientists, public opinion pollsters) obtaining information concerning the system and environmental state and passing it on (usually in
a filtered and distorted form) to the response subsystems (government,
interest groups, citizens) performing the state analysis and policy synthesis. Other important information input into perception, state analysis,
and policy synthesis consists of normative guidelines and constraints,
such as: desire to avoid military conflict, desire to assure economic
growth, valuation of the own system compared to others, valuation of the
near future over the far future, etc. Once an applicable policy has been
determined, the effectors of the system (law enforcement, revenue service, social security office, etc.) are directed to implement the decision.

Hypothesis 8: The s u p e r v i s o r p r o g r a m controls the sequencing of subprograms and the updating of memory content.

Application: Established bureaucratic procedures and the constitutions of national actors are examples of supervisor programs specifying the execution of certain subprograms (policy reviews, planning and budgeting, research programs, elections = updating of normative content, etc.) at certain times or under certain conditions.

Hypothesis 9: The motivation for the removal of (a generalized) c o g n i t i v e d i s s o n a n c e is assumed to be the driving force in all information processing concerning behavior: in the state analysis (e. g. priority assessment), in policy synthesis (e. g. attainability assessment and preference ranking), and in the generation and adjustment of normative statements.

Application: The oil price increase initially resulted in a very strong cognitive dissonance between the new price level and the old level, giving rise to strong pressure to remove the dissonanc e by returning to the old level. After it became clear that there was no way of returning to the old level other than risking the grave consequences of military intervention, the price aspiration level was adjusted to the vicinity of the new level, thus reducing the cognitive dissonance. At the same time however, the economic effects partly resulting from the price increase became clearer: trade deficits, higher prices for energy, industrial products and materials, unemployment. The cognitive dissonance vector resulting from the differences in the perceptions about the actual, resp. projected state of the actor system "consumer countries" and the desired state (state analysis) - clearly evident in a very large number of official and unofficial statements, analyses, reports, publications - then began to set into motion the process of searching for and developing new policies (new sources of energy, energy conservation, new trade agreements, stimulation of export, etc.) (policy synthesis). At the same time, cognitive dissonance between now obsolete normative standards (from building codes to consumer behavior) and not yet established better-adapted norms caused a slow revision of that part of the normative system of the actor bearing on energy issues.

Hypothesis 10: The processing tasks of the response system require s h o r t-t e r m m e m o r i e s for the storage of current information and intermediate processing results, specialized l o n g-t e r m m e m o r i e s for the storage of information, processing routines, and response programs, and proper recall and storage subroutines (including forgetting, updating, learning, etc.).

Application: The memory system of a national actor consists of the memories of those individuals participating in some direct or indirect way in the response process leading to behavior on the level of the actor (i. e. persons in the executive and administrative branches of government, pressure groups, etc.) and of the information recorded in notes, records, files, publications, electronic and other storage devices. All participating natural and artificial memories are subject to information loss ("forgetting") by various processes. Updating and learning are partly informal, partly formal (national statistics, education and re-education).

Hypothesis 11: N o r m a t i v e   i n p u t s from the normative system control the supervisor program, memory handling, perception, state analysis, policy synthesis, and normative change processes proper.

Application: The constitutions of state actors are part of their supervisor program. They require periodic normative adjustment (elections) and state analyses (hearings, parliamentary debates, "state of the union" messages). In most industrial countries, the norm of the "here and now" controls the perception process in a way which keeps out of the attention field most of the problems of Third World countries or of future development, for example.

Hypothesis 12: P e r c e p t i o n is a complex process of decoding, filtering, suppression, bias, and distortion of available environmental and systems information by subprograms of the response system. It is determined by the currently open channels, by codes, classifiers, attitudes, and normative statements in the different memories, and by pattern recognition abilities.

Application: The perception of racial unrest in South Africa by other nation actors, for example, depends not merely on the bias of reporting journalists, but also on censorship or selective reporting, on racial position, on attitudes toward segregation, on political preferences, and on pattern classifiers ("communist infiltration" vs. "struggle for equality" vs. "War of liberation") applied to the situation.

Hypothesis 13: In an on-going process of s t a t e   a n a l y s i s , the perceived system state is constantly or periodically being compared to the (changing) normative reference state. The state analysis generates a cognitive dissonance vector with respect to those system needs and environmental and system state variables which currently lead to system dissatisfaction, and may thus indicate a need for decision and action.

Application: Economic growth, low unemployment, low inflation, are some of the normative reference conditions of industrial countries. The economic recession of 1974/75 caused considerable departure from the reference state, monitored by government agencies, interest groups and citizens. The cognitive dissonance resulting in particular with respect to unemployment and inflation indicated a strong need for action with respect to these state variables.

Hypothesis 14: In the state analysis, the perceived system state is mapped onto the multidimensional orientor space of the system to determine the current and future o r i e n t o r s a t i s f a c t i o n s t a t e. Comparison of the orientor satisfaction state with the current and future orientor satisfaction reference state yields the current dissonance vector containing information on the kind and severity of orientor violations, and, if they can be identified, on the state of the variables causing the violations.

Application: Concerning the oil price raise the relevant set of state variables ("indicators") included energy price and availability, import and export rates and resulting trade deficit, inflation, economic growth, unemployment, change in real per capita income, etc. The system state perceived through these indicators presented an abstraction of a system state which in reality consists of a practically infinite number of state variables. The many indicators characterizing the system state are meaningful to the national actor only if they can be mapped on the space of basic orienting dimensions ("orientors") which guide the response process. In the example the mapping included considerations of the average standard of living, of a measure of national independence and self-determination, of future viability of the actor system, etc. From this mapping - evolving from the interacting cognitive communicative processes (government studies, analyses by individuals, spreading of the results by the media) - an identification of problem areas and of problem variables (price increases, dependence on foreign energy sources, identification of energy waste) ensued and gave rise to a corresponding cognitive dissonance vector.

Hypothesis 15: The perceived state vector and the dissonance vector guide the p o l i c y s y n t h e s i s p r o c e s s. An attempt at classification of state and dissonance patterns is made first: if applicable response programs are available, these are applied. If not, then the search for an applicable policy is initiated.

Application: The perceived state vector embodies the image of a given situation (i. e. oil embargo); the dissonance vector measures the perceived seriousness of the situation for the overall functioning of the system. Depending on the content and adaptivity of the normative system an oil embargo may be classified as anything from an act of war, to a serious economic threat, to a mild annoyance resulting in temporary inconvenience. Corresponding response programs may or may not be available and found applicable, from landing the marines, to diplomatic notes, to counter-embargos. In the oil price controversy applicable standard response programs were not availabe, and the search of applicable alternative policies began and is still continuing in the consumer nations.

Hypothesis 16: Due to the natural limitations of the processing system, the policy synthesis process must be guided by h e u r i s t i c p r i n c i p l e s and programs (incrementalism, satisficing, mixed-scanning, etc.). Only rarely can the process be of an optimizing nature.

Application: The policy synthesis processes connected with real issues like the oil price issue usually involve so many variables, and diverse interests, most of them in very fuzzy and unquantifiable way, that optimization or any other systematic analysis is out of the question, and heuristic principles must be used to handle the task. Some of the heuristic strategies applied in the oil price issue were: temporary reduction of unnecessary consumption (Sunday driving), until effects of the embargo became clearer (cautious retrenchment), wait-and-see until the new price level became more definite, satisficing by settling on energy policies which were satisfactory (but not optimal under the given conditions), mixed-scanning: the search for possible alternatives and a focussing on the more promising ones (energy conservation, nuclear and solar energy).

Hypothesis 17: Trial policies are evaluated for their likely present and future impact by applying them to an i n t e r n a l   m o d e l of the environment (including other actors) and of the actor system itself. The model is normally relatively crude and incomplete and requires constant readjustment through learning.

Application: The internal model of the consumer nation actor system contains concepts concerning the functioning of its economic system, its dependence on oil as a source of energy and raw materials, the socio-economic system of OPEC nations, the interests and influence of the Soviet Union, etc. The internal model which had developed in the days before the oil embargo was often applied unchanged for months, even years after October 1973 (cf. the columns of Milton Friedman in "Newsweek" claiming that "proven" free market principles would soon drive the price of oil back to pre-embargo levels). Trial policies which were evaluated by the internal model - and rejected for their possible consequences - included such proposals as military intervention and occupation of the oil-fields. Only gradually was the internal model of the consumer nations changed to accomodate e. g. the new role and power of the oil producing nations.

Hypothesis 18: The projective p o l i c y   e v a l u a t i o n incorporates subjective risk and probability estimates, projected orientor satisfaction states, future weight (time horizon) functions, and attainability estimates.

Application: The proposals for military intervention following the oil embargo were rejected because the risk of confrontation with the Soviet Union was considered too high, not to speak of the likely reaction of world opinion. The negative results of attainability estimates of large scale liquid fuel production from oil shale, tar sands, and coal eliminated these options from the set of short term solutions. Relatively short term time horizon functions led to an increased reliance on nuclear power, where long term time horizons would obviously favor the development of renewable options (e. g. solar energy). At the same time, rigorous energy conservation was seen as so detrimental to the (current) orientor satisfaction state that it was not seriously considered.

Hypothesis 19: L e a r n i n g of codes, classifiers, norms derivation and adjustment, policy search heuristics, response programs, internal model components, etc. can be both external (perceived reality) or internal (internal model). The required classification and pattern recognition capabilities are gradually built up from a minimal basic set.

Application: In the oil price situation, much of the learning resulted from adaptation to developments in the real system which the original internal model had not correctly predicted. Such external learning tends to be costly, in particular where large national actor systems are involved. Had there been a valid and credible internal model (e. g. a good, and generally accepted computer model), costly external learning could have been avoided by developing applicable response policies through simulation. The classification and pattern recognition capabilities required for the response process concerning the oil trade system (e. g. general knowledge about interaction between the two systems) have been built up over the years since oil first appeared as a factor of industrial development, and they are constantly being revised and expanded, as the situation changes.

Hypotheses concerning the normative system and normative change processes

Hypothesis 20: N o r m a t i v e   s t a t e m e n t s concerning observation and perception, state analysis, policy synthesis, needs satisfaction states, etc. are determined by direct or indirect reference to a set of basic orienting dimensions (basic orientors) reflecting fundamental operational requirements of the causal system and of the response system (i. e. of information processing). Only the causal system needs are system-specific.

Application: One of the basic orienting dimensions of the consumer nation actor system is the need for securing systems viability for at least the immediate future. After the oil embargo of October 1973, this orientor appeared to be threatened, and a whole set of new or revised normative statements was developed in the period following the event: prohibition of Sunday driving, mandatory conservation measures, research on alternative energy sources, change of building codes. Examples of system-specific normative responses are: loans for fertilizer import in some Third World countries, house insulation in Sweden, legislation to increase gas mileage of cars in the United States. On the other hand, the normative adjustments concerning the response systems of the different national actors were not system-specific: All recognized the need for more and better information, and the development of new and adaptive policies, in order to maintain in particular their adaptivity, in order to respond adequately to the new challenges.

Hypothesis 21: The b a s i c   o r i e n t i n g   d i m e n s i o n s of individual or collective autonomous systems are: physiological/physical support needs, psychological needs (where applicable), security, freedom of action,

172

adaptivity, efficiency of control (or their equivalents). Proper attention to all of these dimensions is required for the proper functioning of the system (see Ch. 6).

Application: On the level of the national actor, typical psychological needs such as the need for love and affection play a minor role in rational decisions. Note that in our approach other needs, often considered as psychological, such as that for self-actualization, are recognized as representing functional orienting dimensions of a viable information-processing system (in this case mainly the adaptivity dimension; Bossel 1975b). The response of the consumer nations following oil embargo and oil price increase demonstrate explicit attention to all of the remaining orientors: less important private consumption of energy (Sunday driving) was curtailed in order to satisfy the physical requirements of the economic system considered to be more important, larger stocks of oil were laid in, and the research for alternative sources of energy was intensified in order to better satisfy the security orientor; the freedom-of-action orientor gave rise to "Project Independence", and to accelerated development of Alaskan and North Sea oil resources; the research and development concerning energy conservation and alternative sources of energy was intensified in accord with the requirements of the adaptivity orientor; consideration of the efficiency-of-control orientor led to suggestions of military intervention and to the implementation of bilateral trade agreements between producer nations and various industrial countries.

Hypothesis 22: The normative system of a given actor can be viewed as a h i e r a r c h y   o f   o r i e n t o r s derived from the basic orientors by applying them to increasingly specific contexts. The hierarchy is appended and updated as required (e. g. by processes of ded ction).

Application: The basic orientor "security" together with the concrete situation of the nonavailability of a sufficient oil supply and the observations that (a) driving consumes fuels; (b) hardly anybody works on Sundays; and that therefore (c) Sunday driving does not substantially contribute to essential economic functions, led to the prohibition of Sunday driving in some countries. For a while at least, a new normative statement "Driving on Sundays is not permitted" was introduced into the normative system. Note that once this derivation had been made and as long as conditions remained the same, there was no further need to continuously refer back to the basic orientor "security".

Hypothesis 23: The   b a s i c   b e h a v i o r a l   i n s t r u c t i o n s   are to (1) satisfy first all needs with respect to current system viability (physical/ physiological and psychological needs), and only then to (2) maximize overall needs satisfaction with respect to future viability, i. e. the security, freedom-of-action, adaptivity, and efficiency-of-control orientors. Corresponding to the current orientor satisfaction state, orientor categories and state variables are assigned alarm ("red"), alert ("yellow"), or satisfactory ("green") status.

Application: The curtailment of unnecessary energy consumption immediately following the embargo was a response to assure the continuing
operation of the system on the physical level. At that time, the policy-
making bodies of the consumer countries were fully occupied with their
attention to the immediate physical needs of their respective causal systems. Attention to the future viability concerns was given only after the
immediate crises had subsided. At that time, the consideration of long-
range options and alternatives, of research and development policy and
of readjustment of relationships between consumer and producer nations
could enter the focus of attention.

Hypothesis 24: The results of perception, state analysis, and policy synthesis are determined to a major degree by the t e m p o r a l   a n d   s p a-
t i a l   h o r i z o n of the actor system, i. e. the time horizon as expressed
in (usually fuzzy) future weight functions, and the spatial horizon including
other actor systems ("participating systems") and the domain of the environment whose concerns enter the information processes of the response system.

Application: The time horizon of the consumer nations concerning their
crude oil supplies before the oil boykott was at best of the order of a few
months to a year. As the realization of limited oil supplies and of the
vulnerability of access to them became increasingly recognized, the time
horizon of the consumer nations concerning this policy aspect increased
to something like a few years. Obviously, quite different policies would
result if the horizon were expanded to a few decades hence, when oil resources will be quite scarce, and when therefore the physical base of the
actor systems will have to be based on different sources of energy and
hydrocarbons. The realization that these conversion processes take considerable time would focus attention today on the necessary actions. A
similar effect is present with respect to the spatial horizon: Before the
oil boykott, oil shipments seemed to be assured, their origin was of no
concern, there was no need to look beyond the boundaries of the actor
system as far as the oil supplies were concerned. The oil price raise
forced attention on the specific concerns of the supplier nations, including the consideration of their orientor satisfaction space in the policy
deliberations of the consumer nations. As a result, the post-embargo
policies of the consumer nations with regard to the producer nations are
today radically different from the pre-embargo policies.

Hypothesis 25: Quantitative   m e a s u r e s   o f   o r i e n t o r   s a t i s-
f a c t i o n (indexes of global system performance; orientor measures) can
be established from physiological/physical and psychological requirements,
thresholds and constraints, and from system performance measures using
perturbation analysis of the system (e. g. from error rates, response time,
adaptation lag, overshoot, distances from unacceptable thresholds and constraints, effects of disturbances, cost-effectiveness of control, damping,
stability, redundancy, ets.). (The approach is related to the determination
of indexes of stability and of resilience, see Grümm 1976). This means that
the mapping of the system and environmental state on the orientor satisfac-

tion state can be made without resource to further subjective assessments, once global indexes have been defined and chosen on the basis of subjective assessment.

Application: This approach is important for systematic global assessment of system performance, especially that resulting from application of alternative policies. At present it is usually practiced in an intuitive and fuzzy manner. Some such aggregation takes place in all human non-routine decision-making, as the information content of a large number of state variables (indicators) has to be reduced to meaningful information concerning the system performance. In the oil embargo situation, for example, information concerning the oil cargo of tankers heading for consumer nation ports, the content of storage facilities, daily consumption and the expected length of the embargo were integrated and aggregated to produce an intuitive measure of threat to the security of the system. All policies considered were tested for their effect on improving the security measure (while not adversely and intolerably affecting the other orientor measures).

Hypothesis 26: The processes of derivation (from superior orientors, see Ch. 6) and a d j u s t m e n t   o f   n o r m a t i v e   s t a t e m e n t s can be considered a special case of policy synthesis; they are also driven by mechanisms of cognitive dissonance reduction (see Hypothesis 9).

Application: Once it became obvious to the consumer nations that the available set of normative statements concerning the interaction with the producer countries was no longer applicable, resp. that application of the current normative system would only work to the detriment of the consumer countries (e. g. refusal to pay the higher price demanded), the only way left open for the reduction of the cognitive dissonance between the "Is" and the "Ought" was to change the components of the normative system: adjustment of the aspiration level to the vicinity of the new price level, reduction of excessive consumption expectations, introduction of new policy guidelines for taxation, subsidies, research and development, etc.

Hypothesis 27: The   c o g n i t i v e   p r o c e s s e s   in normative adjustment and change processes represent mostly nonquantitative concept manipulations and require description in linguistic terms and/or the concepts of fuzzy set theory.

Application: Seemingly representing an assemblage of "hard" economic facts, production and consumption figures, tanker tonnage, well capacity and other technical detail, as well as cost figures, the oil issue nevertheless can only incompletely be described by turning entirely to hard facts and figures. Much more influential, especially in the normative context, are unquantifiable concepts such as: quality of life, functioning of the economy, national security and self-determination, historical and cultural traits, etc. In arriving at new or revised normative statements, the non-numerical manipulation and concatenation of concepts in deductive and inductive chains plays an important role (see Ch. 13, 14).

Hypothesis 28: The major p r o c e s s e s o f n o r m a t i v e a d j u s t-m e n t are (1) adjustment of aspiration levels and standards by mechanisms of cognitive dissonance reduction; (2) shifting of preferences and priorities as the result of changes in the system state, and of resulting changes in the orientor satisfaction state which require attention; and (3) mutual modification of system structure and normative structure by adaptive evolution or innovative and purposeful self-modification.

Application: An example for the first process has already been mentioned: the adjustment of the price level aspiration to the vicinity of the new oil price, as well as the temporary adjustment of consumption aspirations. The second process is exemplified by the quick replacement of the environmental concerns of 1973 by concerns about energy policy and economic developments, which thereafter dominated political decision-making. An instance of the third process is an increasing realization - perhaps - of the finiteness of resources, and the gradual adaptation of existing energy systems to renewable energy sources, or even the purposeful and controlled introduction of new systems to cope with the challenge (e. g. solar heating and conservation measures).

Hypothesis 29: A m a j o r a d j u s t m e n t o f t h e n o r m a t i v e s y s t e m will only take place if a failure of adaptation would seriously affect the actor's orientor satisfaction.

Application: Mere exhortation will not impel consumers to conserve energy, as long as energy is still plentiful and cheap and sanctions or incentives for energy waste, resp. conservation are weak or nonexistent. However, it does not follow from this that only threats to current viability will cause changes in the normative system. Believable threats to future viability can be just as effective, provided the actor system routinely considers a longer time horizon in its assessments. I.e. if the concerns of the next generation were to play a major role in the plans and actions of today's generation, then normative changes concerning oil conservation measures would have a stronger backing than they do today.

Hypothesis 30: With increasing security of current viability needs, and increasing satisfaction of future viability orientors, the latitude of possible system responses increases, since the system function now becomes more and more unaffected by competing behavioral policies concerning functional requirements. Unless artificially constrained (with the corresponding build-up of dissonance potential and intra-actor conflict potential) the system will tend towards d i v e r s i t y and pluralism.

Application: To the family assured of sufficient heating energy, it makes little difference whether it comes in the form of oil, gas, or electricity,

as long as costs and convenience are comparable. The investment decision may now be dominated not so much by rational argument, as by whims
of personal taste, mood and affect, or perhaps even chance, and by the
subconscious manipulation of advertisements and fashion appealing to normative components more or less irrelevant to viability. It may also be
that in such decision situations, significant differences in long-term orientor
satisfaction (i. e. use of renewable vs. non-renewable energy sources),
or in the orientor satisfaction of other actors (i. e. purchase of Third
World products) may become decisive, even though the choice would only
benefit future generations, or distant actors.

3. PROCESSING SEQUENCE AND COMPONENT PROGRAMS

Fig. 2 is a coherent summary of the hypotheses; it shows the relationships
between the environment and the different system components
- causal system, including perceptors and effectors;
- response system, including perception, state analysis, policy synthesis,
  normative change, and memories;
- normative system.

The response system processing sequence will now be briefly recapitulated.
The cycle begins at $t = t_o$ with a given memory content.

(1) Current sensor states and filter settings restrict and distort the inform-
    ation input to the system from its environment and causal system. These
    sensor and filter conditions are a function of the system state and of the
    information being received.

(2) The perceived information is classified with respect to its potential
    importance to the system, and a filter adjustment may take place. The
    classification requires either pattern recognition, or projective use of
    the internal model.

(3) The perceived information is used to update the current image of system
    and environmental state, and to add other relevant information to the
    long-term memory ("learning").

(4) The current state is compared to the current reference state standards.
    No action is required if the resulting dissonances are small (go to 9).
    If they are not, the dissonance vector is used as a basis for the policy
    synthesis (go to 6) unless an acquired response is available for the per-
    ceived state and dissonance pattern (go to 5).

(5) The available response is employed (go to 8).

(6) Using the current policy norms, the dissonance vector and heuristics
    as guiding inputs, trial policies are formulated and tried out on the inter-
    nal model of the system and its environment.

177

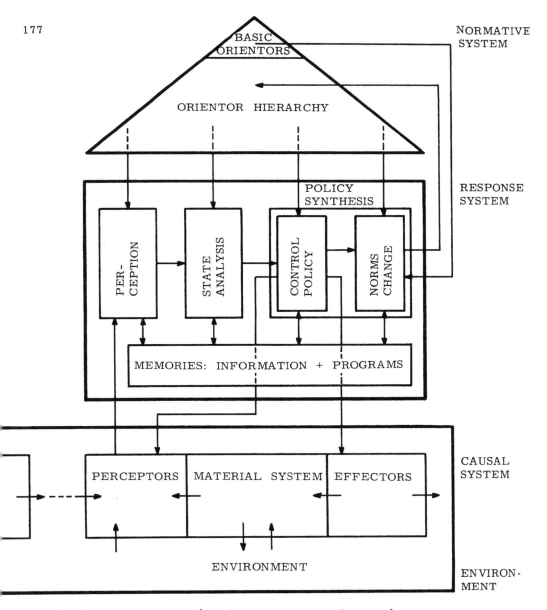

Fig. 2 - Environment, causal system, response system, and
normative system, and their components
and interrelations.

(7) If a successful policy is found in a limited number of trials it is applied via the action subsystem of the causal system (go to 9).

(8) If a successful policy cannot be determined under the given normative conditions, a norms change policy is developed, tested (using the internal model), and implemented (go to 4).

(9) Filter settin gs, reference state standards, policy norms, and emotional state are updated by reference to current conditions and system objectives as derived from the orientor hierarchy.

(10) Successful responses, new pattern classifiers, and relevant information obtained during the cycle are stored.

(11) The process recycles.

Below a comprehensive list of system elements identified previously is presented. A functional distinction is made between memories (short-term, long-term), and programs. In addition to essential elements of any response system (marked by a plus sign +), the list contains optional elements which significantly increase the performance of the advanced systems under consideration in this study.

SYSTEM MEMORIES AND PROGRAMS
(+ = essential components and programs)

Long-term memory components	Short-term memory components
general encyclopaedic information	+ current observations
+ codes and classifiers	observation norms
experience	filter settings and affect
external constraints	
+ normative constraints; orientor hierarchy	
reference state	
orientation	

Programs

+ supervisor program	+ response programs
long-term memory updating and forgetting	learning of response programs
	internal model
+ short-term memory updating	projection
program memory updating and forgetting	norms derivation and adjustment
filter setting, distortion	+ state evaluation
pattern recognition	policy search and modification
pattern learning; classifier buildup	emotional state
	analog/conceptual conversion

While the contributions in this volume adhere to this general framework, they do not cover all aspects of it. The following list gives a survey of how different chapters of this book relate to some of the concepts of the framework:

- Representatioı. of causal system and environment (i. e. of material systems): Ch. 2, 3, 5, 7, 10, 12
- Indicators (of system state): Ch. 2, 5.
- Orientors and normative system: Ch. 2, 6, 15, 16, 17
- Representation of cognitive processes, including normative adjustment: Ch. 6, 13, 14, 16, 17
- State analysis: Ch. 2, 5, 15, 16, 17
- Policy synthesis: Ch. 2, 8, 9, 10, 11, 12, 15, 16, 17
- Internal model: Ch. 13, 14, 16, 17

REFERENCES

BOSSEL, H. 1975a: Framework for the Modelling of Behavioi. Institut für Systemtechnik und Innovationsforschurg (ISI), Karlsruhe.

BOSSEL, H. 1975b: Notes on Basic Needs, Priorities, and Normative Change. ISI, Karlsruhe.

BOSSEL, H. 1976a: Information Processing, Cognitive Dissonance, and Basic Needs: The Modelling of Behavior. In: H. Bossel, S. Klaczko, N. Müller (eds.), Systems Theory in the Social Sciences, Birkhäuser, Basel.

FESTINGER, L. 1957: A Theory of Cognitive Dissonance. Evanston, Ill.

GRÜMM, H. R. 1976: Cefinitions of Resilience. IIASA RR-76-5, Laxenbvrg, Austria.

KIRSCH, W. 1970/1971/1971: Entscheidungsprozesse, Vols. I, II, III. Gabler, Wiesbaden.

KMIECIAK, P. 1974: Auf dem Wege zu einer generellen Theorie sozialen Verhaltens. Hain, Meisenheim am Glan.

KMIECIAK, P. 1976: Wertstrukturen und Wertwrndel in der Bundesrepublik Deutschland. Schwartz, Cöttingen.

MASLOW, A. H. 1954/1970: Motivation and Personality. Harper and Row, New York.

SIMON, Iı. A. 1957: Models of Man. Wiley, New York.

5

SOCIAL INDICATORS AND QUALITY OF LIFE MEASURES

Patrick Bond

I.   INTRODUCTION: THE SOCIAL INDICATORS MOVEMENT

A.   A Brief History of the Movement

The roots of the social indicator movement can be found in early government reports. The first was initiated by President Hoover in 1929. The committee was commissioned to investigate changing social values and interests. Among the many such values they investigated were: farm life, leisure time, criminal justice, health care and government services. As the commission's chairman, Wesley C. Mitchell and the report's director, William Ogburn stated in the preface:

> The primary value of this report is to be found in the
> effort to interrelate the disjointed factors and elements
> in the social life of America, in the attempt to view the
> situation as a whole rather than a cluster of parts[1].

This document was remarkably ahead of its time. Many of the concerns expressed in the volume were those still echoed today in the social indicators literature. Above all, it expressed clearly the interest which government planners had in social welfare and its measurement. It also expressed the interest in the documentation of social trends.

Indeed, the Recent Social Trend volume was so far ahead of its time, that a comparable volume did not follow until thirty years later. This report was commissioned by President Eisenhower. Its focus was slightly different from the one adopted in Recent Social Trends. Rather than attempting to document social trends, it sought to describe the nation's goals (national interest). The commission's major publication Goals for Americans divided national goals in domestic and foreign issues. Within the 'goals at home' category eleven issues were discussed: the individual, equality, the democratic process, the arts and sciences, a democratic economy, economic growth, technological change, agriculture, living conditions, and health and welfare. Under the category 'goals abroad' the commission included four issues: The establishment of a democratic and peaceful world, the defense of the free world, weapons disarmament, and the further development of the United Nations.

The goals, while always in very vague and ambiguous terms, were apparently considered specific enough to warrant several follow-up studies on the feasibility of the efforts then under way to meet them. In fact, the Goals for Americans volume in whole serves as an attempt to justify the then existing public service programs and examine the need for possible further programs.

This in turn was used as a rallying cry for a sizable tax reform. As the commission report states: "If these reforms are made and the minimum growth rate we postulate is achieved, it is the Commission's conclusion that the level of public spending we would need to realize the recommendations of this report are possible".

The Eisenhower Commission report's status as the last official publication on the 'state of the nation' was not nearly as long lived as the Hoover's Commission's. Only five years later in the latter part of 1965 and early 1966 there was a flurry of activity, both governmental and non-governmental, in the area of social indicators.

On the governmental side President Johnson directed the Department of Health, Education, and Welfare to conduct a massive effort to develop a set of social indicators. On the non-governmental side, Wilbert Moore and Eleanor Sheldon published "Monitoring Social Change - A Conceptual and Programmatic Statement[2]." Also at that time, Raymond Bauer published what has turned out to be the seminal work of the movement, <u>Social Indicators</u>. A collection of articles, it contains some of the most cited pieces on the subject. Among the list of contributors were Betram Gross and Albert Biderman.

In the wake of the introduction of large scaled Planned Program Budgeting Systems into the federal bureaucracy, the social indicator proponents disclaimed the 'new philistinism' that characterized PPBS and other forms of economic evaluations technique. The overwhelming message was that economic measures alone could not measure the success of social programs. What was necessary was the development of a comprehensive set of social indicators and the incorporation of such a set of indicators into a rational social systems accounting system. This system, like the economic counterparts of PPBS, would be used to evaluate the wisdom of social programs and social funding.

It has been nearly a decade since the publication of the Bauer reader. In this decade, the literature connected to the social indicators movement has grown tremendously. In 1972 a social indicator study group at Iowa State published an annotated bibliography[3] which contained well over six hundred entries of articles, papers, and books connected with social indicators.

Not only has the relevant literature grown by leaps and bounds, but the level of activity in the movement has raised considerably. In a number of universities, there are projects concerned with social indicators. Indeed the effort expended on social indicators has grown to such an extent that there are major programs concerned only with the coordination of social indicators research. In late 1972 the Social Science Research Council (SSRC) appointed an Advisory and Planning Committee on Social Indicators. This committee is chaired by Otis Dudley Duncan. The committee, in turn, established the Center for Coordination of Research on Social Indicators. Located in Washington, D. C., the center's staff maintains a social indicators library as well as sponsoring symposiums and work shops in the area of social indicators research.

The social indicators movement has grown to such an extent, that just to
document and discuss the present efforts in the field would be a massive effort.
Consequently, such an effort is well beyond the scope and resource of this
work. Rather it will concentrate on providing a general picture of the movement as it stands. Several operational schemes for social indicator systems
will then be discussed.

B.   The Present State of the Movement

As one familiarizes himself with the more recent literature of the social indicators movement, one is impressed with the number of times the same
issues and concerns are repeated, the same problems raised, and the same
obstacles encountered. In general, it seems that there has been a lot of
energy expended and minimal progress made. While this is, at least, partially true, it is certainly not unexpected. Nor, for that matter, is it particularly discouraging. The complexity of the subject matter alone, leads
one to expect a very slow rate of progress in the field. Betram Gross as
early as 1966:

> (In any case) Progress in the collection of social indicators
> will be slow and uneven. It would be utopian to expect that
> any government would set itself to the task of moving from
> economic to social indicators in one comprehensive oper-
> ation. The first social system reports of presidents and
> prime ministers will be fragmentary and exploratory.
>
> Above all, the maturation of social accounting concepts
> will take many decades. Let us remember that it took cen-
> turies for Quesnay's economic tables to mature into national
> income accounting. ... By contrast, the formulation of
> national social accounts is a much more complex under-
> taking. It requires the participation of social scientists
> from many disciplines and the breaking down of many
> language barriers among them. [4]

Probably the most prophetic remark made by Gross is that the progress
will be uneven. This seems to be particularly true. In general the literature
in the social indicators area clusters around two dimensions. On one hand,
there is the level of conceptual issues involved. Discussion at this level tends
to be general and repetitious. On the other hand, there is the operational
level. At this level, the researcher is involved with the actual construction
of a set of indicators, or the use of already existing data to form a set of
indicators. The majority of work on this level has been done in either a
specific geographical area or in regard to the interests of a specific policy
or program. More commonly these are combined, and the indicators focus
on specific interests in a small geographical area. The major problem with
these efforts is twofold. Firstly, the indicators lack any type of comprehen-
siveness, secondly, the criteria which makes the measured phenomena
significant, stem from the goals of the project and not a more general notion
of human welfare.

The current state of the research on social indicators is reflected in the journal Social Indicators Research. A useful brief review of the field has appeared in Science[5].

II. GENERAL CONCEPTUAL ISSUES AND DEBATES

On a conceptual level, schisms within the social indicators movement were present from the beginning. This is most easily seen in the debate which arises over the definition of social indicators. Probably the most cited definition of social indicators is the one which appears in "Toward a Social Report". The definition developed by Mancur Olson and Staff, starts with a somewhat disputed statement. Indicators are defined as 'measures of direct normative interest' which serve as yardsticks to tell us whether things are better or worse off[1]. One need not look far to find an opposing viewpoint. Kenneth Land for example feels that the measures (indicators) themselves can be objective (non-normative).

> (But) we have not imposed any additional structure on our model in the form of normative assumptions about preferred states of social conditions and objective functions to be optimized. For one thing, it should be clear that there is no necessary consensus on preferred social states. For example, some people may prefer a high divorce rate while others prefer a low rate, or some may prefer a high degree of political alienation while others prefer a low degree. Second, for purposes of research and development on social indicators it is not necessary to impose such normative considerations. They add nothing to the scientific development of social indicators and may even be a retarding force.[2]

Land goes on to point out that the policy makers can supply their own normative preferences (value orderings) to the objective measures. The debate over the normative nature of social indicators has produced of itself several articles[3].

Another controversy at the conceptual-definitional level concerns the output issue. To maintain that social indicators must be measures of 'social output' is a distinction[4] which some other writers find overly restrictive. Harland, for example, argues that such a restriction necessarily requires the development of social system models before the development of indicators.[5]

Others object that output measures are often times more difficult to obtain. For example, it is easier to obtain data on the number of doctors per 1000 persons in an area than it is to find data on (or even define a measure of) the quality of health care.

These difficulties are closely related to what seems to be one of the major questions of social indicators research--what criteria can be used to decide which indicators are significant? On this question, social indicator schools are very divided. This division is discussed at length by Otis Dudley Duncan.[6] He identifies the camps as "the theoretical deductive" and the "empirical inductive". Those who fall in the theoretical deductive camp maintain that comprehensive models (theories) of society must precede any serious effort to construct social indicator systems. The argument runs that unless such theories or models exist one does not even know what to look at. Without the basic understanding of the structure of society, it is impossible to construct a state measure.

Such a disagreement has a major effect on the activity of social indicator's scholars. The tasks to which they set themselves are clearly different. Those committed to the deductive school must attempt to develop frameworks from which indicators can be drawn. The effort, as might be expected, focused mainly on the compilation of such a framework. Little time is devoted to the construction of the indicator itself. Such difficulty has led Duncan to observe that in his observation "those who have approached the problem of social reporting with the strongest theoretical presuppositions have possibly made the least impressive contribution, thus far[7]."

The inductive school can concentrate on the development of the statistics themselves, thus providing more effective indicators. The second major advantage available to the inductive proponents is that they can reserve the deductive process and use the highly developed statistics to delineate social models (such an approach is discussed in detail below in Section II;A).

Not surprisingly, these divisions at the conceptual level have produced divergent factions among social indicators researchers. The factions differ not only in approach, but in their major area of activity.

While the divergent factions come out of the conceptual divisions discussed above, the area of activity is as much a characteristic of the faction as the conceptual base itself. Accordingly, I have divided the social indicators movement into two major factions - Social Indicator Modellers and Social Policy Analysts.

A. Social Indicator Modellers

From the preceding discussion one can visualize at least two types of indicators; those suggested by intuition and those suggested by some more explicit model (theory) of society. On another dimension, we can also see two types of indicators; intermediate indicators and output indicators. Land uses a slightly modified view of these dimensions to define three types of indicators.[8]

1) Output descriptive indicators: These are measures of the end pro-

ducts of social processes and are most directly related to the appraisal of social problems and social policy.

2) Other descriptive indicators: These are more general measures of
the social conditions of human existence and the changes taking place
therein.

3) Analytic indicators: These are components of explicit conceptual
models of the social processes which result in the values of output
indicators.

Land then goes on to note that output descriptive indicators and other descriptive indicators have been present in the literature for some time. Analytic indicators are of more recent vintage. Yet, the role which Land attri-
butes to this group of indicators is significant and worth quoting at length.

> Thus, for any particular social condition, social indicators
> are specified when some conception of the relevant social
> process is stated. This criterion is important for at least
> three reasons. First, for a particular social condition, it
> is useful in identifying which output, descriptive, and ana-
> lytic indicators are involved. Second, it allows one to focus
> on the relationship between indicators as these are specified
> in the model. This facilitates a decomposition of changes in
> the output indicators into those changes due to changes in
> other indicators, those due to random disturbances, and
> those due to shifts in the relationships of the output indica-
> tors to other indicators. It may well be the case that changes
> or shifts in such indicator-relationships are as important as
> changes in the output indicators themselves. Moreover,
> since they have been to some extent purged of the purely
> random variation which occurs in direct observations on
> descriptive indicators, these analytic indicators are pos-
> sibly more basic indices of the underlying social condition
> being measured. Third, the position of an indicator within
> a social system model may be of strategic importance in
> determining its construct validity. That is, even though an
> indicator may be defined in the most rational way possible,
> the analyst must still provide evidence that the indicator
> measures what it is intended to measure. One way of making
> such a construct validation of an indicator is to study its
> behavior in relationship to other variables within the context
> of a model. Although such an investigation will in no case
> provide incontrovertible evidence on construct validity, it
> can provide information on how an indicator behaves with
> respect to other indicators.

Land then merges the scheme for categorizing indicators with his perceived
role of analytic indicators to form an overview of the "ideal state of social
indicator research". In this scheme (summarized on Table 1), the usual
distinction is made between those variables which hold endogenous relations

to the model. Within each category of the variables there are two groups of indicators described.

Within the exogenous class there are two types of descriptive indicators: those which are subject to policy manipulation and those which are not.

TABLE 1

Exogenous Variables	Social System Model	Endogenous Variables
	System of relationships connecting all variables and containing analytic indicators	
Policy instrument descriptive indicators $\quad P_1$ P_2 . . . P_i		o_1 o_2 . . . o_m $\quad$ Output or end-product descriptive indicators
		Second order-impact analytic indicators
Nonmanipulable descriptive indicators $\quad d_1$ d_2 . . . d_i		s_1 s_2 . . . s_n $\quad$ Side-effect descriptive indicators

Within the endogenous category there are two types of indicators; those which define social output (in Land's terms; those endogenous variables which define the social condition being measured and are the consequences of the social processes embodied within the model) and those variables which are side effects of the social output.

The model expresses the relationship between the exogenous set and the endogenous set. It contains a third type of indicators, the aforementioned analytic indicators. They are, essentially, the parameters contained in the relational aspects of the model. There is an underlying view in Land's work, that does not emerge clearly. The scheme seems to suggest that a measure of any of the important concepts of society (e. g. a phenomenon which would be included as a variable in a model of the societal system) is necessarily (definitionally) a social indicator. Tautologically, all variation within society would be contained within the category of social indicators. Such a view is open to, at least, two possible difficulties. Firstly, while one might be satisfied that any concept important enough to be included as a variable in a general systems model of society ought properly be classified as a social indicator, such a definition of social indicators is markedly different from that implied by "yardsticks of normative interest". The point is not that the Land definition is desirable or not, rather that such a definition differs sharply from any of the more generally accepted notions of social indicators.

Secondly, there is an implication underlying this scheme that a general model of society is wholly decomposable from its physical environment. Such a notion must either ignore relationships between social and ecosystem variables or expand its view of society to be all inclusive. Yet, if we look on to Land's suggested issue content areas in social indicators, not only do we see physical environment included (I-11), but we see a scheme more typical of general notions of social indicators. Admittedly, the inventory arises in "an almost electric fashion from the topics treated in (such) major social indicator publications". This is hardly an inventory emerging from a general model of society.

TABLE 2

I. Socioeconomic Welfare

1. Population
2. Labor force and employment
3. Income
4. Knowledge and technology
5. Education
6. Health
7. Leisure
8. Public safety and legal justice
9. Housing
10. Transportation
11. Physical environment
12. Social mobility and stratification

II. Social Participation and Alienation

1. Family
2. Religion
3. Politics
4. Voluntary associations
5. Alienation

III. Use of Time

IV. Consumption Behavior

V. Aspiration, Satisfaction, Acceptance, Morale, etc.

Following a scheme similar to the one presented by Land, one might indeed argue from a more inductive perspective that the relationships (i. e. statistical) between already existing indicators might provide or, at least, shed light on a general model of society. Indeed such a position is not unlike the one advocated by SSRC's Center for Coordination of Research on Social Indicators[10], nor is it unlike the position advocated earlier by Sheldon and Land. The major difficulty involved in such a position is the assumption that relationships between presently existing indicators are significant. From a conservative perspective, one might be suspicious of such a supposition. Certainly, there is no assurance that there will be any relationships between indicators as presently defined, nor any assurance that such statistical relationships would capture the dynamics of the forces which determine an indicator (e. g. explain variation in the indicator).

Land states that the scheme he proposes is an ideal state of social indicator research, and that the present state of research is far from this ideal. He says, in fact, "It is impossible to find any one social indicator study which has been successful in incorporating all of these types of indicators into an integrated model of a social process.[11]" He goes on in the volume to look at some of those efforts which are forming the beginnings of such an approach. Indeed by reading through the various modeling efforts, one can see that nothing unexpected arises. Several of the models will be briefly noted here.

The first class of models portrayed in the Land text are replication models. These articles are concerned primarily with survey data. They are non-comprehensive. They do not attempt to define a complete system of social indicators. Rather they deal with a dimension of social indicator research. This might include the use of demographic variables to explain attitudes to-[12] wards Communist and socialist books and speeches. The demographic information in this case, bears a fairly complex relationship to the attitudinal component. A "log linear model" is used. It provides an ability to study the information over time by keeping straight the movement of persons through different age groups as the replicated study moves through time. In one sense, the technique generated is typical of the replication class.

The second part of the Land volume is devoted to longitudinal and dynamic models. Its focus is also on the movement of indicators through time. Again advanced methodological technique (stochastic modeling, differential equation modeling) is employed. While certainly the level of complexity has increased over time, these models are not significantly different from preceding efforts in social science which use mathematical notions to explain social phenomena.

Land maintains that it is a short step from the type of social indicator model he advocated to a social policy model. (Referring back to Table One) one merely optimizes over the set of output indicators. The knowledge provided by the compilation of the model will give an indication of the appropriate changes to be made in the policy manipulable indicators. This is, of course, a clearly straightforward statement which is basic to the notions of any pre-scriptive modeling effort. The advantage which is most frequently claimed for such technique is that it is comprehensive. The models which exist in the social indicators area have not reached this level of sophistication.

This is not to discourage the rigor which such activity produces in the precision of the measures used or the concern it generates over the precise definition of such indicators (i. e. as input versus output measures or output versus side effect measures). Rather, it is to point to the fact that the social indicator models need to move to a more comprehensive state (e. g. therefore models which deal with a number of social indicators).

B. Social Policy Rationale

The preceding section dealt primarily with members of the academic commu-nity. Given such a background, it is not unexpected that they should attempt to formulate indicators which reflect the basic structure of society (in their terms, to provide a state measure). It is also not unexpected that such a group would be interested in the relationships between the various indicators or in the formation of the types of models discussed in the last section. Such a mode of operation provides little comfort for the social policy formulator. While the policy analyst is not opposed to the benefits of such an effort, he is opposed to the time that such an effort would necessarily take.

Policy Analysts have been a part of the social indicators movement from the outset. The earliest works in the field offered great potential. As Robert Parke and Eleanor Sheldon note: "Several of the early proposals for social indicators advanced the rationale that social indicators can help (1) to evaluate specific social programs, (2) to develop a balance sheet, or system of social programs, and (3) to set national goals and priorities[13]." Indeed it is not difficult to guess the type of work which has resulted from such a rationale. In general, it may be said, that the indicators developed by the policy analysts are "ad hoc" in nature. The measures usually attempted to incorporate readily available information such as census tracts or number of persons serviced by a social agency. Usually, the relevance of such measures are generated from intuition.

These points can easily be seen when we bear in mind the role of the policy analyst. He is usually concerned with a policy or set of policies. These policies, in the form of social service programs, are in action in the environment. The analyst's function is to evaluate the performance of each program. Furthermore, they frequently must be evaluated in ways which facilitate comparison. One might think that such a need for comparability would result in the formation of the type of indicators previously discussed. It would certainly be true, that a set of comprehensive indicators based on the "conditions of human existence" would provide the type of flexibility required for comparable data.

Unfortunately, such a result is not found in the literature of public policy analysis. Rather, what seems to happen is that measures like 'number of persons serviced' become comparable indicators of the social performance of programs involved. Indeed, such measures are generally recognized as being so inefficient that they are often times referred to as body counts. This is not to say that the work done in this area is of poor quality. Rather, it is to say that the emphasis which policy analysts place on the need for information now, has a major impact on their effort.

Certainly, it would also be unfair to say that policy analysts and social modelers do not interact. The policy analyst desires to improve the quality of his information and the social scientist desires to provide relevant research to feed such interaction. In fact, the major international efforts at forming a set of comprehensive indicator systems are results of such interaction. The Office of Budget and Management employed a number of leading scholars as consultants when compiling "Social Indicators 1973". There continues to be a call for such interaction in the literature[14], and it appears to be continuing.

Policy analysts have also expended a great amount of energy on attempts to improve the quality of their information. For example, Parke and Sheldon discuss schemes for making data more objective by separating the information gathering function from the actual analysis. They say:

> (There is) a need for a "two-tiered" statistical agency, one part devoted to information collection, the other part to analysis and to communication in the sense in which we have used that term. The separation of function recognizes the fact that in an information-collection agency, the imperatives of information collection and data production invariably take priority over analysis whenever there is a choice, as there always is. The separation of function also recognizes what the Statistics Commission recognized--the disinclination of data-producing agencies to devote time and attention to exploiting the potential of data other than their own.[15]

One might summarize the progress in the policy analysis area by saying it is possibly most susceptible to Biderman's previously mentioned warning. The progress is very slow and very uneven.

III.   INTERNATIONAL EFFORTS IN GATHERING SOCIAL ACCOUNTS DATA

A.   Individual National Efforts

The discussion of social indicators thus far has been delivered from a decidedly American perspective. While the larger part of the social indicator movement has centered in the United States, other nations have been engaged in the collection of social accounts data. In fact, in 1973 and 1974 several nations published social accounts data. Among these were: Canada, France, West Germany, Great Britain, Japan, and the United States, as well as a joint Scandinavian effort including Norway and Sweden.[1]

Previous to this wave of social accounts publications, very little published material existed on an international plane. This can be clearly seen in Ralph Brooks' assessment of international social indicators activities.[2]

Rather than looking at each individual nation's effort, what will be attempted here is a comparison of the various efforts.[3] Also included in the comparison is the Organization for Economic and Cultural Developments publication, 'List of Social Concerns'. This is done primarily as a convenience in that the publication will be discussed later in the chapter.

The first comparison to be made is in the broad area of general concerns. These have usually been included in the publications as goal areas, poles, Lebensbereiche, or chapters. Table 3 presents such a comparison for fifteen social indicators publications.

TABLE 3   191

COMPARISON OF GOAL AREAS, 15 U.S. AND FOREIGN REPORTS

NOTES:

x = represented
(x) = represented in another chap.
0 = not represented

(a) = Bilingualism; native people; immigration
(b) = Aspiration, satisfaction; Alienation and Engagement
(c) = Participation and Alienation
(d) = Le Développement culturel; L'adaptation au changement L'organisation de l'espace rural

Goal Areas		Social Indicators	Social Trends (1972)	Données sociales	Gesellschaftliche Daten	O.E.C.D. List	Soziologischer Almanach	Perspective Canada	Sozialstatistische Trends	Social Intelligence	Political Intelligence	Indicators of Social Change	Human Meaning of Social Change	Toward a Social Report	Indicateurs sociaux	Materialien...Nation
	HEALTH	x	x	x	x	x	x	x	x	x	0	x	0	x	x	0
	PUBLIC SAFETY	x	x	x	x	x	x	x	x	x	0	0	x	x	0	(x)
	EDUCATION	x	x	x	x	x	x	x	x	x	0	x	0	x	x	x
	EMPLOYMENT	x	x	x	x	x	x	x	x	(x)	0	x	x	0	x	x
	INCOME	x	x	x	x	x	x	x	x	x	0	(x)	0	x	x	x
	HOUSING	x	x	x	x	(x)	x	x	x	(x)	0	0	0	(x)	x	(x)
	LEISURE AND RECREATION	x	x	x	x	x	x	x	x	0	0	x	x	0	x	0
	POPULATION	x	x	x	x	0	x	x	x	0	0	x	0	0	0	x
Economy	Manpower	(x)	x	(x)	(x)	0	x	0	(x)	(x)	0	x	0	0	(x)	(x)
	Economic Structure	0	0	0	0	0	x	0	0	(x)	0	0	(x)	0	0	x
	Economic Growth	0	0	0	0	x	0	x	0	0	0	x	0	0	0	(x)
	Infrastructure	0	0	0	x	0	x	0	(x)	0	0	0	0	0	0	x
	Social Security, Welfare	(x)	(x)	x	0	(x)	0	x	x	0	0	x	0	0	(x)	x
Polity	Political Participation	0	0	0	x	x	x	x	0	x	0	0	x	(x)	0	0
	Political Structure	0	0	0	0	0	0	0	0	0	0	x	0	0	0	0
	Public Expenditure	0	x	0	x	0	x	0	0	0	0	0	0	0	x	0
	Interest Groups, Unions	0	0	0	0	0	x	0	0	0	0	0	0	0	0	0
	Elites	0	0	0	0	0	x	0	0	0	0	0	0	0	0	0
	Mass Media	0	0	0	0	0	x	0	0	x	0	0	0	0	0	0
	International Linkage	0	0	0	0	0	0	0	0	0	x	0	0	0	x	x
Society	Stratification, Mobility	0	0	x	0	0	x	0	x	0	0	x	0	x	x	0
	Family	0	(x)	0	(x)	0	x	0	(x)	(x)	0	x	x	0	x	0
	Women	0	0	0	0	0	(x)	0	0	0	0	0	0	0	x	0
	Children, Youth	0	0	0	0	0	0	0	0	0	0	0	0	0	0	x
	The Elderly	0	0	0	0	0	0	0	0	0	0	0	0	0	x	0
	Minorities/ Discrimination	(x)	0	0	0	0	x	0	0	x	0	0	x	0	x	0
	Social Breakdown	0	0	0	0	0	0	0	0	x	0	0	0	0	0	0
Culture	Science, Technology	0	(x)	0	x	0	0	0	0	x	0	x	0	x	0	0
	The Arts	0	0	0	0	0	0	0	0	x	0	0	0	(x)	0	0
	Religion	0	0	0	0	0	0	0	0	0	0	x	0	0	0	0
	Values, Liberties	0	0	0	0	0	0	0	0	x	x	0	0	(x)	(x)	0
Environments	Natural Environment	0	x	0	x	x	x	x	x	x	(x)	0	0	x	0	0
	Urban Environment	0	x	0	x	(x)	(x)	0	(x)	x	0	0	(x)	(x)	x	0
	OTHER	0	0	0	0	0	0	(a)	0	0	0	0	(b)	(c)	(d)	0
	INTERNATIONAL DATA	0	x	0	0	0	x	0	0	0	0	0	0	0	0	(x)

The list of social goal areas has been generated inductively. That is, all areas are included that were mentioned in any of the publications.

In general, Social Indicators 1973, is more devoted to the individual well-being/satisfaction approach. On the other hand, the European counter-parts, are more dedicated to 'social performance' measures. This is particularly apparent when we look at the data included in the various reports. Table 4 displays relevant data by goal areas for six publications.

Another dimension can be added by examining the Scandinavian efforts. Table 5 displays major headings (similar to goal areas) for several of the reports. While it is certainly harder to see from the evidence presented, the American bias to individual well-being is present. As Natalie Ransey noted:

> The impression one gets from reading Social Indicators 1973 at the same time that one reads corresponding publications from European societies, is that the United States appears as a far more privatized society, consisting of quite unrelated households or individuals, to whom allocations of goods or burdens are made by unspecified "forces" working through unspecified mechanisms (with the exception of racial discrimination). The European societies, through the selection of data presented in the reports, appear to have populations and institutions that are far more connected, in the sense that one gets a closer look at the specific mechanisms through which rewards and burdens are differentially distributed, at the countervailing tendencies produced through the "inputs" of highly self-conscious welfare states, and at the composite results of all of these processes on the various socio-economic strata.[4]

While in a sense the European reports seem to give a more connective appearance, it does not necessarily reflect the power of the theoretical underpinnings (or framework) involved. In the final analysis all the compendiums have a way to go in representing a comprehensive view of society. In short, the basic view that one draws when reading the European and American government publications is that they are similar. They start with a number of intuitively based notions on social welfare or quality of life. (Again in the European case the underlying ideas revolve more around governmental service output, and in the American case the underlying ideas are based more around the individual well-being.) The reports go on to present all the relevant statistics available. When possible the statistics are 'output' measures, also when possible, time series data are used. The only underlying thread is the loosely developed underlying (often implicit) notion of social welfare.

Several reports[5] have taken a somewhat different tack. Two will be discussed here. The first[5]: the Japanese effort attempts to tie a number of measures into a 'cost benefit analysis' form. The second[6]: A Scandinavian effort uses a much more explicitly developed social theory framework around which it clusters the data. While these are certainly far from ideal attempts to in-

TABLE 4   193

COMPARISON OF SOCIAL CONCERNS, SIX REPORTS

x = represented (x) = represented in other chapters 0 = not represented		Social Indicators, 1973	Toward a Social Report, 1969	O.E.C.D. List, 1973	Social Trends, 1972	Données Sociales, 1973	Gesellschaftliche Daten, 1973
Goal Areas	**SOCIAL CONCERNS:** Well-being Concerns *System Concerns* SATISFACTION CONCERNS						
HEALTH	Long Life	x	x	x	x	x	x
	Disability	x	0	0	x	x	x
	Mental Health	x	(x)	0	x	0	x
	"Positive" Health	0	(x)	0	0	0	(x)
	Access to Medical Care	(x)	x	x	(x)	x	(x)
	Preventive Care	0	(x)	0	0	0	0
	Rehabilitation	0	0	x	0	0	0
	Organization of the Health System	(x)	0	0	x	x	x
	Medical Cost and Expenditure	0	x	0	0	0	0
	CONFIDENCE IN MEDICAL CARE	x	0	0	0	0	0
PUBLIC SAFETY	Reported Crimes	x	x	x	x	x	x
	Victim, Victimization	x	x	0	x	0	0
	Offenders	x	(x)	0	(x)	(x)	(x)
	Rehabilitation	0	0	0	0	0	0
	Organization of the Justice System	0	0	x	x	0	0
	Safety Expenditures	0	0	0	0	0	0
	FEAR OF CRIME, CONFIDENCE IN JUSTICE	x	(x)	x	0	0	0
EDUCATION	Attainment, Qualification Structure	x	x	x	x	x	x
	Efficiency: Retention, Graduation	x	x	0	x	x	x
	Achievement	x	x	0	0	0	0
	Flexibility	0	0	(x)	0	0	0
	Adult Education	x	0	x	0	0	0
	Impact of Education	x	(x)	0	0	0	0
	Organization of the Educational System	0	0	0	x	x	0
	Cost and Expenditure	0	0	(x)	x	x	x
	SATISFACTION WITH THE SYSTEM	0	0	x	0	0	0
EMPLOY-MENT	Labor Force Participation	x	0	x	x	x	x
	Qualification Structure	0	0	0	0	0	(x)
	Unemployment	x	0	x	x	x	x
	Working Conditions	x	0	x	x	x	x
	Labor Conflicts	0	0	(x)	x	x	x
	Occupational Mobility	0	0	(x)	(x)	x	(x)
	JOB SATISFACTION	x	0	x	0	0	x

TABLE 4

(Continued)

COMPARISON OF SOCIAL CONCERNS, SIX REPORTS

```
x  = represented
(x) = represented in other chapters
0  = not represented
```

Goal Areas	SOCIAL CONCERNS: Well-being Concerns *System Concerns* SATISFACTION CONCERNS	Social Indicators, 1973	Toward a Social Report, 1969	O.E.C.D. List, 1973	Social Trends, 1972	Donnees Sociales, 1973	Gesellschaftliche Daten, 1973
INCOME	Levels of Income	x	(x)	x	x	x	x
	Distribution of Income	x	x	x	x	x	0
	Income Trends, Life-Time Income	x	0	0	x	(x)	0
	Consumption, Standard of Living	x	0	x	x	x	x
	Level and Distribution: Durables, Savings	0	0	x	x	x	(x)
	Distribution of Wealth	x	0	x	x	0	(x)
	Low Income Population, Poverty	x	x	x	0	0	0
	Redistribution, Subsidies	0	(x)	(x)	x	x	0
HOUSING	Housing Quality	x	x	(x)	x	x	x
	Living Space, Crowding	x	x	x	x	0	0
	Property Conditions	0	x	0	0	x	x
	Neighborhood Quality	(x)	0	x	0	0	0
	Segregation	0	x	0	0	0	0
	Housing Construction, Renewal	0	x	0	x	x	x
	Housing Cost and Supply	0	0	x	x	x	x
	Subsidies to Housing Cost	0	0	0	x	(x)	(x)
	SATISFACTION WITH HOUSING/ NEIGHBORHOOD	x	0	0	0	0	0
LEISURE AND RECREA- TION	Time Budget	x	0	(x)	0	x	0
	Leisure Time, Activities	x	0	x	x	x	0
	Transportation Time	(x)	0	0	x	0	0
	Flexibility of Working Time	0	0	x	0	0	0
	Outdoor Recreation: Time, Activities	x	0	0	0	0	0
	Vacation	(x)	0	0	x	x	x
POPULA- TION	*Total Population, Growth*	x	0	0	x	x	x
	Population Dynamics	x	0	0	x	x	x
	Concentration, Agglomeration	x	0	0	(x)	0	x
	Age Structure	x	0	0	x	x	x
	Family, Household Structure	0	0	0	x	x	x
	Urban, Rural Population	x	0	0	0	x	x
	Migration	0	0	0	x	x	0
	Foreign Population	0	0	0	x	x	(x)

TABLE 5

SUMMARY OF CONTENTS OF FIVE SOCIAL INDICATOR REPORTS

COUNTRY:	UNITED STATES	GREAT BRITAIN	FRANCE	SWEDEN	NORWAY
TITLE:	Social Indicators	Social Trends	Social Data	Social Development	Social Survey
AUTHOR:	Office of Management and Budget	Central Statistical Office	Central Statistical Office	Central Statistical Office	Central Statistical Office
LIST OF CHAPTERS	1. Health 2. Public Safety 3. Education 4. Employment 5. Income 6. Housing 7. Leisure and Recreation 8. Population	1. Population 2. Employment 3. Leisure 4. Personal Income and Wealth 5. Personal Expenditure 6. Health and Personal Social Services 7. Education 8. Housing 9. Environment 10. Justice and Law 11. Resources (Public Expenditures) 12. International	I. Active Population 1. Total Population 2. Active Population 3. Employment 4. Working Time and Rhythm 5. Work-Related Accidents 6. Labor Conflicts 7. Wages & Cost of Living II. Life Styles and Cultural Patterns 8. Household Consumption 9. Household Equipment 10. Vacations 11. Leisure 12. Education 13. Housing 14. Health III. Disparities and Equilibria 15. Social Benefits 16. Distribution and Redistribution of Income 17. Private and Semi-Public Salary Levels 18. Family Formation and Dissolution 19. Social Mobility 20. Crime	Base Data 1. Population and Family Structure 2. Economic Structure and Development Data on Components 3. Housing 4. Employment 5. Personal and Household Economic Conditions 6. Private Consumption 7. Health 8. Social Welfare 9. Education 10. Crime and Justice 11. Leisure	1. Population 2. Health 3. Education 4. Housing 5. Employment 6. Income and Consumption 7. Social Services 8. Crime 9. Social Participation

corporate such innovations, nevertheless, they represent initial efforts in such a direction.

The Japanese Economic Planning Agency's "Whitepaper on National Life 1973: The Life and Its Quality in Japan" differs somewhat from other international efforts to gather social accounts data.[7] This difference stems primarily from the economic framework which it uses in presenting the social accounts measures. Such a framework results from the stated purpose of the effort.

> The purpose of this Report, while describing the present state of national life with respect to various welfare objectives, is to choose and examine today's problems so as to contribute to future design and implementation of welfare improvement policies.[8]

The influence of the economic perspective can be seen in the problem definition report. The basic problems on which the report focuses are seen in Table 6. These problems are examined in quite an interesting way. The writers attempt to assess in each case the cost of programs aimed at alleviating the problem and the possible impact that such a expenditure would have on economy. The overriding concern of the Japanese for avoiding inflation has led them to incorporate the most economic perspective so far, in the treatment of social indicators.

On the other end of the spectrum the Swedish publication "About Dimensions of Welfare,"[9] has probably the most developed sociological/psychological theoretic notions behind its data collection and subsequent analysis. The [10] notions were generated largely from Abraham Maslow's needs hierarchy. The author and research team attempt to develop an operational scheme for such a theory under the general headings of having, loving, being. In the context of the earlier discussion on the individual - vs - social well-being, an attempt is made to differentiate the need categories by individual and structural needs. The results of the effort are found in Table 7.

The authors then use a survey instrument to measure the more 'subjective' values, within several Scandinavian communities. Where possible they supplement this information with the appropriate economic data. The information is then used to explore the original (underlying) theoretic notions. This is primarily accomplished by the use of factor analysis tests to see if the hypothesized dimensions (having, loving, and being) do emerge in the analysis as fairly sharp factors.

This effort is clearly the most 'psychologically' oriented of social accounts data collection techniques. Fairly painstaking efforts are made to develop "subjective" measures of well-being such as belongingness, and the feeling of being loved and wanted. The research staff also applies fairly rigorous tests (replicability and reliability) to the measures.

TABLE 6

(1) With respect to family budget, it is recognized that the structure of consumption of
the average household has been remarkably diversified and upgraded. However, the fact
that items which were, in the past, considered "luxury items" have taken on a character of
daily necessity has made the impact of the rise of their prices on family budget very
large and at the same time, is causing to diminish the demand curtailing effect of price
rise. Meanwhile, with regard to those households which are receiving public assistance,
in contrast to the period in which there were many people who could be relieved by the increase of employment opportunities, the number of households with old and/or disabled
people continues to increase. Thus the need for expansion of social security becomes
greater.

(2) Concerning health, the problem of health of old people is considered. Not only are
many old people not blessed with good health, but recently the population as a whole is
aging, and illness of old people is increasing. Meanwhile, accompanying the change in
household structure, the number of old people who cannot hope for care by the family is
increasing. The need for medical care and welfare services for the aged continues to increase, but facilities and attendants for sufficient services for the aged are still
lacking.

(3) With respect to education, we deal with the problem of higher education. In the face
of increased income and rapid rise of enrollment ratio, the capacity of higher educational
institutions has been expanded. Nevertheless, it does not necessarily mean that -- in
economic and/or regional sense -- availability of opportunities for higher education has
been more equalized. Further, the gap in learning environments and burdens between
national/public and private universities is still very great.

(4) With respect to employment, problems concerning the "retirement system" and life after
retirement are dealt with. Employees, in general, have to leave the job at the age of 55
when they are still active, and in the labor market, it is difficult for aged people to
find gainful employment. In addition, the amount of retirement allowance which accompanies
retirement is not sufficient considering the living cost after retirement, and the public
pension system is going to be revised. Measures for stability of life of old people, e.g.,
the prolongation of the retirement age, are called for.

(5) Concerning housing, housing problems in large cities, centering in Tokyo City, are
taken up. The majority of residents of existing housing areas live in private rental
housing, of which the level of quality and rent are the problems. The possibility of getting into public rental housing is small. Many people want to have their own house. But
the price of land in areas close to the center of the city has already become too high for
ordinary workers to purchase. Consequently, owned houses continue to spread outside the
city, making the price of land in the suburb rise rapidly.

(6) With respect to environmental pollution, principles and measures for pollution control
have finally been established, and improvements have been in some kinds of pollutants, but
there are still various fields in which pollution still continues to worsen. Further, to
harmonize the housing development and leisure development with the preservation of nature
will henceforth become an important issue.

(7) With regard to safety, problems of natural calamities, accidents and crimes are discussed. Potential danger in everyday life is rising due to the lag in safety measures both
of physical and human nature, in the face of increased use of transportation facilities and
other man-made facilities. Potential danger of flood from subsidence of the ground or be-
lated urban waterways repair is also increasing. As for crimes, their number is decreasing
but the number of juvenile crimes is increasing, shifting especially to the early teens.
Public aid to those who met unfortunate disasters is insufficient, so individuals are preparing for untimely accidents by means of savings or insurance.

198

TABLE 7

	The Overall Level of Individual Need-Satisfaction	Dispersions Reflecting Structural Patterns	Correlations Reflecting Structural Patterns
Having	Level of Living E.g., GNP/capita, averages, rates or percentages of the level of living components	Economic Equality E.g., dispersion of the level of living components	Economic Justice E.g., percentage differences between regions, races, etc. on the level of living components
Loving	The amount of loving or of reciprocal human relationships, the amount of persons having somebody to care for and love, the amount of solidarity (the amount of "community")	A low degree of coercion (a low degree pressure toward conformity), possibilities to decide about human relations by own choice	
Being	The Amount of Being E.g., indices indicating lack of alienation, feeling of being a person, of having a place in the world (insubstitutability)	Equality in Political Resources E.g., measures of power differences and variations in abilities to influence decisions	Political Justice Measures of discrimination, e.g., measures of isolation from public life

B.   Data Collection Efforts in Less Developed and Developing Nations

Anyone reading through the last section would be impressed that all the national collection efforts described belonged to fairly industrialized, fairly developed, and fairly Western nations. As can be expected, these nations have produced the largest amount of effort in the area. This, of course, is much to the chagrin of researchers trying to gain a sense of regional quality of life or social indicator systems. This discomfort, for example, can be noted several times in the United Nations publication "Report on the World Social Condition"[11]. The basic problem is the general lack of data. As the study notes:

> Generalization about the state of development of the region is there-
> fore a risky business in the best of circumstances, and is apt to
> obscure almost as much as it reveals. Concerning the social aspects
> of development in particular, generalities are rendered all the more
> uncertain by serious gaps and inaccuracies in statistical information.
> For example, no countries other than Japan - and to some extent the
> Phillippines - can offer anything resembling comprehensive time-
> series data on changes in household income distribution, and for
> many countries even much simpler statistical information is either
> entirely lacking or is so suspect as to be practically useless for
> analytical purposes. In the latter respect, a cardinal difficulty is
> the almost total absence of recent statistical information on main-
> land China and its population of over 700 million. This shortcoming
> is obviously one of such enormous dimensions as to divest large
> parts of the following discussion of any genuine regional applicability.[12]

When the data do exist there is the possibility of still other major problems. One of the more pronounced is that of 'creeping Westernism.' Basically, the framers or data collectors in each national effort are leading scholars in the area of social science. The training of these scholars has, in effect, been heavily influenced by Western education. This bias can lead them to ignore or soften somewhat the concerns relevant to their cultures in attempting to compile a quality of life or social accounts inventory. As one Ceylonese social scientist has suggested of such 'scholars':

> The tendency of the best minds to shift to abstract, theoretical re-
> search, rather than grapple with concrete reality is understandable;
> their writings were invariably addressed to an invisible jury in some
> intellectual center of gravity in the West.[13]

This tendency is also very much in action in the Treasury Economic Report, the official Malaysian compendium of economic statistics. In 1973, the Malaysian Treasurer decided to include "a section devoted to quality of life in Malaysia".[14]

C.   Attempts at Devising International Indicator Systems

As one might guess having seen the relatively small number of national social accounting efforts, both the number and quality of schemes for an international accounting system are low. There are of course additional problems introduced at the international level. The problems range from the sheer cost in money and manpower of such an effort to the conceptual problem of determining the dimensions such an effort should include to the methodological problem of constructing measures with cross-cultural (cross-national) validity.

The organizational problems are discussed at some length by Davis Bobrow in his article entitled "International Indicators."[15] The problem of constructing an inventory of international indicators has been, at least, partially addressed. In 1973, the member states of the Organization for Economic Cooperation and Development sent delegates to a conference in Paris. The purpose of the conference was to discuss the possibility of a formation of an inventory of areas of social concern. Such a list was not only discussed, but was actually compiled (Table 8). Several things are apparent from reading the list. The first is that the topics are very general and, consequently, operationalization would not always be straightforward. The second is that, in many ways, the compilation method of the list adds nothing to the removal of qualifications previously made. It is a list compiled by experts (scholars) with similar Western bias. This bias is accentuated by the characteristics of the member states themselves.[16]

Also a number of people involved in the formation of national accounts were the same scholars (such as Mancur Olson) heavily involved in the compilation of the list. Accordingly, the list reflects the same conceptual organization that is found in the individual government publications.

The additional methodological problems which would face a truly international effort have not yet received much attention. This is, obviously, due to the fact that there have not been any efforts to generate such concerns. Nevertheless, one can anticipate the scope and seemingly insurmountability of such problems.

D.   Divising a System of International Indicators

While efforts at constructing an independent system of international indicators have been contained to the fairly primitive stages, it seems appealing to construct such a set from the communality of the various national efforts. To such a construction several points should be made. The first is that the 'creeping Westernism' phenomena already noted would be present, if not intensified. The second is that nations which presently have not developed national social accounting systems would be unrepresented.

The third and probably most significant is that any attempt to use a communality method would capture and intensify the weaknesses already present in the national accounts.

TABLE 8

The Organization for Economic Cooperation and Development

SOCIAL INDICATORS

List of Social Concerns Common to Most Member Countries

FUNDAMENTAL SOCIAL CONCERNS	SUB-CONCERNS
HEALTH	
A-1 THE PROBABILITY OF A HEALTHY LIFE THROUGH ALL STAGES OF THE LIFE CYCLE.	
A-2 THE IMPACT OF HEALTH IMPAIRMENTS ON INDIVIDUALS.	A-2-a The quality of health care in terms reducing pain and restoring functional capabilities.
	A-2-b The extent of universal distribution in the delivery of health care.
	A-2-c The ability of the chronically impaired and permanently handicapped to participate more effectively in society.
INDIVIDUAL DEVELOPMENT THROUGH LEARNING	
B-1 THE ACQUISITION BY CHILDREN OF THE BASIC KNOWLEDGE, SKILLS AND VALUES NECESSARY FOR THEIR INDIVIDUAL DEVELOPMENT AND THEIR SUCCESSFUL FUNCTIONING AS CITIZENS IN THEIR SOCIETY.	B-1-a The extent to which children from economically and socially disadvantaged families reach the basic standards of achievement.
	B-1-b The extent to which the physically and mentally handicapped receive educational services for their individual development through learning and for their more effective participation in social life.
	B-1-c The proportion of other children reaching the basic standards of achievement.
B-2 THE AVAILABILITY OF OPPORTUNITIES FOR CONTINUING SELF-DEVELOPMENT AND THE PROPENSITY OF INDIVIDUALS TO USE THEM.	
B-3 THE MAINTENANCE AND DEVELOPMENT BY INDIVIDUALS OF THE KNOWLEDGE SKILLS AND FLEXIBILITY REQUIRED TO FULFILL THEIR ECONOMIC POTENTIAL AND TO ENABLE THEM TO INTEGRATE THEMSELVES IN THE ECONOMIC PROCESS IF THEY WISH TO DO SO.	
B-4 THE INDIVIDUAL'S SATISFACTION WITH THE PROCESS OF INDIVIDUAL DEVELOPMENT THROUGH LEARNING, WHILE HE IS IN THE PROCESS.	
B-5 THE MAINTENANCE AND DEVELOPMENT OF THE CULTURAL HERITAGE RELATIVE TO ITS POSITIVE CONTRIBUTION TO THE WELL-BEING OF THE MEMBERS OF VARIOUS SOCIAL GROUPS.	
EMPLOYMENT AND QUALITY OF WORKING LIFE	
C-1 THE AVAILABILITY OF GAINFUL EMPLOYMENT FOR THOSE WHO DESIRE IT.	
C-2 THE QUALITY OF WORKING LIFE.	C-2-a Working conditions.
	C-2-b Earnings and fringe-benefits.
	C-2-c Employment-time, employment-related time and paid holidays.
	C-2-d Employment security.
	C-2-e Career prospects.
	C-2-f Industrial conflict.
C-3 INDIVIDUAL SATISFACTION WITH THE EXPERIENCE OF WORKING LIFE	C-3-a Working conditions.
	C-3-b Earnings and fringe-benefits.
	C-3-c Employment-time, employment-related time and paid holidays.

FUNDAMENTAL SOCIAL CONCERNS	SUB-CONCERNS	FUNDAMENTAL SOCIAL CONCERNS	SUB-CONCERNS
	C-3-d Employment security.		E-5-c The extent to which individuals and families perceive themselves as secure against adverse change in their economic status.
	C-3-e Career prospects.		
	C-3-f Relations among and participation by employees.		
	C-3-g Supervision, autonomy and job-challenge.	PHYSICAL ENVIRONMENT	
TIME AND LEISURE		F-1 HOUSING CONDITIONS	F-1-a Cost and availability of suitable dwellings.
D-1 THE AVAILABILITY OF EFFECTIVE CHOICES FOR THE USE OF TIME.	D-1-a The flexibility of patterns of working time.		F-1-b Living space and utilities of dwellings.
	D-1-b The accessibility and quality of leisure time opportunities.		F-1-c Accessibility to neighborhood shops and services, and work-places.
	D-1-c The time available for personal development, family and social obligations, and social participation.		F-1-d Neighborhood and environmental amenities.
COMMAND OVER GOODS AND SERVICES		F-2 POPULATION EXPOSURE TO HARMFUL AND/OR UNPLEASANT POLLUTANTS.	F-2-a Air.
E-1 THE PERSONAL COMMAND OVER GOODS AND SERVICES.			F-2-b Noise.
E-2 THE NUMBER OF INDIVIDUALS EXPERIENCING MATERIAL DEPRIVATION.			F-2-c Pervasive and persistent pollutants.
E-3 THE EXTENT OF EQUITY IN THE DISTRIBUTION OF COMMAND OVER GOODS AND SERVICES.	E-3-a The extent of relative impoverishment.		F-2-d Water.
	E-3-b The dispersion in the structure of income and wealth.		F-2-e Land.
E-4 THE QUALITY, RANGE OF CHOICE AND ACCESSIBILITY OF PRIVATE AND PUBLIC GOODS AND SERVICES.	E-4-a Whether individuals have the information needed to make effective choices.	F-3 THE BENEFIT DERIVED BY THE POPULATION FROM THE USE AND MANAGEMENT OF THE ENVIRONMENT	F-3-a Land management.
	E-4-b Individuals' satisfaction with quality, range of choice, and accessibility of the private and public goods and services they consume.		F-3-b Water management.
			F-3-c Management of the urban and rural landscape.
E-5 THE PROTECTION OF INDIVIDUALS AND FAMILIES AGAINST ECONOMIC HAZARDS	E-5-a The extent to which individuals and families obtain insurance or other compensation for predictable and unpredictable income losses.		F-3-d Housing conditions.
			F-3-e Control of pollution.
	E-5-b The extent to which individuals and families obtain assistance for significant expansions of obligatory expenditures particular to them.		F-3-f Reduction of congestion.
			F-3-g Accessibility among social services and functions.
			F-3-h Environmental contribution to recreation and amenity.
			F-3-i Other aspects of urban and rural life.

FUNDAMENTAL SOCIAL CONCERNS	SUB-CONCERNS		
PERSONAL SAFETY AND THE ADMINISTRATION OF JUSTICE			
G-1 VIOLENCE VICTIMIZATION AND HARASSMENT SUFFERED BY INDIVIDUALS	G-1-a	Involving persons.	
	G-1-b	Involving property.	
	G-1-c	Involving perceptions of danger to safety and security.	
G-2 FAIRNESS AND HUMANITY OF THE ADMINISTRATION OF JUSTICE	G-2-a	In the administration of criminal law.	
	G-2-b	In the administration of civil law.	
	G-2-c	In the administrative practice.	
G-3 THE EXTENT OF CONFIDENCE IN THE ADMINISTRATION OF JUSTICE			
SOCIAL OPPORTUNITY AND PARTICIPATION			
H-1 THE DEGREE OF SOCIAL INEQUALITY	H-1-a	The degree of inequality among social strata.	
	H-1-b	The extent of opportunity for social mobility.	
	H-1-c	The position for disadvantaged groups.	
H-2 THE EXTENT OF OPPORTUNITY FOR PARTICIPATION IN COMMUNITY LIFE INSTITUTIONS AND DECISION-MAKING			

E.   Conclusion

The literature as exemplified in the above discussion of social accounts systems seems to be focused at the level of intermediate and relatively easily
obtainable measures. In short, the level of argument which goes on at the conceptual level is not mirrored at the level of data collection. The concern over
input versus output measures, the debate over the validity of measurement
and the concept of tightly built theoretical models is not found in the pages
of social accounts data, as it presently exists.

Moreover, there is no tightly formulated theoretical backing. Consequently,
no claims can be made that the lists are comprehensive (exclusive or exhaus-
tive) in any way. In fact, while there are several common areas of concern,
some of the studies have very different focuses (i. e. the Japanese and Scandinavian). This suggests that the search for Quality of Life Measures might
be markedly different from one nation to the next.

On a larger and possibly more unsettling note, is the tendency of the less
developed (Malaysia) and more recently developed nations (Japan) to assume
highly economic perspectives in dealing with Quality of Life issues. Seemingly the rallying cries for the Social Indicators Movement are not as clearly
heard. Quite possibly the movements "concern for social conditions" and
attempt to remove the "now philistinism" from policy planning may be an
ethnocentric notion. The less developed nations, who have never shared in
the dubious blessing of technological progress, may be willing to pollute their
air and water and destroy their countrysides as the developed nations have
done for economic growth.

IV.   QUALITY OF LIFE MEASURES

Several things are true about the concept of Quality of Life. Fist, there is
great concern about it. Second, it is not clearly understood nor clearly defined. This difficulty stems from several possible sources. The most apparent is the subjectivity of the concept. It seems to have a duality in its
nature. On the one hand, its nature is unique to each person. On the other
hand elements of it are shared by various groups; religious, national, or
cultural. This duality is reflected in attempts to define the components which
ought to be contained within the conceptual boundary of the term. It seems
that there are components which are generalizable, at least, to a specific
population. It still seems nearly impossible to construct a definition, at
any level, which is applicable to each individual within that population. It is,
therefore, fair to say that no consensus exists as to what quality of life is
or exactly what its components are.

Nevertheless, some scholars have attempted to define the concept. A number of these are found in "Social Indicators" by Anton Schmalz. Also, he
attempted to find common elements within these definitions. Instead of pro-

viding common elements, however, he devised three limitations on the definition of quality of life.

1. The notion that quality of life refers to an indefinite number of states and does not imply an evaluation of life styles.

2. The idea that there are as many different life standards as there are individuals (i.e. there is no single, universal quality of life criterion extant in any society at any given time).

3. The proposition that quality of life refers to a subjective state of the individual and can only be partially explained by using such terms as "trained", "happiness", "educated", "welfare", "self-fulfilled", "satisfied", "reason", "purpose", etc. The same holds true of their opposites: "discontent", "illiterate", "frustrated", "apathetic", "alienated", etc. [2]

Fairly direct economic definitions have been attempted. Nordhaus, for example, suggests a "MEW" index[3]. It would be a measure of the amount of expenditure on welfare programs. Clearly, it falls into the problems expressed in qualification three above, in that no measure of welfare expenditure can be a direct measure of quality of life.

Hornback and Shaw used a somewhat different approach[4]. They maintained that there is an "objective set of conditions" which affects quality of life. It was not these conditions, however, but the "subjective attitude" toward them which actually constituted quality of life. While such a distinction may, in fact, be useful, it does not lessen the difficulty of the definitional problem. It merely divides it into two categories (objective conditions, subjective attitudes) equally hard to define. There is no assurance that either the same set of objective conditions will "affect" each individual's quality of life, or that given the same set of objective conditions they will respond with the same subjective attitudes.

(The next section will deal specifically with schemes for the attempted quantification of quality of life measures. This section, as a preface, will discuss some of the various factors underlying the construction of such measures.)

It was noted above that while each individual might have his own interpretation as to what affects quality of life, there might be some form of sharing of common elements by different groups. One might begin thinking about quality of life by thinking about groups which might hold common viewpoints, as to what is entailed by quality of life. A list, compiled by the Quality of Life Study Group, Environmental Protection Agency, provides a springboard for such an effort. At a conference in 1973, they compiled the following list of eleven.[5]

1. Races (the Negro, Indian, Eskimo, Puerto Rican, Spanish, Oriental, Middle East, Chicano - the obvious minorities, as well as other minorities).

2. Ethnic groups (Greek, Polish, Irish, Italian, German, Scandinavian, Russian, etc.).

3. Religious groups (Protestant, Roman Catholic, Greek Orthodox, Jewish; also Protestant includes over 250 branches, and that there are a myriad of oriental and other cults and sects springing up all over America).

4. Sex oriented groups (such as the homosexual).

5. Special interest groups (sports fans, classical musical fans, rock music fans, country and western music fans, needle pointers, card players, potters, handicraftmen, chess players, etc.).

6. Physical (short, tall, crippled, in wheel chairs, blind, deaf, dumb, ugly, etc.).

7. Geographical (urban, surburban, country, mountain, valley, desert, plains, cold, heat, sun, rain, water, snow, sand, dust, etc.).

8. Economic (wealthy in abundance, just rich, affluent, well-off, poor, destitute, getting by, poverty level).

9. Cultural (highly sophisticated, mildly sophisticated, not sophisticated, gauche, living in a cultural ghetto - i.e. isolated such as Harlem or Scarsdale).

10. Education (lots of formal education, no formal education, a little formal education, lots of practical knowledge, no practical knowledge, wise, sensible, foolish).

11. Age (babies, children, youth, young adults, middle aged, elderly, aged, ancient).

One need not think very hard or for very long to think of some of the different perspectives that these groups might have on the Quality of Life. Such categories might also overlap and combine to form other subgroups and ideologies. The young, for example, as portrayed in such works as Kenniston's The Uncommitted[6] or Reich's The Greening of America seem to attribute an entirely unique set of beliefs to the youth. These beliefs, especially those described by Reich, would have tremendous impact on quality of life assessment. One could also see the "sharing" of these beliefs by older members of the species. Indeed, these beliefs are as old as the picture, "He goes back to his equals" which accompanied Jean-Jacques Rousseau's "Discourse on the Origin and Foundations of Inequality Among Men"[7]. These belief systems which advocate a "return to nature" or "the Revolution against many of the values which Technology has thrust upon us"[8], are basically incompatible with a number of other notions of quality of life. In Hornback and Shaw's terms, we can be fairly certain that a back to nature proponent and the average man on the street would differ sharply in their subjective attitudes toward a number of objective conditions (i. e. level of industrial production, growth rate of technology). That is, when presented with such a set of conditions, indeed, they might differ in their subjective attitudes. However, there is no assurance that such individuals would even select the same set of objective conditions.

Consequently, it seems as though the quality of life concept, while elements of its constitution differ from person to person and are shaped by certain groups, is, in the final analysis, a totally subjective concept. Consider for a moment an argument similar to the "need gratification" argument developed by Abraham Maslow[9]. Once a need level is satisfied, the individual moves on to satisfy another need. If asked what he or she needs, the individual would be likely to concentrate on the present level of needs. This raises an interesting point, in that it might be possible to see an individuals subjective evaluation of his or her needs at a point in time as relative to that time point. This is to suggest that as those needs presently sought are satisfied the individual will find new needs and that the evaluation is not likely to contain those needs already satisfied. (This problem will be discussed again in the context of using survey techniques to measure quality of life.)

Such a view suggests that there are conditions not likely to be included in the individual's assessment of factors affecting quality of life which do directly affect that value. This calls for the use of objective measures in determining those things which the individual needs but is not aware of. One can easily speculate as to the difficulty of defining such measures.

As in the area of social indicators, the definitional problems involved with quality of life are immense. Accordingly, progress in the area has been and probably will continue to be very slow. Scholars, well aware of the above problems, know the difficulties which would surround any effort to quantify quality of life. Yet as the policy analysts, they are convinced of the important need to do so, consequently, several ventures have been made in such a direction. These will be discussed in the next section.

V. ATTEMPTS TO OPERATIONALIZE A SYSTEM OF QUALITY OF LIFE MEASURES

Needless to say, there are not many schemes which attempt to provide either a complete set of social indicators, or an operational definition of quality of life. With the present level of conceptualization it is not even possible to distinguish between them. From the widest viewpoint, it appears that "A measure of any of the important concepts of society ... is necessarily ... a social

indicator'' (see Sec. II A.). Drawing on the previous section, it appears that
a wide range of phenomena fall within the conceptual boundaries of quality of
life. Yet, emerging from the literature is a sort of consensus, though not well
defined, that there are certain elements that are important to look at. Many
efforts have been made to provide inventories of these elements. Still others
have gone on to attempt to provide operational definitions of them. Fewer still
have made an effort to weigh the relative importance of these categories.

This section will attempt to examine several of these efforts. On the subjective
side of the question, we will examine survey instruments constructed to find
an individual's assessment of quality of life. On the more objective side, we
will look at an effort to define social indicators from a behavioral standpoint,
and also from a mixture of the subjective and objective perspectives, an
attempt by 'experts' in the field of quality of life, to construct such measures,
either independently or as a group.

In general, it should be noted, however, that all attempts considered have the
element of 'expert' input. In forming a survey instrument, if one were simply
to ask something like, "What do you feel defines quality of life", one would be
likely to gain useful insights but hardly a complete inventory. This is largely
due to the satisfaction of needs argument presented in the concluding paragraphs
of the last section.

On the other hand, many accounts and anecdotes can be found displaying a
situation in which policy planners were, seemingly, totally ignorant of the
needs of the programs' recipients. Guy Pauker relates such an incident.

> Guy Pauker, Research Associate at Cal Tech's Environmental
> Quality Laboratory presented additional information regarding the
> priorities of the American people. He stated that a survey in Watts
> indicated that the three most serious problems, in order, were
> stray cats and dogs; garbage, and noise. Yet many policy planners,
> viewing Watts from their own value bases or standards, would have
> thought of something else. It is believed that social indicators or
> QOL indicators would provide this kind of information regarding the
> feelings of the people as they actually are, not as planners may
> think they are.

A. Experts and The Quality of Life

In that all operational schemes for quality of life depend somewhere on the
input of experts, it is reasonable that they should be discussed first. We
have already looked at a number of such efforts. The national account measures
were conceived of by the nation's leading statisticians and social scientists.
This is particularly true of the OECD's "List of Social Concerns". Beside
the governmental and the governmentally connected efforts, some scholars
have compiled their own lists. A number of group efforts also exist. Some
of these are conducted by research organizations, such as the Stanford Re-

search Institutes study or the Battelle Study[2]. Also, at the Environmental Protection Agency's symposium on the Quality of Life, Norman Dalkey conducted a Delphi experiment similar to his more detailed earlier efforts[3].

Along the lines of self-compiled lists we find Sheldon and Land's. It is suggested as a list of content areas for social indicators[4].

I. Socioeconomic Welfare

1. Population (composition, growth, and distribution)
2. Labor force and employment
3. Income
4. Knowledge and technology
5. Education
6. Health
7. Leisure
8. Public safety and legal justice
9. Housing
10. Transportation
11. Physical environment
12. Social mobility and stratification

II. Social Participation and Alienation

1. Family
2. Religion
3. Politics
4. Voluntary associations
5. Alienation

III. Use of Time

IV. Consumption Behavior

V. Aspiration, Satisfaction, Acceptance, Morale, etc.

Within the research group compiled category the Battelle Study or Environmental Evaluation System (EES) has gained some notoriety.

Ecology
- Species and populations
- Habitats and communities
- Ecosystems

Environmental pollution
- Water pollution
- Air pollution
- Land pollution
- Noise pollution

Esthetics
- Land
- Air
- Water
- Biota
- Manmade objects

Human interest
- Education-scientific significance
- Historical significance
- Cultural significance
- Mood-atmosphere significance

As it is obvious from the list, it is attempted to be a list of environmental characteristics. Yet, in the last category "Human interest" is included. The first three categories of the EES fall entirely in one subcategory of the Sheldon and hand list. Such an example, clearly shows how a difference in focus can generate lists with great differences.

Another individually composed scheme is offered by Robert Joyce (Table 9). While at a very general level, it offers an interesting comparison of several dimensions. The basic dimensions of the social environment are examined in several specific issue areas. In each cell, the measure (usually already obtainable), which Joyce feels might tap the respective intersection of the dimensions is included.

An interesting list compiled by 'experts' is the one generated at the Environmental Protection Agency's symposium on Quality of Life Indicators. The list was generated using the Delphi technique[5]. The method employed by the Environmental Protection Agency was actually a combination of Norman Dalkey's approach and Robert Joyce's list. The first rounds of the Delphi were designed to construct a list of factors which should be included in a quality of life inventory. Subsequent rounds were used in an attempt to gain an insight as to what measures would successfully tap each factor. The framers were interested in generating four quantities for each factor.

1. The Objective Measure - the level of objective conditions relating to the factor. Where possible, a scalar is provided. For example, measurements of various pollutant concentrations would be combined to an 'air quality' index.

2. The Subjective Measure - the satisfaction or dissatisfaction of the population with the objective conditions.

3. The correlation between the objective and subjective measures (more generally, some mapping of the relationship between the elements).

4. The relative importance (weighting) of the factors.

TABLE 9

Quality of Life Matrix Developed by Joyce (1972)

Manifestations or Aspects	Measures of the Quality of Life in the Area							
	Accessibility	Law Enforcement	Fire Protection	Health Care	Recreation	Education	Housing and Neighborhood	Income Production
Attitudinal	Modal Preference of Transportation	Juvenile Probations per pop. 20-21	Malicious False Alarms	Inoculable Diseases (under 13)	Vandalism $ per Park Acre	High School Dropout Rates	Elementary School Enrollment	% White Collar Employment
Societal.	Traffic Arrests/Total Street Miles	Juvenile Dependencies per pop. age 20-21	Arsons per 100 pop.	Suicides per 100,000 pop..	% pop. for Different Age Groups	Largest Ethnic percentage. % Non-white Enrollment	Elementary School Translency Rates	% Household with Wives Working
Political	Deficient Select System/ Total Select System Streets	Total Arrests per 100 pop.	Fire Engine Companies per 1000 pop.	% Public Hospital Care	5-yr. Proposed Cap. Improv. Program for Parks and Recreation	Voter Participation Rates	Non-residential Uses on Residential Parcels	% Children 4-5 Yrs. Age on Welfare
Economic	% By-passed Employment Due to Lack of Transportation	Losses Due to Burglary and Robbery	No. of Fires Greater than $1000. Loss	Deaths in 25-44 age Group	Private Recreation Investment per 100 pop.	% of People 25+ Yrs. Completed College	Median Imputed Rent per Median Income	Unemployment Rate
Physical	Median Work Trip Time by Private Transportation.	Part 1 Felonics per 100 pop.	Structural Fires per 100 Structures	Infant Mortality Rate	No. of Types of Facilities	Median 6th Crude Reading Achievement	% Stand Housing. % lacking Facilities	No. Householders under $1000. per Capita Income

These quantities could be used to generate a satisfaction index of the form:

$$I = f \left(\frac{\text{Actual Level of Factor}}{\text{Desired Level of Factor}} \right)$$

or

$$I = f \left(\frac{\text{Objective Measure}}{\text{Desired Subjective Measure}} \right)$$

These indices could then be used to form a quality of life index:

$$QOL = F (I_1, I_2, I_3 \ldots I_n).$$

Using the weights (category four above) this index might possibly take the form:

$$QOL = \left(\frac{W_1 I_1 + W_2 I_2 + W_3 I_3 + \ldots + W_n I_n}{n} \right)$$

Such procedures are rather straightforward and hardly complex. Yet, the Dalkey-EPA-Delphi Experiment demonstrated at least that experts were hesitant to perform such exercises. As the EPA Fellows state in a description of the experiment.

> The attempt to introduce the experiment and encourage the conference attendees to participate elicited a surprisingly hostile reaction from a substantial percentage of the group. There were two common themes underlying this dissent: (1) that individuals were (somehow) being "manipulated" by the Federal Bureaucracy, and (2) that the quick rating judgments asked for would (somehow) be professionally demeaning and unacceptable, despite the assurances to the contrary offered by Professor Norman Dalkey, based on his own research experience. The discussion of the experiment's validity and of various concerns about its conduct lasted for over an hour and at times became quite heated. In the end some eighty of the conference attendees (slightly over half) agreed to complete the weighting exercise, and their judgments were used in the data analysis that follows.

The half that did agree to participate were first asked to weigh the relative potency of the three major dimensions (Economic, Social/Political, Environmental) of indications. This was done by "splitting one-hundred" among the dimensions - (e. g. a score was assigned to each dimension such that $D_1 + D_2 + D_3 = 100$). The results showed the scores for each dimension being almost normally (in a statistical sense) distributed about the mean. In each case the mean was close to 33.

Fewer participants took part in an exercise to assign weights of relative importance to the factors within each dimension. This exercise, however, yielded greater differentiation among the factors.

As promising as such procedures might be, the reluctance of so many of the experts to participate makes possibly the strongest point. There simply is no consensus as to what elements are essential to a system of quality of life indicators. It is rather pointless to construct elaborate procedures for measuring, and comparing quality of life factors when no consensus exists as to what these factors are.

This is not to say that individuals of the population do not have ideas about such factors. The next two subsections will examine various methods of drawing such ideas from the population. The first will discuss the use of survey techniques. The second will discuss behavioral or objective methods.

B. Survey Methods for Obtaining Quality of Life Measures

Surveys which tap at least some quality of life measures have been going on for some time. Since the beginning of the 1930s, the Gallup poll has asked questions like "What do you feel is the major problem facing you today?" Since such questions provide a rather open-ended forum for the discussion of those factors which cause the individual a great deal of dissatisfaction, they tap quality of life dimensions. While such questions do not necessarily provide a comprehensive set of quality of life factors (they completely ignore the satisfaction section of the set), the responses provide some view of the nature of such a set. The answers, also, provide a demonstration of some of the conceptual problems already mentioned.

An attempt to deal exclusively with this type of information can be found in William Watts and Lloyd Free's publication, The State of the Action[6]. It was the major publication of a project designed in an attempt "to take the composite temperature and pulse of the American Body Politic". It is probably not desirable to examine this effort at length, yet several types of responses are worth considering.

When asked, "What do you feel is the most important problem facing you today?" several types of responses are given quite frequently. One such type is the very general response. It is likely to be of the form that basically things are getting worse, or to refer to a "basic moral decay" in the nation. While such responses do indicate a basic dissatisfaction, they do little to identify those elements primarily responsible for a feeling. On the other hand, more specific problems are of little additional aid. Consider the response, "Race". Such a response might indeed suggest possible indicators, or valid quality of life concerns. One might want to look at levels of integration. Such indicators are likely to come squarely up against Land's point of the indicator itself being non-normative. Some might feel society is 'better off' when integration increases, while others might believe that an increase would signal that things were 'worse off'.

Such an example, points squarely to some of the major research problems encountered when using a survey approach in constructing schemes for quality of life measures.

There is an assumption basic to the survey method that the population, and hence the sample, will possess a clear idea as to what affects the quality of life. Such an assumption is questionable. There are, at least, two exceptions to be made. First, the respondents are not likely to include elements which, for them, have already been addressed in some way. Possibly, the clearest example of such a point can be provided by viewing the work of Norman Dalkey and colleagues. Working with a group of college students, the researchers used the Delphi Technique to arrive at a list of quality of life factors. The students produced very significant psychological dimensions. These dealt primarily with the need for friendship, love, and challenge in life. Accordingly, there were elements which expressed dissatisfaction with loneliness and boredom. On the other hand, the students did not produce significant dimensions to deal with material comfort or health care concerns. It seems that it would be, at least, highly suspicious to maintain that the students were not interested in such concerns. What seems more reasonable is that their basic requirements for such needs had already been met.

From the decision-making or policy oriented perspective, a more general criticism can be leveled at survey proponents. This is that the population might not be sensitive to certain elements which clearly affect the quality of life because they have not yet reached a sufficient level of providing dissatisfaction. Such a case may be constructed for environmental concerns, in general. If we extend the notion, we can say with some certainty that if a large percentage of the population was becoming ill or dying from pollutants, the level of pollutants would be considered a quality of life factor. However, when the level of pollutants falls below the point at which it causes irritation or dissatisfaction, it is not likely to be perceived in a survey as a quality of life factor.

Such a case presents a real problem to the decision-maker. If at a certain level pollution becomes a quality of life factor, then it is important to monitor it. This argument is more appealing when there is some chance that the pollution level will rise to a significant point. When extended, however, such a notion undercuts the basic rationale for employing a survey method. Its implication is that the sample members aren't capable of identifying the factors which affect the quality of their life. Any suggestion that the decision-makers should provide their own ideas of unrealized factors or, as suggested previously, experts provide lists which include these factors, is met, at best, with suspicion, and, at worst, with cries of technocracy. Yet, it is important to remember that the expert is not providing his value system. Rather, he is attempting to assess the population's value systems.

Such problems have characterized survey attempts to construct quality of life or social indicator systems. In addition to the Watts and Free work, two other notable studies exist. The first is the Scandinavian study previously mentioned. As noted before, this study concentrated on a number of psychological factors derived primarily from Abraham Maslow's work. The questions for the survey were generated by the researchers along the lines of the redefined need categories. This represents a case in which the researchers had already, theoretically, determined what the appropriate factors were. The instrument was used only to provide measures of the factors within the population. Accordingly, it avoids to some extent the above mentioned problems. It may be noted, however, that the Scandinavian study did not include items to measure a number of dimensions which other QOL experts have included.

Another important study has been conducted by the Survey Research Center at the University of Michigan[']. This study contains elements of both using the instrument for identifying and measuring levels of hypothesized factors.

In conclusion, survey efforts fall prey to the same basic questions which plague quality of life and social indicator measures. This is true if one is convinced that surveys can serve as accurate measuring instruments, but are questionable in the role of identifying major components. Such a view falls clearly within the range of those tendencies criticized by the social indicator modellers. There is no underlying understanding of society which dictates the selection of proper factors. Accordingly, progress in the area of social indicator and quality of life measures can be expected to be slow. It can also be expected to lag behind the development of comprehensive lists by expert and other means.

C. Behavioral Attempts to Construct Quality of Life and Social Indicator Systems

As mentioned before, the problems facing policy decision-makers are varied. First, they must identify the factors which form a social indicator or quality of life measure system. After the appropriate factors are identified, operational definitions which allow measurement of the factors must be constructed. After reliable measures can be constructed, it is still necessary to weigh the relative importance of the factors, so that fluctuations in different factors can be compared. Given the state of the literature described this far, it is not surprising that such progress is yet to be made. However, some preliminary thinking has been done in this direction. An example of weighing quality of life factors was discussed before. In the case mentioned, experts guessed at the relative importance of a number of factors. Again, this is a method which is questionable, at best.

In an effort to make the weighing of factors more objective, other techniques have been described in the literature. Essentially when assigning a relative weighting, the expert makes a decision of how many units of one factor are worth how many units of another (on all other) factors. Such a procedure clearly resembles the behavior of an economic (market) decision. Consequently, several authors have discussed the possibility of extending notions from economic theory to the study of social indicators and quality of life measures. This section will examine two such discussions. Also, in both cases, the authors suggest methods of observing behavior to provide estimation procedures for relative factor weights. It must be noted that this discussion is very general and does not capture the full potential of either author's suggested schemes.

The first scheme is one which is drawn from Mancur Olson's monograph, On the Information for Assessing and Improving the Quality of Life[8]. In the major body of the work, Olson turns his attention to the poverty of already existent national accounts data. The argument presented is that a social indicator system is needed, not in addition to, but to refine economic indicators. A simple rendering of this argument makes the point. If say ten percent of the GNP was being spent to combat pollution (a diseconomy), the expenditure on the services and goods used to abate pollution would again be added to the GNP. Not only does this inflate the GNP, but, as Olson argues it should be substracted as it represents the cost of the pollution.

Before such considerations could be used to refine national economic accounts measures, some assessment must be made of the cost of pollution removal. As Olson points out, a very simple way to make such an assessment would be to ask how much one is willing to spend to rid himself of x units of pollution. However, there is a major difference between a respondents verbal willingness to spend and actual spending habits. Accordingly, it would be more appropriate to view actual spending habits (economic behavior). This is, of course, not easily done. Pollution abatement spending, for example, is a public good in that less pollution in the air is less pollution for everyone. The major problem in dealing with behavior on public good expenditure is twofold. On the one hand, were one to ask how much an individual is willing to pay for his share of a public good, he is likely to underrate his willingness. This is because the individual knows if others pay a larger share he will benefit anyway. Secondly, individuals do not provide public goods. Public institutions are responsible for this task. If one is interested in discovering the preference orderings of members of the population, then one cannot look to the behavior of public institutions.

To overcome these difficulties Olson proposes the "sample exclusion" method. This is a procedure whereby a random sample of users are forced to pay prices to receive the good (in return for compensatory increases in their income) and thereby to several of its output and worth to them. Such a scheme obviously has limitations. The indivisibility of public good must be made divisible. Where this is impossible, other procedures for indicators must be developed.

A second and much more elaborate scheme has been developed by Karl Fox[9] in Social Indicators and Social Theory: Elements of an Operational Theory[9]. Like Olson, Fox believes that the language of conventional economic theory can be extended into the social arena. In the volume he begins an effort which he hopes will "facilitate convergence toward an operational system or systems of social accounts and indicators". It is somewhat of a multi-disciplinary effort in that he employs economic notions to weld together a number of concepts developed in sociology. With this effort Fox formulates the measure Total Income (TI). Total Income is a sum of economic and social income. The value purportedly maps "a range of human concerns" into a scalar value. The scalar represents a measure of utility resultant from the individual's "total activity" in a given time period. It is advantageous to look briefly at the development of such a measure. A number of schemes developed in sociology are central to the construction of Fox's measure. The first is Talcott Parsons' "Media of Human Interchange"[10]. There are non-economic means of providing or denying reward. Fox's media include influence, political power, and value commitments, erotic pleasure; affect (including recognition and response); technological know-how and skill; ideology, conscience, reputation and faith. He makes two major points about the media. First, that they have "human capital" aspects or represent social bartering. Second, they tend to be related or confined to specific activities (i.e. faith to religious practice, political power to the policy, and erotic pleasure to a specific type of interaction).

The second major concept is one of behavior setting as developed by Roger Barker. These settings are the major geographical settings in which behavior occurs. One can easily think of such settings: work, church, social clubs, bars and pubs or wherever social interaction takes place. The major task involved is identifying such settings. In the volume mentioned, Barker does this for a small community. He also develops the notion of equivalence of behavior settings.

The third central concept was also developed by Barker[11]. It is called zone of penetration. It represents the level of involvement which one has in a behavior setting. In describing the concept Barker uses a set of six concentric circles. Going from the innermost circle to the outer rim we find the labels (1) single leader, (2) joint leader, (3) active functioning, (4) member or customer, (5) audience, and (6) onlooker. The reward in units of the social media is drawn from interaction within a certain behavior setting. As might be expected, the amount of reward is related to the zone of penetration (role) in which the individual takes part. Supposedly, the higher levels of penetration yield a greater reward.

Having developed this basic notion, Fox moves on to consider the amount of time an individual allocates to each respective behavior setting and each role. Assuming that the individual is maximizing his return in social media over all the relative behavior and time settings, we can draw the basic rationale behind the social aspect (SI) of the total income (TI) measure. Accordingly

$$U_{k,i,j} = f\, T_k(R_i, B_j)$$

Where the utility is a function of time T_k spent occupying role R_i in behavior setting B_j.

The Social Income will be the sum of rewards from all situations or:

$$\sum_{a}^{n} T_k \, (R_i, B_j)$$

Fox goes on to argue that the identification of behavior settings and roles in society will lend itself to the construction of such a system. Furthermore, he argues that such a system will have great flexibility in many ways. Once developed, actual time budget studies could be used to estimate relative weights of a given set of roles and behavior setting. (A unique weight for each ordered pair (R_i, B_j)). Once again, weights would be drawn from actual observed behavior.

There are, of course, shortcomings in both Olson's and Fox's scheme for the development of social indicator systems. Neither seem to rise much above the difficulties which plague the other (survey and expert generated schemes) efforts. Both lack comprehension. The Olson scheme, admittedly, cannot deal with absolutely indivisible commodities. Also there are not likely to be experimental techniques developed which would force an indivi-dual to buy happiness. Also, in Olson's case, an external source is needed to provide a list of what the 'social' commodities are.

In Fox's case, one might be able to arrive at some idea of how people spend their time. Consequently, it might yield insight as to which forms of social interaction are the most rewarding. Such insight, however, has little to do with a number of other concerns (environmental) addressed in the social indicator literature. Given that the techniques presented here are a long way from a workable system, they do provide alternate approaches to the problem of constructing a social indicator system.

VI.   CONCLUSION - SOCIAL INDICATORS AND WORLD MODELING

It is, I think, clear from the preceding discussion that the social indicator movement has not yet progressed to a point where it can be of direct input to global modeling efforts. That is to say, that the literature will not suggest a list of concerns to which decision-makers can focus their attention. There is no consensus as to what a social indicator or quality of life measure ought to be and less agreement as to what elements would be included in a compre-hensive set of measures or indicators. Meanwhile[1], global modellers are de-veloping approaches suited to their specific tasks[1]. Social scientists are be-coming aware of the problem; a recent UNESCO conference was devoted en-tirely to the development of social indicators for world models[2].

There are, however, several worthwhile items to be drawn from the litera-ture as it presently exists. Tables, such as those provided in this paper, indicate the type of concerns which will eventually be included in such a list. Also Mancur Olson's suggestions on the refinement of national accounts data could be partially incorporated into global models. One way this could be accomplished is by subtracting pollution abatement cost from the gross regional product. With a closer look at Olson's arguments, I'm sure, other such innovations could be made.

It seems in general that international attempts to collect social indicators data could do little to shed light on cross-cultural differences on the factors determining quality of life.

The movement, while almost a decade old, has yet a long way to go. As Gross predicted, it will be sometime before social indicators reach the point of even the most primitive economic indicators. What is left is still a challenge to model-builders and policy analysts alike. They must be able to generate intuitively those values which are important to monitor. This will have to be based on an educated guess derived from the modeler and analysts' view of the world.

FOOTNOTES

Sec. I.

[1] President's Research Committee on Social Trends, Recent Social Trends (Government Printing Office, 1933), p. XII - XIII.

[2] Wilbert Moore and Eleanor Sheldon, "Monitoring Social Change - A Conceptual and Programmatic Statement" in Proceedings of the Social Statistics Section, American Statistical Association, pp. 144 - 152.

[3] L. D. Wilcox, R. M. Brooks, G. M. Beal, G. E. Klonglan, Social Indicators and Societal Monitoring. Jossey-Bass Inc., San Francisco, 1972.

[4] Betram Gross, "The State of the Nation: Social Systems Accounting", pp. 270 - 271, Bauer (Editor), Social Indicators.

[5] Eleanor Bernert Sheldon and Robert Parke, "Social Indicators", Science Vol. 188, 16 May 1975, pp. 693 - 699.

Sec. II.

[1] Toward a Social Report (U.S. Department of HEW, 1969:97).

[2] Kenneth Land, "Social Indicator Models , an Overview", p. 20 in Kenneth Land and Seymour Spilerman (editors), Social Indicator Models (Rusell Sage Foundation; 1975).

[3] For example see the above mentioned authors: Kenneth Land, "On the Definition of Social Indicators" in The American Sociologist (Volume Six, November, pp. 322 - 325) and Mancur Olson, "Social Indicators and Social Accounts", in Socio-Economic Planning Science (Volume 2, pp. 325 - 346).

[4] This point has been made by a number of authors. See Kenneth Land, Social Indicator Models, p. 17.

[5] Douglas Harland, "The Content, Measurement, and Forecasting of Quality of Life", Volume I, Social and Human Analyses Branch, Canadian Department of Regional Economic Expansion.

[6] Otis Dudley Duncan, in "Toward Social Reportings: Next Steps." Paper Number 2 in Social Science Frontier Series. Rusell Sage Foundation, 1969.

[7] ibid, p. 9.

[8] Kenneth Land and Seymour Spilerman (eds.), Social Indicators Models, p. 17 (Rusell Sage Foundation, 1975).

[9] ibid, pp. 17 - 18.

[10] "Social Indicators Newsletters",March 1973, Number 1, published by the SSRC.

[11] ibid, p. 19.

[12] James A. David, "The Log Linear Analysis of Survey Replications" in Social Indicator Models, Kenneth Land and Seymour Spilerman (eds.).

[13] Robert Parke and Eleanor Sheldon, "The Need for Social Indicators" from the Proceedings of the 25th Annual Meeting of the Industrial Relations Research Association, p. 99 - 105; 99.

[14] See for example, Robert Parke and Eleanor Sheldon, "Social Statistics for Public Policy" a section entitled "Involvement of University Research" in the 1973 Social Statistics Section; Proceedings of the American Statistical Association, pp. 105 - 112; 111.

[15] ibid, p. 111.

Sec. III.

[1] Please see Appendix - for a complete listing of the publications and agencies from which they are obtainable.

[2] Ralph Brooks, "Social Planning and Societal Monitoring", pp. 22 - 26 in Social Indicators and Societal Monitoring.

[3] This discussion is being generated from two basic sources, Wolfgang Zapf, "Social Indicators, 1973: Comparison with Social Reports of Other Nations", and Natalie Rogoff Ransey, "Social Indicators in the United States and Europe: Comments on Five Country Reports". Both can be found in, "Social Indicators 1973: A Review Symposium",Roxann Van Dusen, ed., obtainable from the Social Science Research Council, Center for Coordination of Research on Social Indicators. I have freely merged these articles and accordingly, the entire discussion minus errors should be credited to them.

[4] ibid, p. 40.

[5] Whitepaper on National Life 1973: The Life and Its Quality in Japan, see appendix for citations.

[6] About Dimensions of Welfare: An Exploratory Analysis of a Comparative Scandinavian Study, see appendix for citations.

[7] See references in the Appendix.

[8] op cit, p. VIII.

[9] About Dimensions of Welfare (full citation in Appendix) Erik Allardt. A shorter discussion of the study can be found under the same title in Scandinavian Political Studies (Volume 7/1972).

[10] Abraham Maslow, Motivation and Personality. (Harper & Row, New York, 1970) see Chapter 7.

[11] Report on the World Social Condition, (United Nations Publication E/CN. 5/456; ST/SOA/110).

[12] Op Cit, p. 3.

[13] Ralph Pieris, "The Implantation of Sociology in Asia: printed in the International Social Science Journal, (Vol. XXI, No. 3).

[14] See reference in the Appendix.

[15] Davis Bobrow, "International Indicators", unpublished study. Obtainable from the Harold Scott Quigley Center for International Studies; University of Minnesota.

[16] The 32 member nations of the OECD are: Argentina, Australia, Austria, Belgium, Brazil, Canada, Denmark, Finland, Formosa, France, Germany, Greece, Iceland, India, Ireland, Israel, Italy, Japan, Lebanon, Netherlands, New Zealand, Norway, Pakistan, Portugal, Spain, Sweden, Switzerland, Turkey, United Kingdom, U.S.A., Venezuela, Yugoslavia.

Sec. IV.

[1] Anton Schmalz, et. al., "Social Indicators" a report to the National Science Foundation, New World Systems, July, 1972.

[2] Environmental Protection Agency, Office of Research and Monitoring, Environmental Studies Division, The Quality of Life Concept: A Potential New Tool for Decision-Makers, p. 1 - 4 (Government Printing Office, Washington, D.C.).

[3] Richard James, "Measuring the Quality of Life", The Wall Street Journal, May 18, 1972.

[4] Kenneth Hornback and Robert Shaw, Jr., "Toward a Quantitative Measure of the Quality of Life". Quality of Life Symposium, Environmental Protection Agency, August, 1972.

[5] Environmental Protection Agency, Office of Research and Monitoring, Environmental Studies Division, The Quality of Life Concept: A Potential New Tool for Decision Makers, p. I-10 (Government Printing Office, Washington, D.C.).

[6] Kenneth Kenniston, The Uncommitted, Harcourt Brace and World: New York, 1965. Or see same author, same publisher, 1968, Young Radicals: Notes on Committed Youth. Charles Reich, The Greening of America, Random House: New York, 1970. Also published in paperback by Bantam.

[7] The First and Second Discourses Jean-Jacques Rousseau, edited by Robert D. Masters, published by St. Martin's Press, New York, Picture appears on page 76.

[8] Justice William Douglas, appears as comment on Reich's Greening of America on the previously cited edition (ibid).

[9] Op cit., p. 35/58, "A Theory of Human Motivation", my apologies for the imprecise rendering of the argument.

Sec. V.

[1] Op. cit. The Quality of Life Concept. (P-I-14).

[2] Ira Whitman and Staff, "Design of an Environmental Evaluation System". Battelle-Columbus Laboratories, June 1971, obtainable by request, and "Toward Master Social Indicators", (Stanford Research Insitute, 1971).

[3] Dalkey, Rourke, Lewis and Snyder, Studies in the Quality of Life, (D. C. Heath and Company: Lexington, Mass. 1972) is a description of this effort. It will be discussed in more detail in the subsection on survey method.

[4] Eleanor Sheldon and Kenneth C. Land, "Social reporting for the 1970's: A review and programmatic statement". (Policy Sciences, 3 pgs., 137 - 151:146).

[5] This technique, especially in regard to Quality of Life Measures, is explained in Dalkey's work cited at the beginning of this section.

[6] William Watts and Lloyd Free, The State of the Nation, (Universe Books; New York, New York, 1973).

[7] Frank M. Andrews and Stephen B. Withey, "Developing Measures of Perceived Life Quality: Results from Several National Surveys,"Social Indicators Research 1(1974), 1 - 26. Frank M. Andrews,"Social Indicators of Perceived Life Quality",Social Indicators Research 1 (1974), 279 - 299.

[8] Mancur Olson, On the Information for Assessing and Improving the 'Quality of Life'. Unpublished Monograph.

[9] Karl Fox, Social Indicators and Social Theory: Elements of an Operational Theory. (Wiley and Sons, New York; 1974).

[10] Talcott Parsons, "Systems Analysis: Social Systems: in the International Encyclopedia of the Social Sciences: Vol. 15. (New York; The Free Press and Macmillan: 1968).

[11] Roger Barker, Ecological Psychology: Concepts and Methods for Studying the Environment of Human Behavior (Stanford University Press: 1968).

Sec. VI.

[1] Carlos Mallmann, "Quality of Life and Development Alternatives", Fundacion Bariloche, Bariloche, Argentina, Sept. 1975.

[2] UNESCO Seminar on "Social Aspects of Economic and Cultural Development and Working Out of Social and Cultural Indicators in World Models" Moscow, 8-11 June 1976. This conference was the third of a series "World Models: Images of Society and Man" organized by the International Social Science Council of UNESCO.

Appendix

NATIONAL SOCIAL REPORTING AND RELATED PUBLICATIONS

(Compiled by Nancy Carmichael, Social Science Research Council, Center
for Coordination of Research and Social Indicators, Washington, D.C.)

CANADA

- Canada. Economic Council.
  Economic Targets and Social Indicators: Eleventh Annual Review.
  Ottawa, Information, Canada, 1974.
  ($ 4.00 from: Information Canada, Ottawa KIA 0S9, or other I.C.
  bookstores.)
- Canada. Statistics Canada. Perspective Canada. Ottawa, 1974.
  ($ 6.75 (Canada); $ 8.10 (Other countries); from Information Canada,
  171 Slater Street, Ottawa, or other Information Canada bookstores).

FRANCE

- Delors, Jacques. Les indicateurs sociaux. Futuribles 15. Paris:
  S. E. D. E. I. S., 1971.
  (S. E. D. I. S., 52 rue des Saint-Pères, Paris.)
- France. Institut National de la Statistique et des Etudes Economiques
  Données sociales. Paris: Imprimerie Nationale. 1973.
  (18 F. from: INSEE, 29, quai Branly, 75700 Paris.)

GERMANY

- Germany (Federal Republic). Bundesministerium für Arbeit und
  Sozialordnung. Gesellschaftliche Daten 1973. Bonn: Presse- und Infor-
  mationsamt der Bundesregierung, 1973.
- Ballerstedt, Eike, and Wolfgang Glatzer. Soziologischer Almanach.
  SPES Arbeitspapiere No. 18, 1973. Frankfurt: Sozialpolitische For-
  schungsgruppe, J. W. Goethe-Universität, 1973.
- Germany (Federal Republic). Bundesminister für innerdeutsche Be-
  ziehungen. Bericht der Bundesregierung und Materialien zur Lage der
  Nation. Bonn, 1971, 1972.

GREAT BRITAIN

- Great Britain. Central Statistical Office. Social Trends, nos. 1-4
  (1970 - 1973). London: Her Majesty's Stationery Office, 1970, 1971,1972,
  1973. (Number 4 is L 2.90 from: HMSO, P.O. Box 569, London SEI
  9NH.)

JAPAN

- Japan. Economic Planning Agency. Whitepaper on National Life 1973:
  The Life and Its Quality in Japan. Tokyo: Overseas Data Service Co.,
  Ltd., 1973.
  ($ 12.00 from: Overseas Data Service Co., Ltd., c/o Mrs. Haneda,
  Shugetsu Building, 3-12-7, Kita-Aoyama, Minato-Ku, Tokyo, 107.)

MALAYSIA

- Malaysia. The Treasury. Economic report, 1974 - 1975. Kuala Lumpur, 1974. (available from: Mohd. Daud bin Abdul Rahman, J. S. M. Director General of Printing, Peninsular Malaysia, Chan Sow Lin Road, Kuala Lumpur 07-03)

SCANDINAVIA

- Allardt,Erik. About Dimensions of Welfare: An Exploratory Analysis of a Comparative Scandinavian Study. University of Helsinki, Research Group on Comparative Sociology. Research Reports, No. 1, 1973. (Research Group for Comparative Sociology, University of Helsinki, Mariankatu 10 A 13, Helsinki 17, Finland.)
- Norway. Statistisk Sentralbyra. Sosialt Utsyn. Oslo, forthcoming.
- Sweden. Statistiska Centralbryan. Social Utveckling. Stockholm forthcoming.
- "Review symposium on the 1968 Level of Living Survey in Sweden", Acta Sociologica, 16 (1973), 211 - 239.

UNITED STATES

- U.S. Department of Health, Education, and Welfare. Toward a Social Report. Washington: U.S. Government Printing Office, 1969. (Out of print)
- U.S. Office of Management and Budget. Social Indicators, 1973. Washington: U.S. Government Printing Office, 1973. ($ 7.80 from: Superintendent of Documents, U.S. Government Printing Office, Washington, D.C. 20402.)
- Van Dusen, Rosann A., ed., Social Indicators, 1973: A Review Symposium. N.W., SSRC, 1974. ($ 3.00 from: Social Science Research Council, 605 Third Avenue, New York, 10016.)

INTERNATIONAL

- United Nations Economic and Social Council. Social Indicators: Current national and international activities in the field of social indicators and social reporting: Report of the Secretary-General. New York: United Nations, January 1975. (U.N.Doc. E/CN. 5/518. General distribution: free, from: United Nations, N.Y., 19917.)
- Organization for Economic Cooperation and Development. List of Social Concerns Common to Most OECD Countries. Paris: OECD, 1973. ($1.00 from: OECD, 1750 Pennsylvania Avenue, N.W., Washington, D.C. 20006.)

6

ORIENTORS OF NONROUTINE BEHAVIOR

Hartmut Bossel

0 - INTRODUCTION: ORIENTATION OF ACTOR SYSTEMS

Human actor systems - individual and collective actors - are capable of an amazing variety of behavioral modes. While some of these modes clearly represent unreflected application of stored behavioral programs, and some result from random choices, others are obviously the end product of complex cognitive processes. This paper is concerned with the latter - here termed nonroutine behavior.

The fact that nonroutine behavior of individual and societal actors is to a great extent intuitively predictable by other actors - else human interactions would be utter confusion - suggests that behavioral decisions are oriented with respect to parameters which are shared by, or at least known to, participants in interactions. We here term these orienting parameters "orientors", in order to avoid some of the connotations commonly attached to the various types of normative parameters playing a role in the behavior of human actor systems: norms, values, goals, objectives, attitudes, priorities, preferences, etc., and in order to have a more general label for all of them.

This report is about the "orientors of nonroutine behavior". An attempt is made to develop a coherent, albeit at the moment discursive theoretical approach and to deduce - and empirically validate - a set of "basic orientors", i. e. a set of orienting dimensions guiding the behavior of human actor systems.

Orientors are meaningful to a system only if the state of the system itself, and that of the environment relevant to the system (i. e. the "system and environmental state") can be assessed with respect to the orientors. This requires first that the system perceive the system and environmental state through a set of indicators, i. e. perceived state variables. The composition of this set may change from moment to moment. It requires second that the perceived system and environmental state can be mapped on the relevant orientor space. The report addresses itself to these questions.

There have been several motivations for this research: First, the desire to improve the description, the understanding, and the simulation of the behavior of human actor systems. This need is evident from the shortcomings of present-day economic and global models. Second, to improve the theoretical base for data collection on societal systems (e. g. social, political, and economic indicators). If societal behavior is indeed guided by a set of orientors and derivative orientors, then a corresponding set of indicators must be observed. Third, to provide a prototype computer-assisted policy analysis tool allowing the assessment of likely priorities and preferences for a given (or projected) system and environmental state with respect to issues, scenarios, and alternatives; i.e. a tool to test not the economic or technological, but the cognitive-normative feasibility of proposed policies and scenarios.

1 - ROUTINE VS. NON-ROUTINE BEHAVIOR

For the purposes of our discussion, it is useful to distinguish between routine and non-routine behavior. While the former requires comparatively little information processing, the latter involves a fairly complex sequence of cognitive processes. As an illustration, consider the decision processes required of a driver approaching a busy intersection: if the intersection is protected by a traffic light, the "green" or "red" signal will evoke an unconditional routine "go" or "stop" response; if the intersection is unprotected, a non-routine response is required. In this case the driver must go through a fairly complicated process of assessing a complex dynamic situation, making projections about vehicle trajectories, assessing accelerations, braking distances and possible impacts, while orienting his actions with respect to an overall goal of something like "getting across the intersection quickly and above all, safely, while not creating a nuisance or hindrance for others". In view of the discussion below, we note in this goal statement the implicit reference of the driver's decision-making to (1) his own safety, (2) his freedom of movement, (3) his efficiency of movement, (4) psychological parameters such as self-esteem, and (5) similar reference dimensions concerning other drivers ("participating systems") approaching the intersection. These dimensions will here be referred to as "orientors" of non-routine behavior.

Certainly the distinction between routine and non-routine behavior cannot generally be unequivocally made by an external observer. Even if - in a given situation - the information-processing were completely known, one would still find a great number of "routine" components even in a non-routine decision situation. Thus the following characterizations of routine and non-routine behavior should be viewed merely as convenient idealizations.

Routine behavior

In routine behavior,
- the situation is familiar to the actor system, and
- a suitable response is available and can be recalled and applied.
The first requirement necessitates a pattern recognition ability, the second the storage and recall of an appropriate response program. The process follows the sequence of steps: (Fig. 1).

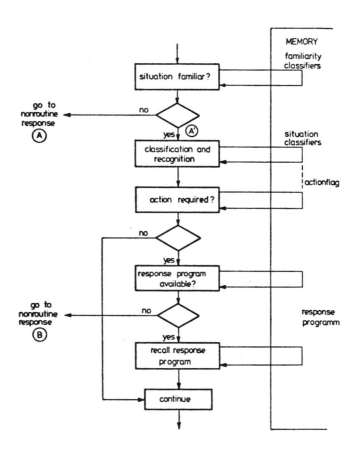

Fig. 1 - ROUTINE BEHAVIOR:
Information processing sequence.

(1) The perceived situation is classified as "familiar" or "unfamiliar" using classifiers in the memory. If "unfamiliar", go to "non-routine behavior".

(2) If "familiar", then find the appropriate classification by reference to classifiers in the memory. This represents the recognition of the situation.

(3) If the recognized situation pattern carries an "action flag", then determine if an appropriate response program exists in memory. If such a program does not exist, go to "non-routine behavior".

(4) If an appropriate response program is available, then recall and apply the program.

(5) Monitor the resulting changes in the environment (feedback).

Routine behavior constitutes the greater part of daily behavior. Examples are: the driver's response at a traffic light; avoidance reactions; enforcement of rules and regulations; adherence to social and organizational roles and norms; etc. If the classifiers and response programs available to a system are known, a reasonably accurate response prediction becomes possible. In fact, empirical knowledge of past behavior suffices for the prediction of routine behavior, as long as it truly remains routine. The success of macroeconomic theories and of behaviorism are examples; the failures of these approaches point to misapplications to non-routine behavior.

Non-routine behavior

In non-routine behavior,
- the situation is not familiar to the actor, and
- a suitable response is therefore not available in the memory, but must be generated ad hoc.

The first implies either that the situation is indeed "new" to the actor, or that he fails to recognize it as familiar. In both cases at least a provisional classification of the situation is required for the guidance of the problem-solving process for the generation of a suitable response. The complete process requires the sequence of steps (Fig. 2):

(1) The perceived situation is classified as "familiar" or "unfamiliar" using classifiers in the memory. If "familiar", go to "routine behavior".

(2) If "unfamiliar", a provisional classification is made and possibly tested and revised. An information search is initiated in an attempt to overcome uncertainty.

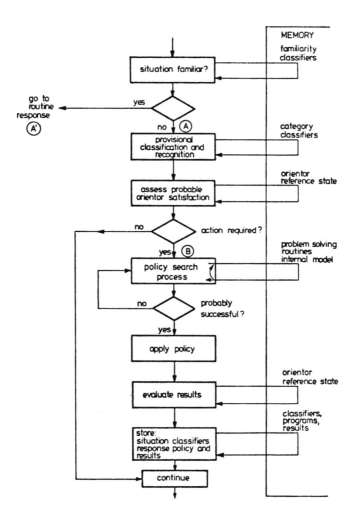

Fig. 2 - NONROUTINE BEHAVIOR:
Information processing sequence.

(3) On the basis of this provisional recognition of the situation the present and perhaps also the possible future orientor satisfaction states are assessed.

(4) If violations occur, or must be expected, a policy search process is initiated, using the expected orientor state as guiding input. The quality and sophistication of the policy search process may reach from immediate application of a randomly chosen policy to careful evaluation of alternative policies using projections by an internal model and assessments of corresponding orientor satisfaction states over a relevant time horizon and spatial horizon (consideration of effects on other systems).

(5) In either case the measure of success is the orientor satisfaction state either attained through actual policy application and possibly trial-and-error refinement, or projected on the basis of projective policy applications, followed by actual application of the selected policy.

(6) If the response led to a satisfactory orientor state, it may be transferred to the stock of routine response programs, together with the appropriate situation classifiers.

It is trivial but important to note that meaningful non-routine behavior (including a trial-and-error approach) can only occur by reference to what have here been called "orientors": standards, norms, goals, objectives, values, basic needs, etc. The possible successes of unoriented non-routine behavior can be nothing more but chance successes. Orientors are thus key elements of non-routine behavior; more space will be devoted to them below. In routine behavior orientors are not needed, as available response programs are applied without concern for their consequences. (As soon as consequences are indeed considered and changes in response programs take place we enter the realm of non-routine behavior.)

Examples of non-routine decision-making are: the driver's behavior at an unprotected busy intersection; search behavior and most scientific research; behavior in emergencies; adaptation to a rapidly changing environment such as changes in consumer behavior or structural change in industry. A better understanding of non-routine behavior is in fact crucial for a better understanding of the complex processes of societal dynamics. Orientors as the basic reference dimensions of behavior provide a certain amount of regularity and predictability in this otherwise confusing picture.

Outline of the paper

Improvements in forecasting methods, in global models, and in policy analysis and impact assessment are contingent upon a better understanding and description of the nonroutine behavior of human actor systems. The following is an attempt to explain and describe nonroutine behavior in terms of the system's orientation by reference to a set of decision dimensions (orientors) (Sec. 2). The set of basic orientors guiding fundamental behavioral changes is of particular significance (Sec. 3).

Finally, the approach requires a mapping of the indicator state representing the system and environmental state on orientor space (Sec. 4). The overall concept is implemented in an interactive computer program presented in Ch. 15.

2 - COMPONENTS OF NON-ROUTINE BEHAVIOR

It is evident from the preliminary discussion of Sec. 1 that the major task of the non-routine decision-making process is the assessment of actual and projected system states with respect to a set of system orientors. The orientor set will for the moment remain unspecified; it will be fully discussed in Sec. 3. The assessment procedure then requires in particular (Fig. 3)
- a perceived system state;
- a set of orientors;
- a mapping function which takes the perceived system state into a corresponding orientor state.

The remainder of this section will be devoted to an informal discussion of these notions; more detailed accounts are presented in the following sections.

Perceived system state

Decisions are made and actions are taken upon consideration of the perceived system state. This state may indeed be an inaccurate and incomplete representation of the real system state. It may contain a set of quantifiable physical state variables ("temperature is 23 deg. C") as well as fuzzy and/ or aggregate quantities ("feeling hungry"); the system state may also be represented by a coherent pattern of individual state variables ("exciting life"), whose individual components would be meaningless if considered individually and out of context.

Those state variables entering into the system's state perception are here termed indicators, irrespective of whether they are quantifiable or not: Indicators are state variables selected to represent the system and environmental state. Except for trivially simple systems, the indicator set is therefore a subset of the set of all observable system and environmental state variables. The perception of system and environment is reflected by the choice; while the chosen set of indicators reciprocally limits the range of perception about the system and its environment. The behavioral response of the system is therefore conditional on the indicator set: problems not perceived cannot be attacked and solved (cf. Ch. 5 on social indicators).

An indicator is characterized by its (state variable)dimension and by its perceived state as determined by some quantitative or qualitative measure. Coherent sets of indicators related to a given system aspect are referred to as issues. Membership in an issue set will normally be a loose one, i. e. there is redundancy; indicators can be replaced by others; different

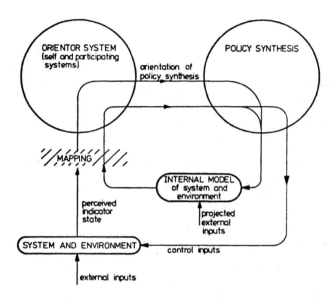

Fig. 3 - ORIENTATION OF NONROUTINE BEHAVIOR

Conditions in the system and the environment are perceived via a set of
indicators. The perceived indicator state is mapped on the relevant orientor
space. The resulting (dis)satisfaction vector guides the choice of control
policy. Before application to the real system, likely results of the chosen
control policy are projected using the internal model. The projected state
changes are again mapped on orientor space in order to produce a new
(dis)satisfaction vector which serves to correct the control policy originally chosen. When the projected dissatisfaction is acceptable, the control
policy is applied to the real system.

indicators are entered at different times and under different circumstances. As an example, consider the indicators belonging to the issue set "exciting life".

It is worth stressing that generally the perceived system state of an actor also contains perceptions about the present and projected system states of other actors and their environment in addition to perceptions about system state and environment of the actor's own system. Those other systems which play a role in the actor's decision-making are termed <u>participating systems</u>.

Orientor state

In the case of routine behavior, the perceived indicator pattern is by definition familiar and a routine response program is available. By contrast, in non-routine behavior the meaning of a perceived indicator state for the operational requirements of the system has to be determined first (state analysis), after which an appropriate response has to be found (policy synthesis) by reference to these operational requirements (see Bossel 1976). For the moment we will not go deeper into the nature of these requirements.

The actor systems which concern us here may potentially perceive a very large number of indicators representing their system state. However, elementary requirements of efficiency of information processing in the state analysis and policy synthesis processes would indicate that the number of orientors being used in a given non-routine decision must be relatively small.

For the state analysis and policy synthesis processes to take place, the perceived system state (i. e. indicator state) must be mapped on the orientor space relevant to the context. As an example, the non-routine decisions of a national actor in the fields of energy policy, national defense, or economic policy require different orientor sets. In issues transcending these limited contexts, however, (e. g. a national emergency), recourse must be made to more basic orientor sets. Obviously one may perceive of a whole orientor hierarchy reaching from very specific orientors which can only be applied to a very limited context (e. g. "speed limit on this road is 100 km/h"; "No smoking in this room") to much more general orientors (e. g. "national self-reliance"). The degree of context-relatedness thus determines the level in the orientor hierarchy. The less routine a given decision situation is, the more it requires the consultation of more context-free and more general orientors (Fig. 4).

In order to insure consistency of orientation, the orientors on the lower levels of the orientor hierarchy must be derivable by application of higher level orientors to specific contexts. Evidently this process stops at the

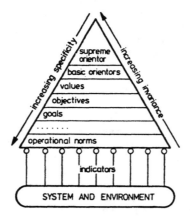

Fig. 4 - ORIENTOR HIERARCHY

Orientors near the bottom of the hierarchy are highly specific, variable, and potentially numerous. They are derivable, for given contexts, from a few more general, and practically invariant, basic orientors near the top of the hierarchy.

top of the hierarchy, where the overall reason for being and behaving of the system (perhaps: "viability") would be located as the supreme orientor. However, this supreme orientor is too general to be of much use in attempts to operationalize the orientor concept. Our study will therefore deal with orientors on the next lower levels.

Of primary concern to our discussion will be the decomposition of the supreme orientor into the dimensions of the basic orientors on the next lower level of the orientor hierarchy. These are the basic operational dimensions which must - in the given overall system and environmental context - enter the decision-making process in order to assure satisfaction of the supreme orientor. Basic orientors have dimensions such as: satisfaction of physical/physiological needs, security, freedom of action, efficiency of control, adaptivity. The set of basic orientors will be discussed more fully in Sec. 3.

If the set of basic orientors is complete, then all orientors guiding the system behavior on lower levels of the hierarchy can be derived by applying increasingly more specific contexts at each successively lower level. In a simulation attempt this can be implemented in two ways:
  (1) The hierarchy of orientors is derived once and for all and updated as necessary. Orientors are then available at all levels of the hierarchy for all conceivable decision cases.
  (2) Derivations are made ad hoc when needed, by direct reference to the basic orientors.

The first approach has been practiced elsewhere (e.g. Zange meister 1975); it requires foresight, advance analysis, and storage and burdens the analysis with considerable inflexibility. Our work takes the second approach; it therefore calls for deduction capability in the computer routines used. We have developed a special routine for this purpose (see the contributions by Rechenmann and Müller-Reißmann in this volume).

Non-routine decision-making requires orientors for two different functions:
  1 - to define a reference state for the guidance of decision-making;
  2 - to evaluate real or projected system states.
The first function (orientor reference state) requires the availability or derivability of the orientor hierarchy (just discussed); the second (orientor satisfaction state) demands a mapping of the perceived system state (indicator state) on orientor space; i.e. an answer to the question "How much does a given improvement of indicator state I_i contribute to an improvement of orientor satisfaction with respect to orientor dimension O_j?" These issues will be dealt with in more detail later.

A given actor system can rarely ever make a decision without simultaneously considering the orientor systems and orientor satisfaction states of other actor systems in addition to his own. The concerns of these 'participating systems' will generally carry a different degree of importance (weight) in his decision than his own system. <u>Participating system weights</u> are therefore important decision parameters.

Equally important parameters of behavior are the <u>orientor weights</u> attached to a given orientor dimension on a given level of the <u>orientor hierarchy</u>. Our analysis will deal with weights attached to the basic orientor dimensions; weights on lower levels can be derived from these.

<u>Mapping indicators on orientors</u>

The state analysis and policy synthesis processes require mappings of the indicator state on the orientor states of the participating systems. These mappings must take into account the following:

(1) A given indicator may load on several orientor dimensions simultaneously (e. g. "energy consumption" loads on both "material standard of living" and "environmental pollution").

(2) Several indicators may load on a given orientor dimension simultaneously (e. g. "energy consumption" and "personal income" both load on "material standard of living").

(3) The loadings themselves may be subject to change with the indicator level (e. g. a loaf of bread is a life-and-death issue to a starving person; it is of little importance to an overfed individual).

(4) Measures of orientor satisfaction should be based on those orientor dimensions that are closest to the respective (physically measurable) indicator dimensions in order to avoid errors introduced in aggregation estimates. This means obtaining satisfaction scales directly for the indicators (e. g. at the level of calorie intake per day).

(5) Neither the indicator satisfaction scales nor the loadings will in general be linear functions of the system state (e. g. with increasing calorie intake per day, the satisfaction scale ranges from "unacceptably low" to "very satisfactory" to "unacceptably high". Similarly, the loading on the "physical needs" orientor will simultaneously range from "extremely high" to "low" to "high" again.)

(6) The satisfaction scales are functions of the indicator state and in particular of the history of the system state (changes in aspiration levels, tolerances, and thresholds, etc.).

The mapping of the indicator state on the orientor state is thus a nonlinear function of the system state, modified by influences of the history of the system state. The present paper is concerned with the former, a companion paper with the latter (Chs. 16, 17). The concepts of the indicator/ orientor mapping developed in this paper apply at all orientor levels;

however, they will here be mainly applied to the mapping of indicators on the basic orientors. For this, the intermediate levels of the hierarchy of orientors will not be considered explicitly.

Section summary

As an introduction to the material in the following sections, the major components in a concept of non-routine decision-making have been presented. The concept is summarized in Figs. 3 and 4;the major components are the following:

(1) A system state is perceived through the observation of (exact or fuzzy) indicators, certain subsets of which may form issue sets relating to particular contexts.

(2) The indicator states are mapped on context-related orientors to produce an indication of orientor satisfaction.

(3) Factors involved in the mapping are the relative weights of the orientors used in the context, the state of each indicator involved, and the loadings of indicators on orientors.

(4) The mapping relationships depend on the state of the system and on the history of system state and are generally nonlinear.

(5) Orientors can be organized in a hierarchy with a single supreme orientor at the top and a usually large number of operational orientors at the bottom. The operational orientors are normative counterparts of the observed indicators.

(6) Lower levels of the hierarchy have more specific orientors. The specificity is obtained by applying more general orientors to more and more specific contexts.

(7) Of particular importance are the orientors just below the supreme orientor, i.e. the basic orientors. The orientor criteria and weights on the lower levels follow from them, though often nonuniquely.

(8) For implementation of the concept an explicit representation of the intermediate hierarchy between operational and basic orientors is not necessary; non-routine decisions can be dealt with by direct mapping of indicator states on basic orientors.

(9) Intermediate or operational orientors can be deduced from basic orientors in an ad hoc fashion when required.

(10) The decision outcome depends partly on the relative weights attached to the different basic orientors. This weight distribution is system-dependent.

(11) An actor system generally has to consider the indicator and orientor satisfaction states of other systems with whom it inter- acts ("participating systems") in its own decision-making.

(12) The processes of state analysis and policy synthesis require the orientor concept in two different functions: (1) to provide a reference state (the aspiration levels of the operational orientors); and (2) to determine the orientor satisfaction resulting from actual or projected system states.

(13) In projective assessments of future orientor satisfaction resulting from probable indicator states the time horizon of assessment ("future weight function") is a crucial parameter.

3 - <u>ORIENTORS</u>

<u>Orientor hierarchy and basic orientors</u>

In Sec. 2 we have postulated the existence of an orientor hierarchy which is capable of supplying very specific orientors for very specific contexts for each of the perceived indicator variables from increasingly more gene- ral orientors on higher levels of the hierarchy, which are applicable to more general contexts. The most fundamental decisions are then made by reference to the orientors at the top of the hierarchy. At the very top the hierarchy reduces to a single supreme orientor (such as system viability) which would be applicable in an y and all circumstances. (The kamikaze pilot is no excep- tion: here the supreme orientor "viability of the state" appears in place of "personal viability").

For our purposes the supreme orientor is much too general to be of much use. We are interested in the next level of orientors ("basic orientors") which follow from the confrontation of the supreme orientor with the basic operational capabilities and limitations of the system and the essential characteristics of the environment. Thus the set of basic orientors derives from the question: "Given the global features of the system and of its environ- ment, what basic orienting dimensions must the system refer to in its non- routine behavior, and in particular in fundamental behavioral decisions in order to fulfil the global instruction of the supreme orientor?"

This process is repeated on all levels of the orientor hierarchy. On the next level, for instance, more specific orientors are derived from application of one or several of the basic orientors to a more restricted system and environ- mental context. Finally, at the bottom of the hierarchy, one orientor (operating norm) is derived for each indicator (or perhaps a fuzzy aggregate orientor for each issue) by application of orientors on higher levels to individual indicators or issues representing the perceived state of the system, resp. of its environment.

The foregoing is not meant to imply that systems have a fully derived and updated orientor hierarchy available to them at all times. In reality, this will rarely be the case, although some industrial and military organizations may come close. What instead we mean is that for any indicator or issue which may at some time confront the system, appropriate orientors can be derived by reference to higher level orientors, and in particular, if necessary, by reference to the basic orientors. We are thus talking of a potentially constructable, not an actual hierarchy of orientors.

There is an extremely important consequence inherent in the concept of the orientor hierarchy: The time constants of validity of each orientor increase as one moves up the hierarchy. Time constants at the very bottom of the hierarchy, where indicator sets and indicator levels are constantly changing, are also small. As orientors on higher levels are applicable to more general and varied contexts, their time constant of validity also increases. The time scales of the basic orientors are determined by the factors which determine the basic orientors themselves: the overall characteristics of the system and of the environment and the supreme orientor. As the time scale of the supreme orientor is at least of the order of the life-time of the system, it will be too long to cause significant changes in the basic orientors. All changes in the basic orientors, if any, must therefore come from fundamental changes in the system itself, resp. of its environment. If there are no fundamental changes in the global character of either the system or its environment over the system's life-time, then the set of basic orientors remains constant[+]. In any case, if one looks for invariants, or quasi-invariants in a system's behavior, one has to look at the level of the basic orientors. They are the factors which ensure system viability (or more generally, satisfaction of the global requirement of the supreme orientor) despite constant and even drastic changes in system and environmental state.

There is an apparent contradiction in this argument which must be discussed: how can quasi-constant orientor sets characterized by very long time constants deal successfully, through the orientor hierarchy, with the often very rapid changes in the system and environmental state having very short time constants? The answer lies in the threshold feature of orientors, which introduces a highly nonlinear coping capability into the system: as indicator states surpass certain thresholds beyond which an orientor is no longer applicable, this threshold violation is reported to the next higher orientor level. Given the new system and environmental conditions, new orientors at the lower

---

[+] The life cycle of a butterfly from larva to pupa to adult is an example for abrupt changes in the individual global system characteristics, with resulting changes in the basic and derived orientors.

level may become activated in order to fulfil the still unchanged requirement of the higher orientor level. The system may thus pass into entirely different modes of behavior without changing any of the orientors at the higher levels of the hierarchy.

As an example, consider a person on a cold day in a room heated by an electric heater. An operational-level orientor would tell him to "keep warm by turning up the heater". This orientor is applicable as long as there is a supply of electric current. Now assume a power failure: obviously the operational orientor is now inappropriate, and the system's actions have to be oriented by the next higher orientor level in conjunction with an appraisal of the system and environmental state. The orientor on the next level merely prescribes "keep warm"; in conjunction with the current state this may give rise to a new operational orientor "keep warm by putting on that sweater". Note that an entirely different mode of behavior has resulted by reference to a higher level orientor ("keep warm") which did not change at all.

It is thus the i n v a r i a n t or quasi-invariant orientors of the upper levels of the orientor hierarchy which enable a system to respond adaptively and often very dynamically to environmental challenges by activating often totally different modes of behavior. It is impossible to understand, let alone predict, the vagaries of non-routine system response without a knowledge of the upper level orientors, and in particular the basic orientors. It is for this reason that we focus our attention on the basic orientors: they are the key to understanding system behavior.

The concepts discussed are equally valid for autonomous and non-autonomous systems, except that for autonomous systems, the supreme orientor will usually be something like "viability", while for non-autonomous systems it is usually a task set by the super-system in which the system is embedded (e. g. "supply fuel to the furnace" for a fuel pump or "collect data on the economy" for a statistics office). However, the term "basic orientors" will in this report be used generally to denote orientors directly derived from the supreme orientor "viability" (or its equivalent) of autonomous systems.

For the operationalization of the concept, it is important to obtain basic orientors which are
- complete; i. e. they must be able to account for all normative aspects of behavior;
- irreducible, in the sense that they cannot be mapped onto even more basic orientors except the supreme orientor;
- each independent of the other orientors in the set, in the sense that none of the basic orientors can be represented by a combination of other basic orientors.

Properties of orientors

Orientors are characterized by (1) a dimension, (2) an aspiration level, and (3) thresholds. In the following, we consider only "active" orientors, i. e. those that currently apply in a given context.

Orientor dimensions are labels characterizing aggregates of system and environmental state variables. These aggregates are composed of the (weighted) contributions of all indicators which are connected to the orientor via the orientor hierarchy. On the lowest level of the operational orientors, the appropriate orientor dimension is that of the corresponding indicator.

For the guidance of decision-making, and the evaluation of real or projected system states, the desired system and environmental state with respect to the orientor dimension must be expressed by some aspiration level. The higher the degree of aggregation of the orientor dimension is, the fuzzier will be the definition of this aspiration level. A clear definition of the minimum aspiration level is possible through the threshold concept:
> The minimum aspiration level of an orientor is reached when all connected orientors on the next lower level are within their respective permissible range between thresholds.

(since this statement is recursive, it implies that all connected active orientors on all lower levels of the hierarchy are within their permissible ranges).

Once the minimum aspiration level has been reached for a given orientor, the aspiration level can be expected to rise in accordance with the rules of cognitive dissonance theory and its extensions (see the article by E. Gruber in this volume).

With changes in the system and environmental state, the orientors in the active orientor set also change. (In the example given previously, the orientor "keep warm by turning up the heater" became inactive after the power failure, while the orientor "keep warm by putting on a sweater" became active.) In the following, the terms orientor, orientor hierarchy, etc. are used to denote the currently active orientors, resp. the active orientor hierarchy etc.

In addition to dimension and aspiration level, orientors are characterized by lower and/or upper thresholds, beyond which the aggregate variable corresponding to the orientor dimension should not fall, resp. rise. In many cases this will simply be "satisfactory/unsatisfactory" classification. An "unsatisfactory" classification or threshold violation of an orientor will only result in a threshold violation of the next higher orientor if all possible means of substitute satisfaction are exhausted (see Fig. 5). (In the previous example, if the power goes off, and if there is no sweater, and if there is no possibility of leaving the cold room, then there will be an unsatisfactory state with respect to the higher level orientor "keep warm".)

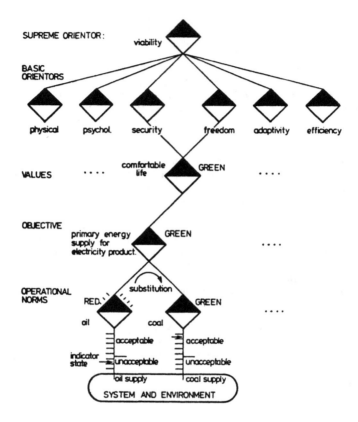

Fig. 5 - CHANGE OF BEHAVIORAL MODE THROUGH LOWER LEVEL
ORIENTOR SWITCHING

The example illustrates the segment of the orientor hierarchy connecting
to the state indicators "fuel oil supply" and "coal supply" for the production of electricity. The production of electricity loads strongly on the value
"comfortable life", which again is related to the basic orientors "security"
and "freedom" of the individual. As the "oil supply" indicator drops to an
unacceptable level, the corresponding operational orientor signals the threshold violation to the connected orientor on the next higher level ("secure
fuel supply for electricity production"). In the given context, this orientor
can be satisfied by switching to coal. Hence orientors on higher levels remain unaffected.

Basic orientors of human actor systems

We use the term "human actor system" to denote systems in which human behavior plays a major role, i. e. nation actors, political actors, interest groups, organizations, and individuals as a special case. Our task is to contribute to the formalized description of such systems, in particular computer simulation of aspects of their behavior. A knowledge of the basic orientors of these systems is crucial to this work.

We have stated before that basic orientors are determined by the supreme orientor, and by the global characteristics of the system and the environment.

In the case of human actor systems, the supreme operator is here taken as "viability". The environment is that of the socioecology with a relatively long time constant of change. The human systems component has the extremely long time constant of genetic change, while that of groups, political actors and other collective systems potentially introduces more rapid changes.

Basic orientors of human actor systems have been studied before under various headings such as "basic needs" (Maslow 1954), "quality of life vector" (Dalkey 1972), "terminal values" (Rokeach 1973), "basic needs and values" (Christensen and Nørgaard 1974), "measures of perceived life quality" (Andrews and Withey 1974), "human space" (Mallmann 1975) and others. The present research owes much in particular to the "basic needs" concept of Maslow 1954. However, for the purpose at hand it was considered necessary to independently obtain a list of basic orientors satisfying the criteria of completeness, irreducibility and independence mentioned above.

Three approaches were used for this purpose:
- clustering of a collection of some 200 concepts taken from decision-making contexts in human actor systems;
- consideration of the basic operational requirements of an autonomous system in a difficult environment (robot);
- analysis of the global response and constraint characteristics of an autonomous system in a difficult environment.

The results obtained could be mapped on each other (except for the psychological dimension) and in this way provided a check on the completeness.

The majority of the concepts used in the clustering approach were obtained by analyzing some 30 political and some 15 individual, resp. social decision-making contexts. The list of concepts was augmented by the terms in the lists of Maslow (1954), Dalkey (1972), Rokeach (1973) and Christensen and Nørgaard (1974).

Taking a completely different point of view, an attempt was made in the second approach to consider the question of basic orientors as a design problem by specifying the set of basic orientors required to allow hypothetical robots to survive and prosper in a difficult environment. The questions which had to be answered in the thought experiment were as follows (Bossel 1976, p. 454):

"Assume that you can construct a robot which will have the physical and information processing capabilities to survive (until it breaks down by material wear and tear) in an environment containing the resources necessary for its survival, but in diffuse form.

(1) What systems features would the robot have to possess if it were to survive as a single individual?

(2) What systems features would a group of more or less identical robots have to possess individually and collectively in order to survive as a group, in particular under circumstances (diffuse resources, adverse environment) which require group action or specialization for survival?

(3) What systems features would be required individually and collectively if two or more groups of robots (whose members have distinct features making them not easily interchangeable between groups) were to survive while competing for the same resource?"

Obviously this approach will not yield any emotional or affective components; however, the list of orientors found corresponded to the functional subset of the orientors identified in the clustering approach.

In the third approach, the topology of the system response and of the constraints were considered. An attempt was made to define global performance indexes which capture the basic dimensions of the global behavior of the system. The approach is in the spirit of stability criteria and performance measures of optimal control theory, resilience indexes (Holling 1973, Grümm 1976) and the topological approach of catastrophe theory to global systems behavior (Thom 1975). The reasoning behind this approach is the following: If it were possible to describe the global features of system behavior completely by a complete, irreducible and independent set of performance indexes, basic orientors could be defined in terms of these. If valid global indexes could be defined, this would have the important consequence that a quasi-objective mapping of the system state on the basic orientor state would be possible (as weighting functions have to be chosen in these indexes, the approach is not fully objective). In our present approach we have not followed up on this possibility; instead the mapping of indicator state on orientor state is established by subjective assessment (see below).

The global measures of system behavior were derived by considering the question:

"Given the topology of actual and possible behavior, and the topology of actual and possible constraints and perturbations in the system and environmental state space, what mathematical combinations of the quantities involved can serve as a set of indexes that would reflect the actual and possible future response topology?"

This approach again resulted in orientor dimensions which could be mapped on the sets derived by the two approaches (with the exception of psychological components). Possible mathematical measures for the set of orientor dimensions derived earlier are described below.

The two latter approaches for the development of the set of basic orientors were of a general nature and did not make specific reference to human actor systems. With the exception of the psychological dimension, the basic orientor set found should therefore also apply to other autonomous systems which have to remain viable in a dynamic and perhaps hostile environment, in particular biological systems and advanced automata.

The initial analysis yielded the following set of orientor dimensions (Bossel 1976, p. 455 - 459) : basic physiological/physical support need satisfaction, basic psychological needs satisfaction, and adopted needs satisfaction as orientors of current viability; security, freedom of action, preparedness, robustness, predictability, success, and ability to influence the environment as orientors of future viability.

Subsequently it was found during data reduction of empirical assessments of value importance using these orientor dimensions, that the orientor pairs security and predictability, preparedness and robustness, and success and influence correlated strongly. These were therefore collapsed into the dimensions security, adaptivity, and efficiency of control, respectively. It was further decided to eliminate the somewhat troblesome adopted needs dimension, as this represents internalized needs which can then be represented by the functional and psychological components.

Empirical evidence (see below) suggests that the resulting orientor set given below may qualify (with some reservations) as a complete, independent, and irreducible basic orientor set for rational non-routine behavior of human actor systems.

Basic orientor dimensions for individual and societal systems

current viability:
    PHYSIOLOGICAL/PHYSICAL SUPPORT NEEDS
    PSYCHOLOGICAL NEEDS
future viability:
    SECURITY
    FREEDOM OF ACTION
    ADAPTIVITY
    EFFICIENCY OF CONTROL

The system has to attend to all of the basic orientor dimensions in order to be viable. However, the first two categories (physiological/physical and psychological needs) refer to current viability and must therefore be secured before the system will pay attention to the remaining categories (security, freedom of action, adaptivity, and efficiency of control) which pertain to future viability. Once minimum threshold levels of all of these are satisfied, the system can be expected to attempt to increase the satisfaction levels with respect to all basic orientor dimensions.

A brief explanation of these basic orientors is required. We shall also indicate possible mathematical performance measures for each component. The measures of future viability are of necessity future-weighted integrals over time.

Physiological/Physical Support Needs: All aspects required for viability and maintenance of the health of the material system and the information processing system.

Possible measure: Normalized sum of weighted distances from survival thresholds of the individual aspects in this category. Direct threats to survival are weighted very heavily.

Psychological Needs: All system-specific affective or emotional aspects. The set does not include psychological needs which must predominantly be counted as future viability requirements of the information processing system (e. g. exploration activity, self-actualization, desire to know and understand, etc.).

Possible measure: Normalized sum of weighted distances from minimal levels of the individual aspects. Direct threats to emotional health and to the self-concept are weighted very heavily.

Security: All aspects of short-, medium, and long-term security of adequate needs satisfaction to ensure future viability under changing external constraints.

Possible measure: Future-weighted probable distance of projected state from viability thresholds, integrated over possible system and disturbance states and over the system's operational time horizon and normalized.

Freedom of Action: All aspects enhancing freedom of action and motion of the system.

Possible measure: Future-weighted probable distance of projected state from constraints, integrated over possible action states and over the system's operational time horizon and normalized.

Adaptivity: All aspects enhancing the coping capability of the system with respect to presently undefined future challenges.

Possible measure: Future-weighted probable distance of possible response states (resulting from possible disturbances) from viability thresholds, integrated over the spectrum of possible disturbance states and over the system's operational time horizon and normalized.

Efficiency of Control: All aspects which allow successful and efficient manipulation of the environment to the benefit of the system.

Possible measure: Future-weighted probable benefits (weighted vector sum) resulting from possible system activity, related to the implementation costs to the system, integrated over the spectrum of possible control activity and over the system's operational time horizon and normalized.

Application of the basic orientor concept to value rankings

In our orientor approach values occupy a natural position as orientors on a level just below the basic orientor level. Values are certainly not basic orientors as they are very much a function of man's particular social systems and of social interaction: the family, the group, the nation, power, conflict and competition. The 36 terminal and instrumental values of Rokeach (1973) demonstrate this point:

Terminal values	Instrumental values
a comfortable life	ambitious
an exciting life	broadminded
a sense of accomplishment	capable
a world at peace	cheerful
a world of beauty	clean
equality	courageous
family security	forgiving
freedom	helpful
happiness	honest
inner harmony	imaginative
mature love	independent
national security	intellectual
pleasure	logical
salvation	loving
self-respect	obedient
social recognition	polite
true friendship	responsible
wisdom	self-controlled

Rokeach (1973) obtained importance rankings for his value lists from a large number of individuals in the United States in the years around 1968, with some additional international samples. The measurement technique consists of providing the subject with the list of values and asking him to rank the items "in order of their importance to YOU, as guiding principles in YOUR life". (One may consider this as an assessment with respect to the supreme orientor "individual viability".)

Within the logic of the present approach, values would then follow from an application of the basic orientor dimensions to more specific features of human life. The importance of a given value to an individual would then be a function of the contribution to the satisfaction of the basic orientors which would result from satisfaction of the value in the specific circumstances the individual finds himself in.

If indeed individuals determine the importance of a given value to them by intuitively assessing its impact on their basic orientors, then the 'intuitive' value ranking by Rokeach's method should give more or less the same result as a formal 'rational' assessment procedure using explicit assessments of value impact on an individual's situation and on his basic orientor satisfaction. Such a 'rational' assessment procedure was therefore developed by us.

Used simultaneously with the "intuitive" Rokeach procedure, it produces two value rankings, which can then be compared. In the "rational" assessment, the individual is asked to scale the significance of each of the values with respect to each of the basic orientor dimensions on a scale from 1 to 10. Following this, the results of the assessment are sealed and the individual is asked to intuitively rank the same list of values by the Rokeach method. In the evaluation, this rank order is compared with the results of the "rational" rank ordering by the same individual. The "rational" rank order is obtained by summing the significance numbers for each value and rank ordering the · resulting sums. The "rational" assessment method is designed in such a way that the result is not obvious to the individual, unless he knows the evaluation method. Hence an influence of the "rational" assessment on the "intuitive" assessment is unlikely.

In an initial application, the test was taken by 26 persons (all of them ISI employees with academic degrees), 21 of whom returned fully completed assessment forms. All individuals were completely unfamiliar with the procedure and its purpose when they took the test.

The results seem to confirm the hypothesis that values and their importance ranking derive from a mapping of their potential impact on the individual's basic orientor satisfaction. The mean correlation of the 'rational' versus the 'intuitive' assessments of the 21 individuals was 0.44, with a standard deviation of 0.33 (with 13 out of 21 respondents having correlations greater than 0.44). Several individuals had correlations as high as 0.86.

Of the 357 individual assessment pairs of the sample, 55 percent showed a difference of 3.0 rank order points or less (out of a possible 17) between the 'intuitive' and the 'rational' rankings: 75 percent had differences of 5.5 points or less. This means that the odds of correctly predicting an individual's value rank ordering (and hence his behavioral inclinations) on the basis of a projection of his particular situation and background on the set of basic orientors are relatively high.

The test also produced 'rational' assessment rankings of the items 'mature love' and 'true friendship' which were significantly lower than the 'intuitive' rankings by about two points. This may indicate either (1) a missing orientor dimension, or (2) an undervaluation of the psychological orientor dimension in the 'rational' assessment, or (3) an intuitive application of common stereotypes on these items. As our task is mainly that of studying aspects of the behavior of collective human actor systems, i.e. social, political, or national actors for whom this dimension is not very relevant, we are at the moment not overly concerned about this possible deficiency. It can be remedied - we think - without invalidating the overall approach. The results seem to indicate that the basic orientor set used is probably complete with respect to r a t i o n a l decision-making.

In order to provide a better feel for the relative accuracy of the basic orientor assessment method, the rankings by the two methods and their correlations for the full sample are presented in Tab. 1.

Summary of results concerning the orientor concept

(1) Application of the supreme orientor to the global characteristics of the system and of its environment results in a set of basic orientors. All non-routine systems behavior is oriented directly or indirectly by reference to this set.

(2) The dimensions describing orientor space (orientor dimensions) at a given level must be (1) basic (irreducible to even more basic dimensions); (2) complete (all actual dimensions must be represented); independent (no dimension should be obtainable by combinations of other dimensions).

(3) For autonomous systems depending on an environment with diffuse resources the basic orientor dimensions have been tentatively identified as: physical support needs, security, freedom of action, adaptivity, and efficiency of control. In human actor systems the psychological dimension joins the set. These dimensions were derived independently through (1) clustering of decision aspects; (2) study of design requirements of autonomous systems; (3) study of the topological features of systems behavior and environmental constraints.

Table 1 - COMPARISON OF "RATIONAL" (I) AND "INTUITIVE" (II) RANKINGS OF 17 ROKEACH TERMINAL VALUES BY 21 INDIVIDUALS.

		01	02	03	04	05	07	08	09	10	12	13	14	15	16	17	18	19	21	23	24	25
comfortable life	I	9.5	4	1.5	9	2	11	10	8	13	12	9.5	12	3	8	4.5	3	1	9.5	1	4	9
	II	16	15	2	16	12	12	8	16	11	14	16	9	5	17	16	11	5	11	12	14	2
exciting life	I	3	6.5	12	3	7	8	16	11.5	3.5	5	5	4	11	7	11	1.5	7	3	4	16	6
	II	4	2	9	6	3	11	17	12	7	3	14	6	2	7	6	15	7	1	2	2	12
sense of accomplishment	I	16	12.5	8.5	10.5	5	4	6.5	14.5	5.5	6	9.5	3	5	2	9	14.5	6	7.5	2	14.5	10
	II	11	12	6	8	7	8	4	14	4	11	11	2	10	5	4	12	15	6	13	8	4
world at peace	I	9.5	2.5	10.5	14	3.5	9	12	2.5	14	14	1	8.5	13.5	12	9	4.5	4	4	4	6	3.5
	II	12	10	16	13	2	17	11	6	17	12	1	5	16	13	17	5	10	12	1	11	13
world of beauty	I	10	17	16	17	14	14	14	14.5	17	15.5	16	17	17	17	17	17	17	13	17	17	15
	II	15	5	17	14	13	9	14	11	15	15	9	16	17	10	11	13	17	13	17	10	16
equality	I	5	5	8.5	13	16.5	7	11	5.5	16	8	12	8.5	13.5	6	2.5	10.5	10	7.5	11	8	7.5
	II	2	17	12	15	16	10	12	9	16	9	7	15	13	11	8	7	11	5	7	16	9
family security	I	8	11	7	12	6	10	3	5.5	10	13	6	8.5	2	2	2.5	9	2	13	5	3	11
	II	9	6	5	11	4	4	2	7	8	10	5	3	1	2	9	6	3	14	3	4	10
freedom	I	1	2.5	6	2	1	3	5	5.5	10	2	3	2	1	5	6	1.5	4	2	3	3	5
	II	1	9	14	3	1	3	6	10	8	4	12	14	9	8	10	3	1	9	6	7	3
happiness	I	12.5	9.5	14	14	14.5	1	8.5	5.5	1	10	4	12	9	3.5	14	12	16	13	16	12	12
	II	8	1	1	3	9	1	3	1	10	8	6	12	3	3	14	10	9	10	15	1	15
inner harmony	I	12.5	6.5	4	7	9.5	1	6.5	5.5	1	3.5	8	12	6	8	11	6.5	12	5.5	8.5	3	3.5
	II	10	14	1	10	9	2	13	1	6	6	10	11	12	4	7	4	9	3	11	9	5
mature love	I	4	16	10.5	7	9.5	16	11.5	9	5.5	3.5	2	15	4	8	9	8	12	5.5	14	10	17
	II	3	3	5	10	5	3	3	5	3	2	2	4	6	1	3	1	4	4	9	3	6
national security	I	15	8	4	15.5	16	15	1	9	5.5	11	14	8.5	16	14.5	1	14.5	4	16.5	13	14.5	7.5
	II	17	3	4	12	8	16	1	17	3	16	8	8	15	14	2	8	13	17	10	12	11
pleasure	I	6	14.5	13	15.5	16.5	17	17	16	12	17	17	14	11	14.5	15	16	13	15	15	13	13.5
	II	6	8	11	17	17	14	16	13	9	13	17	10	8	15	13	17	12	16	16	17	17
self-respect	I	2	12.5	4	1	9.5	2	8.5	13	2	1	2	1	7	3.5	13	10.5	8.5	16.5	8	11	1
	II	7	11	1	1	7	7	5	3	1	1	2	1	4	9	1	11	8	15	4	5	1
social recognition	I	14	9.5	15	5	14.5	12	13	17	15	15.5	15	5.5	11	10	7	13	14.5	11	11	9	13.5
	II	14	16	17	7	14	15	10	15	14	17	13	13	11	16	15	16	14	8	14	13	8
true friendship	I	7	14.5	17	7	12	13	13	10	7	7	11	16	15	16	12	6.5	8.5	9.5	11	6.5	16
	II	13	4	2	2	11	5	13	2	5	5	4	6	8	6	5	2	6	7	8	6	14
wisdom	I	17	1	1.5	4	3.5	6	15	2.5	3.5	9	7	5.5	8	12	4.5	4.5	11	1	6.5	1	2
	II	13	13	10	9	10	15	15	8	13	7	15	17	14	12	12	16	16	2	5	15	7
correlation r (I/II) for each individual		.77	-.47	.22	.76	.70	.64	.73	.45	.72	.86	.36	.19	.54	.33	.00	.38	.35	.80	.52	-.16	.47

(4) The application of basic orientors to more specific features of the individual and socio-ecological system and environment results in values: more specific orientors on a level below that of the basic orientors.

(5) The hypothesis that behavior is oriented by reference to basic orientors has been tentatively confirmed by good agreement of value rankings obtained by "intuitive" and "rational" assessments.

(6) The time constant of orientor change increases as one moves up the orientor hierarchy. The basic orientors are practically invariant.

(7) Basic orientors are the major invariants of systems behavior and are as such the key to the understanding, description, and simulation of systems behavior.

(8) Even with invariant orientors at a given level, the orientor satisfaction state at this level together with the system and environmental state may result in abrupt changes of attention given lower level orientors, even the ad hoc derivation of new orientors adapted to the problem at hand. The invariance of basic orientors together with the nonlinear feature of orientor switching provides the system with the ability to cope flexibly and adaptively with a widely and quickly changing state of system and environment.

(9) Orientors are characterized by (1) a dimension; (2) an aspiration level of orientor satisfaction; (3) upper and/or lower satisfaction thresholds, beyond which control is transferred to connecting orientors on the next higher levels.

(10) Orientors on a given level will generally be of different relative importance to the system; i.e. they will be weighted differently.

(11) Systems will generally also consider the orientor sets of other systems with whom they are in interaction.

(12) The behavioral instructions concerning given orientor sets appear to have two dimensions; one of urgency, and one of satisfaction. In a given situation, attention will first focus on immediate or pending threshold violations. Once these threats are removed, attention will shift to improving the overall satisfaction level of the orientor set.

(13) The orientor approach is closely related to the topology of the systems response at a given level; in particular, basic orientors are related to the topology of global systems behavior, and of overall behavioral constraints.

Some of the concepts are illustrated in Figs. 5 and 6.

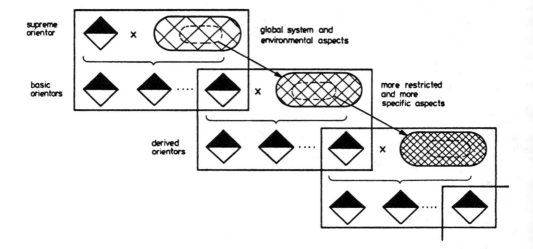

Fig. 6 - RECURSIVE PROCEDURE OF ORIENTOR DERIVATION

Orientors applicable to specific contexts are derived by applying a more
general orientor (e. g. "security") to the specific situation (e. g. "car approaching in an unprotected intersection") to produce a situation-specific
normative guidance (e. g. "decelerate", "give a warning", etc.). Each of
these orientors (e. g. "decelerate") applied to the relevant circumstances
(e. g. "ice on the road"), gives rise to even more specific orientors (e. g.
"brake cautiously and intermittently").

Some critical comments

The discursive study presented here can and must be augmented by a formal mathematical description. In particular, the relationship of basic orientors to global features of systems response and environmental constraints can better be studied in a more formal analysis.

It is evident that thorough empirical research, both on natural and on artificial systems (models) is required to firmly establish (or reject) many of the conjectures made here on the basis of not always complete or fully validated, though perhaps plausible evidence.

4 - MAPPING INDICATORS ON ORIENTORS

In the following it will be assumed that indicators are mapped directly on a set of orientors relevant to the decision context. This set of orientors may be at any level of the orientor hierarchy, including that of the basic orientors. The orientor set is considered invariant with respect to the given decision context. The discussion therefore applies in particular to state analysis and policy synthesis made by direct reference to basic orientors; however, it also applies to decision-making with respect to lower level orientors as long as they can be considered invariant; resp. as long as the system and environmental state do not require higher level orientors as a behavioral reference.

For indicators of systems and environmental state to provide any input to the information processes of non-routine decision-making, they must be mapped on corresponding orientor dimensions at the appropriate level of the orientor hierarchy. This section will develop the components of a mapping concept which has been implemented in our computer programs.

A given indicator represents one aspect of the system and environmental state of interest to the system - or else it would not be in the set of observed indicators. This 'interest' is expressed by the fact that the indicator connects to one or more orientors at the lowest or at higher levels of the orientor hierarchy. Through the hierarchy, it ultimately directly or indirectly connects to the basic orientors. The strength of the connection to orientors may be very much a function of system state - hence we have to consider state-dependent loadings of the indicators on orientors.

The loadings do not carry information on the state of the system however (resp. that of the indicator), hence a second requirement is the transformation of the state information available through the indicator into information relevant to the orientors connected to it. This latter information must carry a measure of the resulting orientor satisfaction or dissatisfaction. Hence a transformation of perceived indicator state, measured in the applicable dimension, into a satisfaction scale is required. Thirdly, some orientors may be more important to the system than others, hence orientor weights must be considered. Fourthly, a system in direct or in-direct interaction with other systems must also to some degree consider the impact of a given state and of state changes on the orientor hierarchies of the other 'participating' systems. This 'concern' for other systems will be weighted differently for each participating system.

The present section will therefore have to concern itself in particular with
  - the loadings of indicators on orientors;
  - the transformation of state information into orientor satisfaction or dissatisfaction;
  - relative weights of orientors;
  - participating systems and their weights.
Subsequently the total mapping concept will be summarized in preparation for the discussion of its implementation in an interactive computer program.

Loading of indicators on orientors

Consider a set of indicators I_i (i = 1, 2, ..., I) representative of a certain aspect of the system and environmental state, and a set of orientors O_j (j = 1, 2, ... J) on which the given state aspect has, or may have, an impact. A first step of the required mapping must be to establish how strongly, if at all, each indicator connects to each of the orientors. It is important to note that the strength of this connection ('loading') is general-ly not constant, but may instead vary very strongly with the system and environmental state. Even for a constant system and environmental state, it may change as perception changes about the strength of the connections.

It is possible in principle to determine the loading 1_{ij} of indicator i on orientor j for a given system and environmental state by a perturbation analysis, provided (1) relevant satisfaction indexes exist for the orientors (i.e. mathematical expressions representing system performance with respect to a given orientor, see the earlier discussion), and (2) a valid model exists of the system and of its environment, which can produce a valid description of the system and environmental response following a perturbation. In fact, this is the procedure applied intuitively in judging the impact of an indicator on given orientors. The present report deals with methods of implementing intuitive loading assessments; the formalized loading assessment using a full mathematical model will be left to future work.

Orientor satisfaction scales

At the orientor level, the information about the state of the system received through the indicators must be available in a common dimension in order to allow comparative assessments and to provide the proper guidance to the decision-making process. As an illustration, let the number of apples and oranges on a table be two independent state indicators perceived by an individual. Both indicators connect to an orientor like 'pleasure of eating'. The fruit that promises to provide better satisfaction of this indicator at this particular moment will be eaten. The incomparable physical indicator units must therefore be transformed into comparable satisfaction units (or a similar measure like utility etc.).

It has previously been stressed that behavioral mode changes can result even where orientor sets remain invariant. The reason lies with the possible threshold character of the satisfaction function corresponding to a state indicator. As the state changes smoothly on the physical scale, the satisfaction classification may switch from a "satisfactory" to an "unsatisfactory" or even "unacceptable" rating, causing alarm at the proper orientor level, and resulting possibly in a major change in the behavioral mode.

An indicator state may be unsatisfactory because it is either too low or too high. If we assume that the orientor satisfaction varies monotonic with the indicator state, then three types of satisfaction functions result which are outlined in Fig. 7:

Type I: As the indicator state measure increases, the satisfaction rating changes from 'unsatisfactorily low' to 'satisfactory' to 'unsatisfactorily high'. Example: satisfaction of "physical needs" by calorie intake.

Type II: As the indicator state measure increases, the satisfaction rating changes from 'satisfactory' to 'unsatisfactorily high'. Example: satisfaction of "security" orientor by increasing pollution level.

Type III: As the indicator state measure increases, the satisfaction rating changes from 'unsatisfactorily low' to 'satisfactory'. Example: satisfaction of "freedom of action" orientor by personal income.

In actual assessments, more refined satisfaction/dissatisfaction scales are used (see Ch. 15).

Relative weights of orientors

It is obvious that in many contexts the different orientors in the applicable orientor set may carry different importance ratings, i.e. weights. The empirical studies of Rokeach (1973) have clearly established such ratings on the level of the value orientors. The overall concept must therefore include the possibility of assigning different relative weights to different orientors. As a result, an indicator whose state is "unsatisfactory" and which loads on a heavily weighted orientor will receive priority attention over an unsatisfactory indicator loading on an orientor of lesser relative weight.

Participating systems and their weights

Our concern lies mainly with autonomous systems which may interact with other systems at certain times. We are interested in "considered interaction",

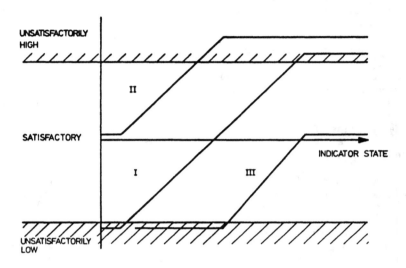

Fig. 7 - TYPES OF SATISFACTION FUNCTIONS

As an indicator measure increases, the corresponding orientor satisfaction
may go from either
- unsatisfactorily low to unsatisfactorily high (type I); or from
- satisfactory to unsatisfactorily high (type II); or from
- unsatisfactorily low to satisfactory (type III).
Examples: Food (type I), pollution (type II), income (type III).

i. e. interactions that have been foreseen and whose consideration has affected the behavior towards the other system(s). Such a consideration of the possible effects on, and the actions of, the other system means that its needs, i. e. representative orientors, play a role in the decision-making process leading to behavior affecting the other participating system. The relevant orientor sets of these participating systems enter the decision-making process with certain weights, depending on their relative importance to the system (e. g. power relationships, family relations, courtship, conflict, etc.).

The satisfaction functions concerning a given indicator will generally be different for the different participating systems. A zero-sum game is the classical illustration: one system's losses are the other system's gains.

State assessment using the orientor concept

We shall now consider the assessment of an actual or projected system state for a single system. If participating systems are involved, their respective relative weights enter the assessment process, but otherwise the approach remains the same.

Assume that (Fig. 8)
- the set of relevant indicators I_i is given;
- the set of relevant orientors O_j^i is known;
- the loadings l_{ij} of each of the indicators on each of the orientors have been determined as a function of the indicator state;
- the satisfaction classifications of each indicator state (satisfaction function for each indicator) have been established[+];
- the relative weights w_j of orientors are known.

With these data available, an assessment of the perceived state can be made. There are several possible approaches; we shall here outline the approach which is currently being used in our computer program.

Let there be three categories of satisfaction classification:
- GREEN: the indicator state is satisfactory with respect to the orientors involved;

- YELLOW: the indicator state is unsatisfactory and only temporarily tolerable and should be brought to GREEN status as soon as possible;

- RED: the indicator state is unacceptable; it must be brought to YELLOW or GREEN status immediately, if at all possible.

[+] In the following, the assumption is made that an aggregate satisfaction function can be obtained with respect to each relevant (or one dominant) orientor; i. e. we will not deal with individual satisfaction functions of indicator I_i, with respect to orientors O_j.

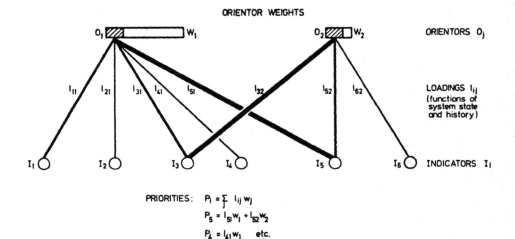

ORIENTOR WEIGHTS

$$P_i = \sum_j l_{ij} w_j$$

$$P_5 = l_{51} w_1 + l_{52} w_2$$

$$P_4 = l_{41} w_1 \quad \text{etc.}$$

$$P_5 > P_3 > P_1 > P_4 > P_2 > P_6$$

Fig. 8 - INDICATOR PRIORITIES

An indicator priority index is computed from (1) the weights of the orientors to which it connects, and (2) the state-dependent loadings of the indicator on each orientor. In the example, the indicator I_5 has the highest priority index. The indicator attention depends in addition on the (dis)satisfaction classification of the indicator. If I_5 were in the RED category, it would receive top priority. In the GREEN category, it would merely show that the system obtains considerable satisfaction from the current state of I_5.

If there are several indicators in one category, a priority ordering will be established according to (1) the weights of the orientors to which the indicator connects, and (2) the strength of the loadings on these orientors at the given system state. The priority index of indicator I_i is then

$$P_i = \sum_j w_j l_{ij} \qquad \text{where } l_{ij} = f \text{ (indicator state)}$$

P_i establishes a priority order for the indicators within each satisfaction category. The system focusses its attention on the indicators according to some attention rule, a likely candidate for which would be the rule:

(1) RED status has priority over YELLOW status;
YELLOW status has priority over GREEN status.

(2) Within each status class, the indicator with the higher priority index P_i has priority over that with a lower P_i.

It is to be expected that this simple rule will not be adequate in many applications, mainly for two reasons:

- It is likely that a very important YELLOW issue will receive priority over a relatively unimportant RED issue; the attention rules should be so modified.

- Status classification and priority ranking within a status class are subject to modifications due to psychological mechanisms such as the desire for the removal of cognitive dissonance (see the article by E. Gruber in this volume).

Corresponding modifications can easily be inserted into a formalized model.

Assessment of issues

In the present context, we understand an "issue" as an aggregate of fuzzily defined indicators concerning a certain aspect of the system and environmental state. As no quantifiable scales are available, an explicit satisfaction classification cannot be made. It is possible, however, to establish clear priority ratings by again using loadings and orientor weights as before to calculate a priority index. The loading l_{ij} of issue I_i on orientor O_j is now constant, since the issue name (e. g. "equality", "construction of a power-plant at a town", "national security", etc.) is taken to refer to an invariant aggregate.

Summary of the model concept

(1) The various possible dimensions of indicator states have to be mapped on a common dimension at the orientor level. Orientor satisfaction or dissatisfaction is a natural dimension for this purpose.

(2) Mapping the indicator state on the orientor state requires specification of (a) the amount of orientor satisfaction produced from a given indicator state (satisfaction assessment), and of (b) which orientors are affected how much be a given indicator state (loading assessment).

(3) In the satisfaction assessment, satisfaction ratings with respect to the orientor set are obtained for the whole range of possible states of the given indicator.

(4) In the loading assessment, the strength of the connection l_{ij} of the given indicator I_i to each of the orientors O_j is assessed as a function of indicator state.

(5) The attention rank of indicators is established from a consideration of their satisfaction rating, the weights of orientors on which the indicator loads, and from the state-dependent loading of each indicator on the orientors.

(6) If the action or reaction of other systems must be considered in the decision-making process, then the points of view of these participating systems are taken into account by adding appropriately weighted indicator and orientor sets and the corresponding mappings.

(7) Aggregates of indicators, characterizing a certain state aspect ("issues") are assessed with respect to their impact on the orientor set by considering the loadings of the issue on the different orientors. From this and the relative weight of the orientors involved, a priority ranking can be established. Treatment of participating systems is analogous to the case of indicator assessment.

Some points of criticism

The approach is an exploratory one. The validity of the overall concept appears to have been confirmed by its application to value rankings (see Sec. 3) and in computer simulations (see Ch. 16). Nevertheless, some deficiencies require attention. We are aware of the following:
- The satisfaction and loading assessments for a given indicator are now made under ceteris paribus conditions, changing only one indicator state at a time.

- The simple approach outlined above assumes that indicators are independent of each other. This means that there can be only one indicator for each relevant state dimension, e. g. the indicators "bread"
and "cake" cannot appear simultaneously, unless their possible sub-
stitution effect for the supply of carbohydrates is introduced explicitly,
or "bread" stands strictly as an indicator for food, and "cake" for
luxuries, or if the respective "food" and "luxury" components are
clearly separated in both. In a situation where plenty of cake is
available, but no bread, the present approach would, unless modified,
still signal an overriding need for bread.

- Strictly speaking, a satisfaction curve with respect to each of the
orientors should be obtained for each of the indicators. Consider the
case where the indicator "money spent" connects to the orientors
"pleasure" and "thrift". An increase in the amount spent would increase the satisfaction due to pleasure, while reducing that due to
thrift. In the present implementation, we are using only a single
satisfaction curve for each indicator. The reason is that the present
method was intended to be used mainly with the set of basic orientors,
whose dimension "physiological/physical support needs" is the only
one for which a satisfaction relationship for most indicators is well
defined. Once in the "satisfactory" range on this dimension, the
indicator can also be assumed to be satisfactory with respect to the
other dimensions. Its final impact on the priority ranking is then determined predominantly by the indicator state-dependent loadings and
the weights of the connecting orientors.

- Changes in indicator and loading perceptions, in aspiration levels,
satisfaction ratings, weights etc. due to psychological processes such
as cognitive dissonance reduction have not been considered, as noted
previously. A combination of the present approach with that of E.
Gruber (see article in this volume) is necessary.

- Because of the many assessments necessary, the approach becomes
unwieldy for complex problems. An upper practical limit exists around
10 orientors, 20 indicators, and 5 participating systems.

5 - CONCLUDING REMARKS

The analysis presented was based on the hypothesis that non-routine decisions
are made by direct or indirect reference to a set of basic orientors, whose
dimensions are identical across human actor systems, and are probably identical (with the exception of the psychological dimension) for all autonomous systems, animate or not, relying for their physical support on an environment with
diffuse resources. These dimensions were identified as: physiological/physical
support needs, psychological well-being, security, freedom of action, adaptivity, and efficiency of control (or their functional equivalents). Fundamental

decisions are oriented by direct reference to these dimensions, minor decisions may be oriented by indirect reference through a multilevel hierarchy of orientors of increasing specificity. More general orientors, having longer time constants of change, are found nearer to the set of basic orientors at the top. The quasi-invariance of the basic orientors, together with the threshold switching property of lower level orientors (control is transferred to higher level orientors, if lower level orientors cannot maintain the required orientor satisfaction) guarantees maximum response flexibility while maintaining the global viability of the system even under rapidly changing circumstances. The set of orientors was derived by three different approaches; supporting empirical evidence was presented.

Even though the set of basic orientors may be identical in human actor systems, significant differences of non-routine behavior may still result from (1) differences of time horizon, (2) differences in spatial horizon (consideration of other "participating" systems), (3) differences in orientor weights, and (4) differences in participating system weights.

The mapping of a perceived system and environmental state (indicator state) on the orientor space to determine orientor satisfaction provides a way to assess how a system will be affected by a given system and environmental state, and how it is likely to respond. In practical terms, the approach provides a way to determine likely priorities and preferences and it promises a sounder foundation for the simulation of the behavior of systems in general, and of human actor systems in particular.

To facilitate exploratory investigations, the concept was implemented in an interactive computer routine, making extensive use of interactive computer graphics (light pen on display screen). This routine assists the user in constructing and using policy analysis models of a particular class (i.e. mapping of system and environmental state on orientors). The routine enables the user to make systematic and structured assessments having some theoretical and empirical foundations in an area where previously one had to rely on vague hunches (see Ch. 15 for a full discussion).

In an entirely different nonnumerical approach, a routine for logical deduction has been developed to deal in particular with the ad hoc situation-specific derivation of normative statements from more general orientors (see Chs. 13 and 14).

The concepts and applications presented here are merely first steps. Questions raised concerning the indexes of global system response, the study of basic orientor sets, satisfaction functions, and mappings of the system and environmental state on orientor space, point to many challenging research problems.

REFERENCES

ANDREWS, F. M. WITHEY, S. B. 1974: Developing Measures of Perceived
    Life Quality: Results from Several National Surveys. Social Indicators
    Research 1, 1 - 26.
ANDREWS, F. M. 1974: Social Indicators of Perceived Life Quality.
    Social Indicators Research 1, 279 - 299.
BOSSEL, H. 1976: Information Processing, Cognitive Dissonance, and
    Basic Needs: The Modelling of Behavior. In: H. Bossel, S. Klaczko,
    N. Müller (eds.): Systems Theory in the Social Sciences, Birkhäuser,
    Basel.
CHRISTENSEN, B. L.; NØRGAARD, J. S. 1974: Social Values and the Limits
    to Growth. Thayer School of Engineering, Dartmouth College, Hanover,
    N. H., DSD-17.
DALKEY, N. C. 1972: Studies in the Quality of Life. Delphi and Decision-
    Making. Heath, Lexington/Toronto/London.
GRÜMM, H. R. 1976: Definitions of Resilience. RR-76-5, International
    Institute of Applied Systems Analysis, Laxenburg, Austria.
HOLLING, C. S. 1973: Resilience and Stability of Ecological Systems.
    RR-73-3, International Institute of Applied Systems Analysis, Laxenburg,
    Austria.
MALLMAN, C. 1975: Quality of Life and Development Alternatives.
    Fundacion Bariloche, San Carlos de Bariloche, Argentina.
MASLOW, A. H. 1954/1970: Motivation and Personality. Harper and Row,
    New York, N. Y.
ROKEACH, M. 1973: The Nature of Human Values. Free Press, New York.
THOM, R. 1975: Stability and Morphogenesis. Benjamin, Reading, Mass.
ZANGEMEISTER, C. 1975: Zur Methodik systemanalytischer Zielplanung -
    Dargestellt am Beispiel des Bildungsbereichs. Zentrum Berlin für Zu-
    kunftsforschung.

I

analog computer, 141
analogy, 467
absenteeism, 114
access channel, 100
action alternative, 487
action primitives, 470
action unit, 147
active society, 34
actor, 12, 25, 53; see also: actor system,
  human actor, human actor system
actor, inconsistent, 166
actor, rational, 166
actor, simulated, 572
actor system, 12, 15, 17, 142, 162, 227, 235
actuality, 104, 105, 106, 113, 114
adaptation, 34, 143, 149, 580
adaptation, anticipative, 459
adaptation of normative principles, 7
adaptation to user, 313
adaptive behavior, 59
adaptive capability: defects, 479
adaptivity, 249
affect, 165
aggregated model, 447, 449, 450
aggregation of actors, 165
aggregation of input parameters, 310
alarm classification, 172, 259, 543; see
  also: RED classification
alert classification, 172, 259, 543; see
  also: YELLOW classification
alibi concept, 525
alienation, 187, 209
a-logical phenomena, 515
alternative futures, 143
branching, 143
alternative, 53, 444, 483, 539, 542
alternatives assessment, 18, 444, 538, 540,
  543, 551, 552
alternative system states, 54
alternatives, testing of, 589
AND, 472, 489
approximate solution, 396
artificial intelligence, 57, 488
Ashby's Law, 97
aspiration, 9
aspiration level, 43, 175, 562-581, 603-609
aspiration level: change, 607
aspiration level: lowering, 570
aspiration level: raising, 570
assembly list, 329
assessment, 467
assessment of alternatives, 556, 559
assessment of value rankings, 250
assessment output, 539, 542
assessment output record, 542
atomic predicate statement, 493, 494
atomic statement, 489
attainability, 170
attainability assessment, 167
attention focus, 474
attention priority, 543
attention rank, 262
attention rating, 538
attention rule, 261
attenuator of variety, 99

attitudes, 9, 555
attitude change, 39, 40
authoritative distribution, 589
autonomous system, 242-251
autonomy, 85, 102, 121

back to nature, 207
balance, internal, 565
balance theory, 37, 38
balancing, 38
basic behavioral instructions, 172; see
  also: orientor
basic needs, 245, 558; see also: orientor
basic norms, 484; see also: orientor
basic operational dimensions, 237; see also:
  orientor
basic orienting dimensions, 240; see also:
  orientor
basic orientors, 15; see also: orientor
basic reference dimension, 232; see also:
  orientor
batch processing, 268
bahavior, 7
behavioral change, 464
behavioral diversity, 479
behavioral equation, 52
behavioral failure, 458
behavioral instruction, 163
behavioral latitude, 458, 478
behavioral limitation, 462
behavioral mode, 141, 165, 227
behavioral mode change, 257
behavioral model, 82
behavioral procedures, 467
behavioral program, 227
behavioral program, inadequate, 458
behavioral tendency, 487
behavior, guidance, 479; see also: orientation
behavior, overt, 555
behavior, nonroutine, 227-231
behavior, routine, 228, 229, 230
behavior setting, 217, 218
being, 196, 189
belief system, 207
best compromise, 395
bidding-allocation, 154
block diagram, 16, 270-273
block diagram construction, 276
body count, 189
bond, 470
bounds, 415
branch-and-bound, interactive, 427
branching, 143

calculation phase, 399
capability, 104, 105, 106, 113, 114
catastrophe theory, 246
catastrophic behavioral failure, 465
cathode-ray screen, 128
causal level, 148
causal loop diagram, 272

AFFILIATIONS OF AUTHORS

Patrick Bond, Political Science Department, Case Western Reserve University, Cleveland, Ohio, U.S.A.

Hartmut Bossel, Institut für Systemtechnik und Innovationsforschung (ISI), Fraunhofer Gesellschaft, Karlsruhe, F. R. Germany.

Christophe Deissenberg, FB Wirtschaftswissenschaften und Statistik, Universität, Konstanz, F. R. Germany.

Edelgard Gruber, Institut für Systemtechnik und Innovationsforschung (ISI), Fraunhofer Gesellschaft, Karlsruhe, F. R. Germany.

Pieter van der Hijden, Social Science Research Group, Department of Psychology, University, Nijmegen, The Netherlands.

Walter Hudetz, Institut für Systemtechnik und Innovationsforschung (ISI), Fraunhofer Gesellschaft, Karlsruhe, F.R. Germany.

Karl-Friedrich Müller-Reissmann, Institut für Systemtechnik und Innovationsforschung, Fraunhofer Gesellschaft, Karlsruhe, F.R. Germany.

Eduard Pestel, Deutsche Forschungsgemeinschaft (DFG), Bonn, und Institut für Mechanik, Technische Universität, Hannover, F.R. Germany.

Francois Rechenmann, Ecole Nationale Supérieure d'Informatique et de Mathématiques Appliquées, Grenoble, France, and European Nuclear Research Center, Ispra, Italy.

Hermann Schwember, Industrial Sociology Unit, Imperial College of Science and Technology, London, U.K.

Karl-Heinz Simon, FB Philosophie, Universität, Erlangen-Nürnberg, F. R. Germany.

Michael G. Strobel, Psychology Department, Université de Montréal, Montreal, Canada. ·

Interdisciplinary Systems Research
Birkhäuser Verlag, Basel und Stuttgart

GPSR Compliance
The European Union's (EU) General Product Safety Regulation (GPSR) is a set
of rules that requires consumer products to be safe and our obligations to
ensure this.

If you have any concerns about our products, you can contact us on

ProductSafety@springernature.com

In case Publisher is established outside the EU, the EU authorized
representative is:

Springer Nature Customer Service Center GmbH
Europaplatz 3
69115 Heidelberg, Germany